The Provision of Public Services in Europe

The Provision of Public Services in Europe

Between State, Local Government and Market

Edited by

Hellmut Wollmann

Professor Emeritus of Public Policy and Public Administration, Social Science Institute, Humboldt-Universität, Berlin, Germany

Gérard Marcou

Professor of Public Law, Université Paris 1 Panthéon–Sorbonne, and Director of GRALE, Paris, France

Edward Elgar
Cheltenham, UK • Northampton, MA, USA

© Hellmut Wollmann and Gérard Marcou 2010

All rights reserved. No part of this publication may be reproduced, stored in a retrieval system or transmitted in any form or by any means, electronic, mechanical or photocopying, recording, or otherwise without the prior permission of the publisher.

Published by
Edward Elgar Publishing Limited
The Lypiatts
15 Lansdown Road
Cheltenham
Glos GL50 2JA
UK

Edward Elgar Publishing, Inc.
William Pratt House
9 Dewey Court
Northampton
Massachusetts 01060
USA

A catalogue record for this book
is available from the British Library

Library of Congress Control Number: 2009942850

ISBN 978 1 84844 809 4

Printed and bound by MPG Books Group, UK

Contents

List of figures	vii
List of tables	viii
List of contributors	x
Preface and acknowledgements	xv

1 Introduction 1
  Hellmut Wollmann and Gérard Marcou
2 The multi-level institutional setting in Germany, Italy, France and the UK: a comparative overview 15
  Hellmut Wollmann, Enzo Balboni, Jean-Pierre Gaudin and Gérard Marcou
3 New public management in continental Europe: local government modernization in Germany, France and Italy from a comparative perspective 49
  Sabine Kuhlmann and Paolo Fedele
4 The local government role in pre-school child care policy in France, Germany, Italy and the UK 75
  Michael Hill, Martine Long, Anna Marzanati and Frank Bönker
5 Towards marketization and centralization? The changing role of local government in long-term care in England, France, Germany and Italy 97
  Frank Bönker, Michael Hill and Anna Marzanati
6 Health services: issues and trends in Italy, France and Germany 120
  Dieter Grunow, Francesco Longo and Martine Long
7 Comparative study of a local service: waste management in France, Germany, Italy and the UK 146
  Magali Dreyfus, Annette Elisabeth Töller, Carlo Iannello and John McEldowney
8 From public service to commodity: the demunicipalization (or remunicipalization?) of energy provision in Germany, Italy, France, the UK and Norway 168
  Hellmut Wollmann, Harald Baldersheim, Giulio Citroni, Gérard Marcou and John McEldowney

9	Neither state nor market: municipalities, corporations and municipal corporatization in water services – Germany, France and Italy compared	191
	Giulio Citroni	
10	Comparative aspects of institutional variants for local public service provision	217
	Giuseppe Grossi, Gérard Marcou and Christoph Reichard	
11	From public sector-based to privatized service provision. Is the pendulum swinging back again? Comparative summary	240
	Hellmut Wollmann and Gérard Marcou	

Index 261

Figures

3.1	Effects of privatization and contracting out in German local government	53
7.1	The amount of waste in the main EU member states	147
8.1	Net production of energy by type of producer (GWh)	173
9.1	Water service providers by model of management (% of the population)	197

Tables

2.1	Intergovernmental structure (data for 2006–9)	16
2.2	Public employment by levels of government (in %)	19
2.3	Subnational public expenditure in 2005 by economic function (in %)	22
2.4	Subnational expenditure in 2005	24
2.5	Development of total number of public sector personnel by level of government over time (in %, respective period in parentheses)	25
3.1	Modes of local service delivery in the French water sector, 2000	54
3.2	Modernizing local service provision: implemented NSM elements in German local governments	58
5.1	The situation of elderly people in about 1990	99
6.1	Health system indicators	124
6.2	Contextual factors of local health services provision	126
6.3	Local service-related activities	129
6.4	NPM reforms	142
7.1	Directives on waste	148
7.2	Waste management under the responsibility of *communes* in France	150
7.3	Competency framework according to Act 152 (2006)	158
7.4	UK institutions and responsibilities for waste	161
7.5	Municipal waste recycled (kg) per capita	164
8.1	Number, size and ownership of public and public–private energy companies in Italy, 2003–5	183
9.1	Uses of water	192
9.2	Water prices for households in selected European countries: prices, investments and trends in the 1990s	195
9.3	Forms of water services management	196
9.4	Provision models of different public utilities in a sample of cities over 50 000 inhabitants	198
9.5	Models of water service provision	199
9.6	Water service providers in Italy, by subsector	202
9.7	Models of aqueduct operation (number of providers and amount of water carried)	203

9.8	Incidence of water service models in France, 2000	209
9.9	Incidence of *gestion déléguée* in water delivery	210
9.10	Market share of water companies in France (%)	210
10.1	The variety of legal forms of local utilities	231

Contributors

Enzo Balboni is Professor of Constitutional Law in the Faculty of Law at The Catholic University of Milan, Italy. His main research interest is comparative public law.

Harald Baldersheim is Professor of Public Administration in the Department of Political Science, University of Oslo, Norway. His research interests include comparative local politics and government, e-government and European regionalism. He has edited (with Hellmut Wollmann) *The Comparative Study of Local Government and Politics: Overview and Synthesis. The World of Political Science Series* (Opladen: Barbara Budrich, 2006).

Frank Bönker holds a PhD in Political Science and teaches at the University of Cooperative Education, Leipzig, Germany. His main fields of research are welfare state reform, local social policy, post-communist economic reform and the Europeanization of East Central Europe. His most recent book publications include *The Political Economy of Fiscal Reform in East-Central Europe* (Cheltenham: Edward Elgar, 2006) and *Postsozialistische Transformation and europäische (Des-) Integration* (co-editor, Marburg: Metropolis, 2008).

Giulio Citroni holds a PhD in Political Science, is a researcher and is Visiting Professor of Political Science and Public Policy Analysis at Università della Calabria in Cosenza, Italy. His research interests lie in the transformation of the exercise of political power at the local level, privatization of services, participatory policies, and local and regional political elites. His most recent work is *Mai più soli! Note sulla democrazia partecipativa* (Rome: Bonanno editore, 2010).

Magali Dreyfus holds a PhD in Law from the European University Institute, Florence, Italy. Her fields of research are local public services (public transport, waste management) and services of general interest in European law.

Paolo Fedele is Assistant Professor in the Department of Finance and Financial Markets, Udine University, Italy. His main research fields are public management reform, management of supranational organizations and business–government relations. He recently contributed an article, 'Le autorità amministrative indipendenti: centralità nel dibattito italiano', to E. Ongaro (ed.), *L'organizzazione dello Stato tra autonomia e policy capacity* (Roma: Rubbettino).

Jean-Pierre Gaudin is Professor at the Institut d'Etudes politiques d'Aix en Provence, France. His main research interests are public policies, governance and participation. Recent publication: *La démocratie participative* (Paris: Armand Colin, 2007).

Giuseppe Grossi is Associate Professor of Public Financial Management, University of Siena, Italy, and a Visiting Professor in International Accounting and Public Administration at Kristianstad University, Sweden. His main research interests are public management and governance, government financial reporting. He recently wrote a paper, 'New development: consolidated financial reporting as stimulus to change in Italian Local Government', in *Public Money & Management*, **29** (4), 2009, 261–4.

Dieter Grunow is Professor of Political Science and Public Administration, Institute of Political Science, University of Duisburg-Essen, Germany. His fields of research are public administration (local level, implementation), social policy, health policy and system theory. He recently co-edited Vereinbarte Verbindlichkeit im administrativen Mehrebenensystem, *Kommunalisierung im Sozialsektor* (Wiesbaden: VS Verlag, 2009) and edited *Verwaltungshandeln in Politikfeldern* (Opladen: UTB, 2003).

Michael Hill is Emeritus Professor of Social Policy, University of Newcastle upon Tyne, and Visiting Professor at Queen Mary College, University of London and at the University of Brighton. Publications include *Understanding Social Policy* (1980, 8th edition with Z. Irving, Chichester, UK: Wiley-Blackwell, 2009) and *The Public Policy Process* (latest edition Harlow, UK: Longman, 2009).

Carlo Iannello is Associate Professor of Public-Law Institutions at Seconda Università degli Studi di Napoli, Italy. His main field of research is public economic law. Recent publications include: *Poteri pubblici e servizi privatizzati. L'idea di servizio pubblico nella nuova disciplina interna e comunitaria* (Torino: Giappichelli, 2005); and G. Marotta, *I lavori pubblici tra etica e diritto* (Napoli: La scuola di Pitagora editrice, 2008).

Sabine Kuhlmann is Professor of Comparative Public Administration/ Public Administration in Europe at the German University of Administrative Sciences, Speyer, Germany. Her main fields of research and publication are comparative public administration, public sector reforms, local government and evaluation. Her recent publications include *Politik-und Verwaltungsreform in Kontinentaleuropa: subnationaler Institutionenwandel im deutsch-französischen Vergleich* (Baden-Baden: Nomos, 2009).

Martine Long is Maître de Conférences en Droit Public (HDR) at the University of Angers, France, and a member of GRALE. Her field of research is public law in the health and social sectors. Recent publications include: 'Intérêt public local et clause générale de compétence', in N. Kada (ed.), *L'intérêt public local* (Presses Universitaires de Grenoble, 2009);'Le département, chef de file de l'action sociale vers de nouveaux espaces de solidarité', in J.-F. Brisson (ed.), *Les transferts de compétences de l'Etat aux collectivités territoriales* (Paris: L'Harmattan, 2009); 'Les compétences en matière sanitaire et sociale des collectivités territoriales', *Encyclopédie Dalloz des Collectivités Locales* February 2009.

Francesco Longo is Associate Professor of Public and Health Care Management at the Bocconi University of Milan, Italy, and Director of CERGAS (Bocconi's Research Centre for Health and Social Care Management). His research fields are public, health and social care management; public strategy; and public networks governance. He recently edited, with D. Cristofoli, *Strategic Change Management in The Public Sector: A European Case Book* (London: Wiley, 2007).

John McEldowney is Professor of Law at the School of Law, University of Warwick, UK. His research interests include public law, regulation and legal history. His recent publications include a jointly authored textbook on environmental law (Longman Pearson, 2009).

Gérard Marcou is Professor of Public Law at the University Paris 1 Panthéon–Sorbonne, Director of GRALE (Research Network on Local Government in Europe), and Editor of *Annuaire des Collectivités Locales* Paris. His main research fields are comparative public law and comparative regional and local government. He acted as scientific director of the *First Global Report on Decentralization and Local Democracy in the World*, UCLG: (Barcelona: United Cities and Local Governments, World Bank, 2008) (in English, French, Spanish and Catalan – French edition, Paris: L'Harmattan).

Anna Marzanati is Professor of Public Law at the University of Milan–Bicocca, Faculty of Economics, Italy. Her main fields of research are regional and local government law; environmental law; social rights and social care services.

Christoph Reichard is Emeritus Professor of Public Management and a board member of the Institute of Local Government Studies, both at Potsdam University, Germany. His main fields of research are (new) public management, governance issues, public financial management and public personnel. He has published widely in these fields.

Annette Elisabeth Töller is Professor of Public Policy at Fern Universität Hagen, Germany. Her main research fields are environmental policy, Europeanization of public policies, and cooperative approaches to public policy. Publications: *Warum kooperiert der Staat? Kooperative Umweltpolitik im Schatten der Hierarchie* (Baden-Baden: Nomos, 2010)

Hellmut Wollmann is Emeritus Professor of Public Policy and Public Administration at the Social Science Institute of Humboldt-Universität Berlin, Germany, and a member of the scientific council of GRALE. His main interests are comparative local government and administration, and evaluation research. Recent publications: *Reformen in Kommunalpolitik und -verwaltung, England, Schweden, Frankreich und Deutschland im Vergleich* (Wiesbaden: VS Verlag, 2008); *Comparing Local Government Reforms in England, Sweden, France and Germany*, Internet publication available at www.wuestenrot-stiftung.de/download/local-government.

Preface and acknowledgements

This volume is the result of a collective and interdisciplinary effort of researchers from five European countries (France, Germany, Italy, the UK and Norway). The concept of the underlying project emerged from discussions in the Scientific Council of the Paris-based Groupement de Recherche sur l'Administration Locale en Europe (GRALE). In view of the massive changes that the delivery of social and public services has undergone in most European countries, the international group of scholars set out to perform a comparative analysis of these changes and the factors that have shaped them.

The joint work that has produced co-authored chapters was carried forward in a sequence of three research conferences held between 2006 and 2008 in the Villa Vigoni, located at Lago di Como, Italy. Villa Vigoni is a research centre jointly funded by the German and Italian governments. Its programmatic aim is to facilitate discourse and cooperation among European scholars.

Hence our thanks go, first of all, to the Villa Vigoni programme, to the German Research Council (Deutsche Forschungsgemeinschaft, DFG) and to Maison des Sciences de l'Homme (MSH), Paris. Besides the financial and logistical underpinning, the beautifully located villa and its amiable staff provided a unique environment and atmosphere in which to pursue the collective and collegial work.

Further thanks are owed to GRALE, which was instrumental in organizing and co-financing the research conferences and has subsequently generously supported the publication of the volume.

Last but not least, we are grateful to Edward Elgar for publishing this volume.

Hellmut Wollmann
Gérard Marcou
Berlin/Paris, October 2009

1. Introduction
Hellmut Wollmann and Gérard Marcou

BACKGROUND

This book is the final output of a series of workshops organized by GRALE[1] between 2006 and 2008 with major support from the Villa Vigoni programme[2] at the Villa Vigoni (Menaggio, Lake Como, Italy). The research has been extended beyond the limits of the Villa Vigoni programme triad (Italy, France and Germany) to include the UK and Norway as thematically particularly relevant.

IN FOCUS: SOCIAL SERVICES, PUBLIC SERVICES

This book offers an international comparison of local government responsibilities and functions in providing public services to the local population. It examines the provision of both social and economic services by local authorities, mainly city governments. Although these categories of service differ strongly, they have been subject to increased market pressure after a long period under the more or less exclusive responsibility of local government, and when local authorities decided to contract out services to private enterprises. This has determined the sample of services selected for cross-country comparison

Social services are services for people and families. They include child care, long-term care for the elderly and frail, and health services; and they can include basic education, basic cultural amenities (e.g. public libraries) and sports facilities (e.g. swimming pools). Such services are usually financed by budgetary appropriations or social security contributions, and only to a limited extent by user contributions. This is also the case when service delivery is contracted out.

The terminology of economic public services differs from country to country. This may cause confusion but also reflects conceptual differences between countries.

'Public utilities' is a term commonly used in the UK and in the USA.

It focuses on the industrial dimension of the service and the idea of duties imposed on the public authority, whereas services are generally offered by enterprises on a market basis. This notion has been adopted by a number of European countries, notably Italy, where the English expression, translated as *servizi di pubblica utilità*, is, by Law 491/1995, which organizes the regulation of such services, preferred to the classical expression *servizi pubblici*. In France, similar services are called *services publics industriels et commerciaux*; this term relates such services to the broader notion of *service public*, which is central to French public law. In this conception, a *service public* is always a legal competence of a public body to satisfy basic needs. This means that the competent body (central or local government authority) is required to establish, organize, regulate and supervise the service, as when it takes the form of 'public service obligations' imposed on enterprises operating in the market. In Germany, the expression *Daseinsvorsorge* (which can be translated as 'provision for existence') was introduced by Ernst Forsthoff in the 1930s in a context that has limited the possible scope of this notion. Very close in essence to the French notion of *service public*, it has never attained the status of the French term because of the political context in which it appeared. But it has still been used in case law to determine the subject matter and the limits of local government competence. There is nevertheless an important difference: *Daseinsvorsorge* does not include social services, which now derive from the constitutional concept of the 'social state', whereas the French notion of *service public* covers both *services publics administratifs* (which include 'social services' in the above meaning) and *services publics industriels et commerciaux* (see Moderne and Marcou, 2001; on Germany specifically, see Marcou, 2001a). Whatever the conceptualization, economic public services include local public services such as water supply, sewage disposal, energy supply, public transport, and waste collection and treatment.

With the process of European integration, EC law has developed its own concepts in liberalization policy, aiming to establish the single market by removing all barriers to the market, including those in public service sectors still under state control. The concept of 'services of general economic interest' is laid down in Article 106 (2) Treaty on the Functioning of the EU (previously EC Treaty Art.86 (2)), which requires governments to remove all exclusive or special rights and prohibits the establishment of new rights except when the general economic interest makes it necessary to deviate from competition law. However, with the development of the single market and progressive liberalization, the EU (Commission, Court of Justice, member states) has had to face the need to ensure service provision under given conditions, and in the newly competitive framework being established. The directives on electronic communications (2002,

2008), gas and electricity (2003, 2009) and the 2007 regulation on transport reflect this contradiction and the search for an acceptable trade-off between competition and guarantee. The broader notion of 'services of general interest' was later proposed by the European Commission for services not economic in nature that are not subject to competition law. The protocol of the Lisbon Treaty on 'services of general interest' confirms this orientation and supports the role of member states in this field, recognizing their 'exclusive competence' to establish, organize and fund such services. Although the borderline between economic and non-economic services is blurred, it is clear – especially after the Lisbon Treaty – that liberalized public services in the economic field cannot operate in a pure market regime and that member states should regain responsibility for public services of all kinds, albeit depending on the government structure and traditions of each country.

Beyond country differences and political assumptions by the EU, the comparison also reflects the universal nature of the notion of 'public service'. This notion is not specific to French public law, although it has been conceptualized at a much deeper level in French public law than in that of any other country that has endorsed this notion. It has not become obsolete because of public policies that acknowledge the role of market mechanisms in the provision of public services. It reflects much more a basic feature of all modern governments. 'Public service' exists, and can be identified in one way or another, as soon as government acknowledges that it has to achieve a certain level of coverage of collective needs considered as essential, and that that level cannot be attained merely by matching supply and demand on a market. The government may be central, local or even European; the needs considered essential may vary from one country to another, and even more the level of coverage the government considers it has to guarantee, and all this can change over time, but these variations will not change the core; that is, what is in essence a public service. This explains why, even in countries where the legal system does not use the notion of 'public service', the legal regime of services guaranteed by government to citizens is always to some extent specific; that is, it includes some rules or institutions that deviate from the current legal relations between privates (Marcou, 2001b; Prosser, 2005, 2008). It is obvious that the means of providing public services is changing under the influence of liberalizing policies, which such services submit to the market, whereas in the past the public service regime always implied the exclusion of market mechanisms. Also, the coverage area of the public service has become smaller than in the past, but this shift does not invalidate the conceptual and heuristic value of the notion of public service. On the contrary, the new notions introduced by EC law, such as 'public service obligations' and 'universal service' reflect the core idea of the public service as summarized above, albeit in the context of a new economic policy based on the competitive legal order of the European 'single market'. The thesis of the withering away of the *service public* is based on a confusion: the *service public* is considered as an instrument to impose public purposes on private subjects, whereas its meaning is to guarantee the coverage of collective needs based on the requirements of 'social interdependency' (Duguit); the fact that users are facing market behaviours and are induced by the new legal regime to adopt such behaviours will provide no answer to issues of social solidarity and sustainable development. It is therefore wrong to present as a basic change the 'universal service' of EC law as a guarantee for the users, instead of the *service public* as a guarantee for state interests (see Napolitano, 2005, p. 41). The shift to private-law mechanisms, which is not new, is also no argument for the obsolescence of the public service; it has been admitted for a long time that public service duties may be discharged under private-law regimes.

This book will show how local governments have become involved in the services covered here, and why and how they have been induced to give more space to market regulations in the provision of these services. Nevertheless, even in contracting-out procedures or public–private partnerships, they have to keep involved, since they bear the final responsibility for the provision of services, and they are accountable to citizens for that. This explains the reluctance of local governments in all countries reviewed to support privatization policies, since they imply a loss of control on the substance of the service, and why some trends to a return of local governments to the forefront can be observed in several countries.

For the purpose of this research, specific services were selected. Among social services, child care, long-term care and health care were chosen as services with varying local government involvement in health services and a general competence of local government in social care in all countries of the survey, albeit with different degrees of interaction with central or regional governments, and subject to important changes regarding service provision. Among economic services, three have been selected: water supply, waste management and electricity supply. The last is most subject to EU regulations enforcing competition, and also reflects very different starting points in the countries of the survey; the former two are not dependent on networks on a wide scale; they are part of the core responsibilities of municipalities in all countries, although withdrawn from local authorities in the UK several decades ago. Again, we can observe here very different starting points, with a strong municipal public sector in several countries, and on the contrary a traditional involvement of private industrialists in France.

COUNTRY SELECTION

Italy, France, and Germany were selected not only because they were the subject of the Villa Vigoni programme, but also because remarkably few comparative studies of the three countries have been undertaken. This book can therefore fill the gap. The UK/England was included as one of the 'prototypes' both of local government and of social and public service provision. Finally, Norway was included with regard to energy provision because it is a conspicuously 'deviant' case.

HISTORICAL APPROACH

From a historical point of view, the provision of social services and public utilities has been part and parcel of the development of the modern welfare state.

Since the nineteenth century and earlier, responsibility for providing such services was shared at the local level by local authorities and charitable organizations. The growing involvement of local government amounted to an incipient 'local welfare state', which conservatives branded 'municipal socialism'.

With the advance of the modern welfare state, which, largely with a social democratic stamp, made considerable progress after 1945 and peaked during the 1960s and early 1970s, some services were nationalized in certain countries, shifting provision and ownership from local to central government (the most conspicuous cases being electricity, water and health care during the late 1940s in the UK under a Labour government). While other services remained in local government ownership and responsibility, they were increasingly regulated by national legislation and treated as the local level of the national welfare state. In some countries, again most markedly in the UK, social services were delivered almost entirely by local government personnel. Thus, in the advanced postwar welfare states, social services and public utilities were largely 'public sector centred', operated either directly by central government agencies and local authorities or by non-public actors closely related to, if not functionally integrated into, the public sector.

Since the 1980s, this concept and structure of the public sector-centred welfare state have been undermined by various interrelated forces. Neoliberal policies, developed and adopted in the UK after 1979, sought to cut back the expanded and expansive 'social democratic' welfare state; the aim was 'lean government' reduced to 'core functions'. Second, 'new public management' (NPM) concepts, essentially drawn from private sector principles, sought to revamp the traditional hierarchical ('Weberian') welfare state bureaucracy bound by legal rules on the basis of managerialist principles such as cost efficiency and internal flexibility. Third, the public sector focus of service provision was to be overtaken by competitive tendering and 'marketization'. These changes were driven initially by political shifts in national government and the internationally increasingly dominant NPM discourse. From the 1990s they were promoted by drives for EU market liberalization. The ensuing shifts in the operation of social services and public utilities have shown that direct provision by the public sector has been shrinking in favour of competitive 'outsourcing', 'marketization', if not 'asset privatization', to non-public, not-for-profit and commercial organizations and companies.

It has been a sobering experience that 'marketizing' services can raise rather than lower consumer prices and reduce competition between providers rather than increase it by fostering oligopolistic market concentration. This has weakened the role of local authorities as defenders of the public interest against a multitude of providers intent on their own economic objectives. In response, a new conceptual, mental and practical development appears to be gaining momentum to bring the public sector back in by reinforcing its regulatory and instrumental influence and by 'remunicipalizing' service provision. The recent global financial and economic crisis to which national governments, not least the USA, have responded by state interventionism in unprecedented dimensions is likely to redefine and 'bring back in' the role of the public sector in the subnational and local domain as well.

It is this fascinating development of the provision of social services and public utilities paralleling the evolution of the welfare state that has imposed a historical approach on this comparative study, and the relevant shifts, forces and currents to be identified.

INSTITUTIONAL(-IST) APPROACH

In political-science-based 'policy research' it has become conventional wisdom to make a distinction between 'policy, politics and polity'. In this linguistic triad, policy is the content (concepts, programmes, goals etc.) of policy-making. Politics denotes the conflicts and interactions between actors involved in policy-making. Finally, polity is the institutional setting in which politics is carried out and policies are determined and implemented – with a wide understanding of institutions and institutionalization that encompasses not only formal organization and legal regulation, but also informal institutions and actor networks.

In discussing the different sectors of services and public utilities, although chapters in this volume take a broad policy perspective of the subject matter, policy, politics and polity, they focus chiefly on the polity dimension, on the institutionalization of the services and utilities.

ANALYTICAL FRAME

The dependent variable to be identified and explained in examining the institutionalization of service sectors from the developmental perspective comprises institution-building and institutional choice.

In order to conceptualize the explanatory factors (independent variables) in respect of changes or the lack thereof, some help may be gained from the 'neo-institutionalist' debate that has recently attracted the attention of social scientists (see Peters, 1995; Schmidt, 2006 for overviews).

Three of the main factors assumed to influence institutional development are considered:

1. Institutional development is assumed to be influenced by historical institutional givens (traditions, legacies stressed by the 'historical' variant of institutionalism; see Thoenig, 2003) Historical, entrenched institutions and legacies may set the course for institutional development in what has been called 'path-dependence' (see Pierson, 2000).
2. 'Actor-centred' institutionalism (see Scharpf, 1997, 2000) directs the analytical spotlight on actors, actor constellations and coalitions. In analysing and explaining the occurrence or non-occurrence of institutional change, this variant of institutionalism primarily considers the constellation of political, economic and other actors, their interests, policy goals, 'will and skills' that drive their decisions on institution-building/formation/change. The institutional trajectory can be assumed to be strongly influenced, if not radically deflected from its path, if and when a shift (change of government or regime) occurs in the ruling actor constellation that goes hand in hand with a far-reaching change in policy (as in the UK in 1979). More recently, the EU and European Commission have positioned themselves by pushing for market liberalization by the single European market.
3. 'Discursive' institutionalism (see Schmidt, 2002) emphasizes the salience of ideas, or discourses, of the discursive processes and interactions that may mentally and conceptually prepare the ground for institutional change. Discursive institutionalism may serve as a vehicle for transporting dominant international debates (also through institutional isomorphism, see Di Maggio and Powell, 1983). A major

example in our context is the 'new public management' debate, which, by promoting the outsourcing and marketization of services since the 1980s, has had a major influence on national debates (see also Wollmann, 2002).
4. The national and international socioeconomic and budgetary context may weigh heavily on institutional change and development.

No one of these or other factors as identified by the different variants of institutionalism can explain the institutional developments under discussion: a somewhat 'eclectic' explication is needed (Katzenstein and Sil, 2005).[3]

COMPARATIVE APPROACH

The studies presented in this volume are comparative in at least three dimensions. First, in examining the historical development service delivery in the countries under review they take a longitudinal comparative perspective. Second, in examining the differences between national service sectors they adopt a cross-country standpoint. Last, in looking at how service sectors within a country differ, they engage in cross-policy comparison.

The analytical potential of this triple approach seems promising. But the three dimensions plus the multitude of possibly explanatory variables make for such analytical complexity that any rigorous, let alone quasi-experimental, design is out of the question.

Instead of aspiring to a methodologically conclusive comparative logic, a heuristic approach has been adopted in formulating hypotheses on six service sectors in four countries in discussion both within each sector study and in the entire group. Corroboration of findings and interpretations was then sought. The analytical and methodological approach was essentially what might be called 'processual–genetic' in analysing institutionalization processes; it also relates closely to 'figurative analysis' (Verba, 1967), the attempt to identify constellation of factors through 'soft' case studies that can plausibly explain institution-building.

COOPERATION AND CO-AUTHORING IN THE INTERNATIONAL GROUP OF RESEARCHERS

In order to make the best use of the analytical competence and empirical knowledge assembled in the group of researchers from four (respectively five) countries, it was decided that, unlike most similar collective publication projects, which end as country-by-country accounts by individual national rapporteurs, the sector chapters should be prepared and written collectively by author groups composed of researchers from each of the countries.

CONVERGENCE OR DIVERGENCE?

One of the guiding questions of our research was whether the institutional development of the service sectors has shown convergence or divergence.

The convergence hypothesis is supported by the assumption that both national and local decision-making arenas have come under the influence of powerful forces and currents, among which those vaguely subsumed under the terms 'globalization' or 'internationalization' loom large. Such factors may drive national systems towards convergence at both the national and subnational level. As we have seen, this may also be the case with major international (neoliberal) policy shifts, internationally influential modernization discourses (NPM), and the EU moves towards market liberalization.

By contrast, the divergence hypothesis may be grounded particularly in country-specific institutional, cultural and other traditions that exercise a 'path-dependent' influence on institutional development by fostering institutional inertia, resistance to change or even adaptation on the basis of inherited structures and discourses.

The following chapters seek to provide empirically supported answers to this guiding question.

OVERVIEW

After the preceding introductory chapter by the editors, Chapter 2 (Wollmann, Balboni, Gaudin and Marcou) maps out the vertical, multi-level intergovernmental setting in Italy, France, Germany and the UK, setting the institutional stage for the coming chapters on policy and identifying the levels and actors to which functions and responsibilities are assigned in the policy and service fields under consideration. The key features of the regional/meso level are discussed in order to shed light on the vertical, intergovernmental dynamics. Second, the territorial and functional profile of local government is outlined, including variance in territorial reform (amalgamation/consolidation versus integrated intermunicipal cooperation/*intercommunalité*).

Chapter 3 (Kuhlmann and Fedele) addresses the modernization of municipal administration inspired by new public management, examining both internal and external reforms. In the internal dimension, the reorganization of administrative structures, the introduction of performance management and new steering, controlling and accounting instruments are considered. In the external dimension, the reorganization of local service provision is discussed in relation to private and non-profit actors and the resulting 'fringing out' of local government activities and 'satellitization' of local government structures. The chapter puts particular emphasis on the impacts and effects of these reforms in the three countries concerned.

Chapter 4 (Hill, Long, Marzanati and Bönker) deals with an area of policy that displays strong similarities across the four countries (e.g. similar approaches in child protection involving the courts and key roles for public agencies; a low level of child care provision in the early years with strong independent sectors; strong emphasis on pre-school education, with the main institutional provision linked with the regular education system, except in Germany).

In many respects, dissimilarities arise from differences in local government systems and/or the relationship between central and local government, such as relatively uniform systems in France and the UK (with different kinds of control and monitoring in the two countries, and stronger emphasis on this kind of service in France), variations between *Länder* in Germany, and greater autonomy at the regional and local levels as a source of diversity in Italy. The strong central policy drive towards pre-school education and child care to facilitate parental labour force participation is causing some convergence. In this respect, developments in Italy, the UK and Germany may be reducing differences between their systems and that of France (action against *de facto* diversity in Italy despite central legislation, increased central control of local authorities in the UK, federal government intervention in family policy in Germany).

Chapter 5 (Bönker, Hill and Marzanati) traces changes in the provision of long-term care in England, France, Germany and Italy since the early 1990s. While policy reforms have differed substantially, a common trend towards centralization and marketization/commercialization is apparent. The role of central government and/or social insurance funds in financing and regulating services has increased, as long-term care has become too important an issue for economic, social and political reasons to be left to local government. On the other hand, commercial service providers have gained ground, partly replacing public or non-profit providers or meeting the increasing demand for services from ageing populations.

Chapter 6 (Grunow, Longo and Long) discusses health services in Italy, France and Germany. After describing the rather similar starting conditions in the three countries, the authors examine development paths towards the decentralized, tax-based public system in Italy; the centralized, insurance-based public system in France; and the insurance-based, mixed system of self-organization and public responsibility in Germany. Service production and delivery design are influenced by financing systems, the system of medical and paramedical professions, and service organization (outpatient, inpatient). Despite different path-dependencies, convergence is apparent in the variously exercised, increased central control over the system to curb health expenditure. In contrast, there is notable diversification of service delivery agencies and actors, and regional governments in Italy have broader responsibility. In all three countries these changes are propelled by the health systems' ongoing financial problems.

Chapter 7 (Dreyfus, Ianello, Toeller and McEldowney) considers the institutional framework for waste management in four countries – France, Germany, Italy and the UK in a development that has been increasingly influenced by the EU. The main focus is on how local agencies and institutions are coping with new arrangements that have transformed their role through public contracts, private finance initiatives and other devices. These changes come at a time when public perceptions about waste have become more acute.

Waste management accordingly places local authorities at the apex of control in contributing to environmental protection and also influences the way in which local authorities deliver goods and services. The outcome of waste management strategies is to revitalize the role of local authorities as pivotal actors in making policy, enforcing good practice and managing resources.

Chapter 8 (Wollmann, Baldersheim, Citroni, Marcou and McEldowney) focuses on the role of local government in energy supply in France, Germany, Italy, the UK and Norway. The starting conditions for local energy supply differ strongly, ranging from monopolistic local authority ownership and operation of local power plants (the 'deviant' case of Norway included for this reason) to early outsourcing of local energy supply in France. Nevertheless, energy supply has commonly been regarded as a local service on a protected local market or even as a local monopoly. Since the 1990s, the local energy sector has experienced profound changes, largely driven by the EU market liberalization policy designed to open national energy markets, particularly by ensuring discrimination-free and competitive access to distribution and transmission networks for all providers. Local distribution areas have of course been affected. Despite remaining institutional differences, there has been a general trend towards universal access under a concept of electricity as a commodity, the quality and price of which is determined by national and international markets. The question is whether splitting up national energy monopolies to build up a market will give a new opportunity to local government, which has lost control over electricity in countries such as the UK and France. The problems caused by liberalization might offer government at all levels the opportunity for a 'comeback', as in Germany moves towards some 're-communalization' of local energy provision (through a renewed expansion of the traditional municipality-owned multi-utility companies, *Stadtwerke*) seem to indicate. Whether such re-entry and 'comeback' of the public/municipal sector in energy provision is a marginal and passing phenomenon or a momentous and permanent change remains to be seen.

Chapter 9 (Citroni) discusses water management in Italy, France and Germany, describing the history, organizational structures and legal framework of the sector. For each country, specific issues defining the nature and evolution of water service politics are addressed, including public–public (intercommunal) partnerships, public–private partnerships, principal–agent relationships in concession contract management, corruption and environmental protection. On the whole, the pendulum in all three countries has swung from private management in the nineteenth century to municipalization in the twentieth century and back to privatization, combined, however, with persisting concern for water as a 'special' good (merit or common good) that should not be left to the market as such. Conspicuous differences between countries exist in the instruments and success with which local authorities control service management units.

Chapter 10 (Grossi, Marcou and Reichard) examines the different organizational forms of local government service delivery. One major focus is 'corporatization' in Germany and Italy; that is, corporations still fully or partly owned by municipalities but which enjoy organizational, legal and financial autonomy. The authors also discuss the consequences of corporatization for steering and controlling municipal holdings, and argue that the existing structures and mechanisms of public corporate governance are insufficient for effective control. However, this trend has little relevance for France, where the municipal public sector has always been smaller because of the widespread and ancient practice of contracting out major municipal economic services (water supply, gas and electricity supply, public transport, and even street lighting) to private companies, and the postwar establishment of national public enterprises. Nevertheless, French law recognizes two types of corporatization for municipal services within the public sector: the public corporation (*régie personnalisée*) and the 'local mixed economy company' (SEML), recently supplemented by companies in the full ownership of local authorities. Over and above the variety of solutions adopted, this demonstrates the attempt in all three countries to introduce industrial and entrepreneurial dynamics to the local public sector.

Chapter 11 (Wollmann and Marcou) offers the editors' comparative conclusions. Taking up the volume's guiding question as to whether the developments have been convergent of divergent from sector to sector and country to country, they argue that the chapters of the book invite ambivalent, if not contradictory conclusions. On the one hand, the (advanced welfare state-typical) public/municipal sector-centred model of public service delivery has been profoundly impacted by the combined onslaught of neo-liberal concepts ('lean government'), NPM tenets ('marketization') and EU policy ('market liberalization'). Hence, on the one hand, a (convergent) 'mega-trend' is apparent from public sector-based service to 'privatized' service provision, be it through 'formal' ('organizational'), privatization ('corporatization'), or wholesale ('material', asset) privatization. One the other hand, within and notwithstanding these general trends, there is a significant divergence between the countries under study in developments on the 'micro' scale due to country-specific historical, institutional and political factors and particularities.

Recently, reflecting the sobered assessment of effected privatization of public services, particularly by way of wholesale material/asset privatization, some rethinking of this strategy had set in among local authorities concerned, as is evidenced for instance, by German local authorities recently embarking upon the 'remunicipalization' of previously sold off public utilities.

Finally linking up with the 'governance' debate, the summary chapter discusses whether and how the role of ('traditional') local government has been effected by the pluralization and 'satellitization' of 'governance-type' institutions and actors in the wake of the formal of material privatization of service provision.

NOTES

1. GRALE (Groupement de Recherches sur l'Administration Locale en Europe) is a multi-disciplinary scientific network on local government and local public policies, backed by the French CNRS and a partnership of public institutions and enterprises, and located at the University Paris 1 Panthéon-Sorbonne, which is also a member of this partnership.
2. The Villa Vigoni programme is funded by the three 'anchor' countries: Italy, Germany (Deutsche Forschungsgemeinschaft, DFG) and France (Maison de Sciences d'Homme, MSH). Additional financial support for the conferences came from Groupement de Recherches sur l'Administration Locale en Europe (GRALE).
3. For the application of a similar analytic frame for an international comparative study of public sector reforms see Wollmann (2003, p. 231).

REFERENCES

Di Maggio, Paul J. and Walter W. Powell (1983), 'The iron cage revisited: institutional isomorphism and collective rationality in organizional fields', *American Sociological Review*, **38** (2), 147–60.
Katzenstein, Peter and Rudra Sil (2005), 'What is analytic eclecticism and why do we need it? A pragmatist perspective on problems and mechanisms in the study of world politics', accessed at www.allacademic.com/meta/p41957_index.html.
Moderne, Franck and Gérard Marcou (eds) (2001), *L'idée de service public dans les Etats de l'Union européenne*, Paris: L'Harmattan.
Marcou, Gérard (2001a), 'Les services publics en droit allemand', in Frank Moderne and Gérard Marcou (eds), *L'idée de service public dans les Etats de l'Union européenne*, Paris: L'Harmattan, pp. 83–192.
Marcou, Gérard (2001b), 'De l'idée de service public au service d'intérêt général', in Frank Moderne and Gérard Marcou (eds), *L'idée de service public dans les Etats de l'Union européenne*, Paris: L'Harmattan.
Peters, Guy B. (1995), 'Political institutions, old and new', in Robert Goodin and Hans-Dieter Klingemann (eds), *A New Handbook of Political Science*, Oxford: Oxford University Press.
Pierson, Paul (2000), 'Increasing returns. Path dependence and the study of politics', *American Political Science Review*, **94** (2), 251–67.
Prosser, Tony (2008), 'Self-regulation, co-regulation and the Audio-Visual Media Services Directive', *Journal of Consumer Policy*, **31** (1), 99–113.
Scharpf, Fritz W. (1997), *Games Real Actors Play. Actor-centred Institutionalism in Policy Research*, Boulder, CO: Westview Press.
Scharpf, Fritz W. (2000), *Interaktionsformen. Akteurzentrierter Instititutionalismus in der Politikforschung*, Opladen, Germany: Leske + Budrich.
Schmidt, Vivien A. (2002), 'Does discourse matter in the politics of welfare state adjustment? ', *Comparative Political Studies*, **35** (2), 168–93.
Schmidt, Vivien A. (2006), 'Give peace a chance. Reconciling four (not three) "New Institutionalisms"', paper presented to annual meeting of APSA August/ September 2008.
Thoenig, Jean Claude (2003), 'Institutional theories and public institution: traditions and appropriateness', in Guy B. Peters and Jon Pierre (eds), *Handbook of Public Administration*, London: Sage, pp. 127–37.
Verba, Sidney (1967), 'Some dilemmas in comparative research', *World Politics*, **20** (1), 111–22.
Wollmann, Hellmut (2002), 'Verwaltungspolitische Reformdiskurse und -verläufe im internationalen Vergleich', in Klaus König (ed.), *Deutsche Verwaltung an der Wende zum 21. Jahrhundert*, Baden-Baden, Germany: Nomos, pp. 489–524.
Wollmann, Hellmut (2003), 'Evaluation and public sector reform: trends, potentials and limits in international perspective', in Hellmut Wollmann (ed.), *Evaluation in Public Sector Reform*, Cheltenham, UK and Northampton, MA, USA: Edward Elgar, pp. 231–59.

2. The multi-level institutional setting in Germany, Italy, France and the UK: a comparative overview

Hellmut Wollmann, Enzo Balboni, Jean-Pierre Gaudin and Gérard Marcou

This chapter reviews the multi-level institutional architecture of Germany, France, Italy and the UK. This 'mapping' provides institutional orientation and guidance for the following studies on the provision of public and social services in the four countries under discussion.

GERMANY

Federal Level

Germany's two-tier federal system comprises the federal level and 16 *Länder* or states, including three city states (Berlin, Hamburg, Bremen). The *Länder* have an average population of 5.2 million, ranging from 18 million (North Rhine–Westphalia) to 550 000 (Bremen) (see Table 2.1, line 1).

Under the Federal Constitution (*Grundgesetz*) of 1949, the 'social state' (*Sozialstaat*) revolves around 'human dignity' (*Würde des Menschen*) and the 'equality' (*Gleichheit*) of every citizen, and is at the core of the 'democratic and social federal state' (Article 20).[1] Federal legislation is constitutionally mandated (Article 72 II) to 'ensure equal living conditions (*gleichwertige Lebensbedingungen*) on the territory of the Republic'. This has been widely interpreted as laying the foundations for what has been termed a 'unitary federal state' (*unitarischer Bundesstaat*) (Hesse, 1967).

Under the complicated constitutional distinction between exclusive legislative competence (assigned either to the federation or the *Länder*) and concurrent (*konkurrierende*) legislative powers (which the federal level has generally come to exercise), the federal level has attained and held the primacy in legislation and policy-making. However, federal predominance is somewhat curbed by a vertical division of power and 'checks and balances'. For example,

Table 2.1 Intergovernmental structure (data for 2006–9)

County		Levels	Number	Population ⌀
1 **Germany**	Federal	Federal states (*Länder*)	16[a] (of which 3 city states: Berlin, Hamburg, Bremen)	Average 5.2 million
	Local	(*two-tier*) counties (= *Kreise*)	323	170 000
		municipalities (*within counties*) (= *kreisangehörige Gemeinden*)	12 196[b]	6 690[c]
		(*single-tier*) cities (= *kreisfreie Städte*)	116	
	Intercommunal	Intercommunal bodies	1 708 'administrative unions' (= *Verwaltungsgemeinschaften, Ämter* etc.[d]	
2 **France**	Local	*Régions*	21 + Corsica + 4 (*d'outre-mer*)	2.3 million[h]
		Départements	96 + 4 (*d'outre-mer*)	550 000
		Communes	36 569[e]	1 560
	Intercommunal	*Intercommunalité*	12 840 *syndicats*[f] 2 601 *communautés* (*à fiscalité propre*)[g]	
3 **Italy**	'Quasi-federal'	*Regioni*	20 (15 *statuto ordinario* + 5 *statuto speciale*)	2.9 million[h]
	Local	*Province*	103	570 000
		Comuni	8 101	7 270
	Intercommunal	Intercommunal bodies	356 *comunità montane* (made up of 4201 *comuni*)	32 700
			278 *unioni di comuni* (made up of 1240 *comuni*)	16 700
			Numerous *consorzi* and *conveni*	

16

4	UK	'Quasi-federal'	Regions		Scotland, Wales, Northern Ireland	Scotland 9%, Wales 5% England 85% of total UK population
		Local	(two-tier) counties	34		720000
			Districts/boroughs (within counties)	238		140000
			London boroughs (within Greater London Authority)	33 + Corporation of London		
			Single-tier authorities		36 metropolitan councils 47 unitary authorities	170000

Notes:
a Varying in size between North Rhine–Westphalia with 18 million inhabitants and Bremen (city-state) with 550000 inhabitants.
b Of which over 75% have fewer than 5000 inhabitants.
c In North Rhine–Westphalia : ∅ 45 000 inhabitants, in Rhineland–Palatinate: ∅ 1700 inhabitants.
d In Rhineland–Palatinate 95% of the municipalities are affiliated with an intercommunal body (such as *Verwaltungsgemeinschaft*), in Bavaria 62%, but in North Rhine–Westphalia and Hessen none.
e Of which 93% have fewer than 3500 inhabitants.
f As of 1 January 2009 comprising *syndicats à vocation unique*, SIVU; *syndicats à vocation multiple*, SIVOM, *syndicats mixtes or syndicats 'à la carte'*.
g As of 1 January 2009: 16 *communautés urbaines*, 174 *communautés d'agglomération*, 2406 *communautés de communes*, 5 *syndicats d'agglomération nouvelle*.
h Varying in size between 124000 (Valle Aosta) and 9.5 million inhabitants (Lombardie).

Source: Mainly Dexia (2008), own compilation + calculation, own table (Wollmann).

a constitutional peculiarity of Germany's federal system enables *Länder* governments to participate directly in federal legislation and policy-making through the upper chamber of parliament, the Federal Council (*Bundesrat*) (Wollmann and Bouckaert, 2006; Wachendorfer-Schmidt, 2004).

While the federation dominates in legislation and national policy-making, it is constitutionally almost entirely barred from maintaining field offices at the subnational level[2] (another speciality of the German federal system). As a result, federal public servants constitute only 12 per cent of the entire public sector workforce while almost 90 per cent are employed by the subnational levels: 53 per cent by the *Länder* and 35 per cent by local authorities (see Table 2.2, line 1).

Länder

The *Länder* hold exclusive legislative powers in education, police and local government, including local territorial reform. In a recent reform of the federal system (under the heading 'federalism reform I') designed to 'disentangle' intergovernmental decision-making, the *Länder* traded in some Federal Council-based veto powers in the federal legislative process for a significant extension of their exclusive legislative powers with respect, for instance, to universities, *Land* and local government personnel systems, and practical everyday matters such as shop opening hours. These constitutional changes have been hailed by some and criticized by others as a departure from the traditional 'homogeneous' federalism and the overture to a 'heterogeneous' or 'competitive' federalism (*Wettbewerbsföderalismus*) (see Wollmann and Bouckaert, 2006, p. 29).

Due to the vertical functional division between legislation, exercised predominantly by the federation, and administration, almost exclusively in the hands of the *Länder* and local authorities, a significant degree of functional interlocking and interdependence between the federal and *Länder* levels has ensued (see Benz, 2005), often referred to as 'cooperative federalism' (*kooperativer Föderalismus*), involving negotiation between multiple vertical and horizontal actor networks (*Verhandlungsföderalismus*). This institutionally 'untidy' situation at the federal/*Länder* interface has been characterized as 'co-financing' (*Mischfinanzierung*) and 'co-administration' (*Mischverwaltung*) and conceptualized as 'policy interdependence' (*Politikverflechtung*, Scharpf, et al., 1976).

Local Government Levels

In 2006, Germany's two-tier local government structure (see Table 2.1) comprised:

Table 2.2 Public employment by levels of government (in %)

Country	Central/federal 85	94	05	Regional/Land 85	94	05	Local 85	94	05	Special sector 85	94	05	Distribution within local level (100%)	
1 Germany	9.9	11.6	**12.0**	55.6	51.0	**53.0**	34.5	38.1	**35.0**				Municipalities	37.2
													County-free cities	32.8
													Counties	25.6
													Intermunicipal	4.7
2 France	54.9	48.7	**51.0**				27.1	30.7	**30.0**				*Régions*	0.7
											Hôpitaux		*Départements*	16.3
										18.0	20.6	**19.0**	*Communes*	68.7
													Intermunicipal	10.3
3 Italy	63.0	**54.7**				**3.8**		14.0	**13.6**				*Province*	13.0
											Aziende		*Comuni*	87.0
											Sanitarie Locali			
										17.0	19.0	**20.3**		
											Enti pubblici			
												7.6		

19

Table 2.2 (continued)

Country	Central/federal 85	94	05	Regional/Land 85	94	05	Local 85	94	05	Special sector 85	94	05	Distribution within local level (100%)	
5 UK	21.9	21.4	16.8				55.0	53.0	56.0	National Health Service 17.6	20.8	26.0	Counties Metropolitan Councils London boroughs Unitaries	36.0 25.6 12.0 19.0

Sources: Data from Dexia (2006), pp. 202 and 167; Dexia (2008), p. 64; data for 1985: Lorenz and Wollmann (1999), p. 505; for Italy 2007: Ministero dell'economia e delle finanze, conto annuale 2008, for distribution between *province* and *comuni* courtesy Luigi Bobbio, data for distribution between counties etc. for England 2004, Wilson and Game (2006), p. 280, own compilation + calculation, own table (Wollmann).

- 12 312 (two-tier) municipalities (*kreisangehörige Gemeinden*, municipalities 'within counties'), with an average population of 6690;
- 323 (two-tier) counties (*Kreise*) – averaging some 200 000 inhabitants;
- 116 (single-tier) 'county-free' cities (*kreisfreie Städte*, combining county and municipal functions like English single-tier 'county boroughs').

Territorial Reforms and Intermunicipal Bodies

During the 1960s and 1970s, the German *Länder* embarked upon territorial reforms on the county and municipal levels in line with the contemporary wave of territorial reform particularly in England and Sweden. The German *Länder*, being solely responsible for local government matters, shared a common 'carrot and stick' approach, initiating the reform drive with a 'participatory' and 'voluntary' phase during which the views, cooperation and agreement of local authorities were sought. Where their consent was obtained, the *Land* government introduced the planned reforms by, as it were, coercive legislation.

The *Länder* adopted two different strategies (see Wollmann, 2004).

In some, for instance North Rhine–Westphalia, the large-scale amalgamation of municipalities produced local authorities with an average population of some 40 000. In opting for large municipalities, these *Länder* adopted what has been termed the 'North European' pattern (see Norton, 1994, pp. 40 ff.). Most *Länder*, by contrast, opted for a 'two-pronged' strategy providing for little or no amalgamation of the municipalities while establishing a new layer of intermunicipal bodies (*Verwaltungsgemeinschaften, Ämter* etc.) in which, again in a 'carrot and stick' approach, small municipalities were induced to obtain the administrative resources they lacked. Rhineland–Palatinate offers a good example, where municipalities have an average population of 2800 inhabitants and 97 per cent belong to an intermunicipal body. After German Unification in 1990, four out of five of the newly established East German *Länder* also retained small municipalities and introduced a layer of intermunicipal bodies, again in 'carrot and stick' fashion.

Recently, some East German *Länder* have begun to reverse this reform strategy, abolishing intermunicipal bodies and establishing territorially enlarged, 'unified' municipalities (*Einheitsgemeinden*). The reason has been growing concern about the lacking political and operational viability of intermunicipal bodies; they are judged to have produced 'institutional overcrowding' and economically inordinate coordination and transaction costs, while the small member of municipalities have been steadily bleeding dry politically and demographically. The German *Länder* thus appear to be intent on further local government amalgamation (for details and further references see Wollmann, 2010).

Functions

German local government traditionally follows a 'dual-task' model, with local authorities performing both local self-government functions and tasks delegated to them by the state (that is, the *Land*).

On the one hand, the delegation modality has widened the functional scope of local authorities, encouraging *Länder* to reduce the number of local field offices and to retreat to some extent from the local administrative space by transferring further public functions to the local authorities (see Kuhlmann, 2009a, pp. 119 ff., 2009b). On the other hand, it has had the problematic effect of making local authorities, in the conduct of delegated business, subject to comprehensive (merits/opportunity) technical supervision (*Fachaufsicht*) – and merely legal supervision (*Rechtsaufsicht*) by state authorities, thus almost integrating them into state administration and, thus, to a certain degree 'etatizing' them (*verstaatlichen*) (see Wollmann, 2008a, pp. 33 ff., 2008b, pp. 38 ff.). Of the local government

Table 2.3 *Subnational public expenditure in 2005 by economic function (in %)*

Function		Germany[a]	France	Italy[b]	UK[c]
1	General public services	11.4	19.2	14.6	8.1
2	Social protection	32.2	15.8	4.6	29.0
3	Education	11.0	16.2	8.3	30.0
4	Health	1.8	0.6	43.0	0.0
5	Economic affairs	21.0	13.0	14.0	8.2
6	Culture, recreation	8.9	10.2	3.0	3.3
7	Housing	12.1	15.2	4.7	5.9
8	Public order	6.2	2.8	1.5	10.0
9	Environmental protection	0.0	6.9	4.6	4.5
	Total 100%	100.0	100.0	100.0	100.0

Notes:
[a] Germany: municipalities + counties (without *Länder*).
[b] Italy: *comuni, province* and *regioni*.
[c] UK: two-tier county and district/borough levels as well as single-tier unitary authorities.

Source: Data from Dexia (2008), own compilation + calculation, own table (Wollmann).

functions dealt with in this volume, the provisions of social services have traditionally been writ large (see Table 2.3, line 2 for a somewhat rough indicator).

The provision of social services has traditionally been a prime responsibility of local government that can be traced back to medieval times. Under the so-called 'subsidiarity principle', rooted in nineteenth-century Catholic social teaching and confirmed by the Federal Social Assistance Act of 1961, local authorities largely bear an 'enabling' responsibility (to use current NPM terminology), with personal social services (elderly care, kindergartens etc.) being primarily delivered by non-profit organizations (so-called 'free welfare organizations', *freie Wohlfahrtsverbände*) (see Bönker and Wollmann, 2006, 2008; Bönker, Hill and Marzanati, Chapter 4 in this volume). In a consequent shift of policy under the 1994 Federal Care Insurance Act, the provision of care for the frail and disabled has been opened to market competition with private/commercial providers now increasingly entering this market.

In the provision of health services, the role of the local authorities is all but minimal as Germany's health care system is premised on a ('Bismarckian') contribution-based insurance scheme under which primary (outpatient) health care is essentially delivered by private general practitioners, while secondary (inpatient) health care is provided by hospitals operated by a whole array of institutions, including cities and counties. For the rest, local authorities, particularly counties and county-free cities, are the site of health offices (*Gesundheitsämter*), responsible for epidemic disease prevention, food control and preventive health measures. By and large, however, the operational and financial involvement of local authorities tends to be low (see Table 2.3, line 4) (see Chapter 6 in this volume).

Furthermore, since the nineteenth century, municipalities have been deeply involved in the production and supply of public utilities (*Daseinsvorsorge*), including water, sewage disposal, waste management, public transport and energy (see Wollmann, 2003). In the past, public utilities were predominantly provided (directly or indirectly) by local authorities themselves, particularly in the organizational form of (municipally owned) 'city works' (*Stadtwerke*). In a recent development, also prompted by EU market liberalization policies, the provision of public utilities has been increasingly corporatized, outsourced, or even, under budgetary pressure, sold entirely to private companies (asset privatization) (see Chapter 10 in this volume). There are recent indications of a trend, for instance in the energy sector, towards remunicipalization, with *Stadtwerke* staging a 'comeback' (see Chapters 8 and 11 in this volume).

In sum, German local government has a comparatively broad,

Table 2.4 Subnational expenditure in 2005

	Germany			France			Italy			UK	
	Munici-palities[a]	counties	Land	Com-munes	Départe-ments	Régions	Comuni	Province	Regioni	Single-tier[b]	Counties
1 Per capita expenditure (€)	1498	314	3150	1211	790	286	1040	200	2320	3930	
2 Total subnational expenditure per capita (€)	4967 (without Länder) 1802			2286			3590 (without regioni) 1240			3930	
3 Level expenditure in % of total public expenditure	11.7	2.4	24.6	8.2	5.4	1.9	8.8	1.6	19.6	29.5	
4 Subnational expenditure in % of total public expenditure	38.7 (without Länder) 14.1			15.5			30.2 (without regioni) 10.4			29.5	
5 GNP per capita (€)	27200			27300			24200			29600	

Notes:
[a] Municipalities (within counties, kreisangehörige Gemeinden) + county-free cities (kreisfreie Städte).
[b] Single-tier local authorities (unitaries and so on) + two-tier districts, boroughs.

Source: Data from Dexia (2008), own compilation + calculation, own table (Wollmann).

multifunctional profile. Average per capita spending by municipalities (including county-free cities) amounts to €1500, notably higher than in French *communes* (at €1211) and very much more than in Italian *comuni* (€1040) (see Table 2.4).[3]

Personnel

Local government personnel constitute 35 per cent of the total public sector workforce as compared to the *Länder* with 53 per cent and the federal level with 12 per cent (see Table 2.2, line 1). The fact that county-free cities and counties combined employ almost 60 per cent of all local

Table 2.5 Development of total number of public sector personnel by level of government over time (in %, respective period in parentheses)

Country	Central/ federal	Regional/ Land	Special sector	Local	Total public sector personnel
1 Germany	−24	−18		West German local authorities: −30.0[a] East German local authorities: −53.3	−23
	(91/04)	(91/04)		(91/04)	(91/04)
2 France	+7		+15[c]	+24.0	+13
	(94/03)		(94/03)	(94/03)	(94/03)
3 Italy	−11		+5[d]	−16.0[b]	−7
	(92/04)		(92/04)	(92/04)	(92/04)
4 UK	−36		+16[e]	−5.0	−4
	(90/03)		(90/03)	(90/03)	(90/03)

Notes:
[a] Data from Kuhlmann and Röber (2006), p. 101.
[b] *Regioni, province, comuni* (Dexia, 2006, p. 167).
[c] *Hôpitaux publics*.
[d] *Aziende Sanitarie Locali e enti ospedalieri* (local health agencies and hospital units).
[e] National Health Service (NHS).

Source: Data from Dexia (2006), own compilation + calculation, own table (Wollmann).

government personnel shows the salient role they play as the 'workhorses' of local government.

Since the early 1990s, local government personnel have seen dramatic reductions that reflect the financial straits of local authorities and the determination of local politicians to cut costs. While cutbacks in West German *Länder* amounted up to 30 per cent between 1991 and 2004, the figure was no less than 53 per cent in East German *Länder*, where, following the restructuring of public administration and local government after 1990, an 'avalanche' of personnel from the former German Democratic Republic's state administration and state economy had to be absorbed by local authorities.[4]

FRANCE

Central Government

Historically, France offered an example of a unitary ('Jacobinist') and centralist ('Napoleonic') state (*république une et indivisible*) in which Paris was the uncontested national hub of policy-making and where public tasks were essentially carried out by the vertically organized state administration. The 89 *départements* and some 36000 *communes* (*collectivités territoriales*) at the local government level were under comprehensive supervision (*tutelle*) by *préfets* appointed by the central government. However, until the First World War, local government played a far from minor role in the performance of government functions, and local expenditure was even higher (compared with central government expenditure) than in the 1950s. Specific to the French case is that administrative developments generated by the new public functions have been absorbed by the state administration or withdrawn from local government, or subjected to pervasive central government control even where although local government has taken the initiative (e.g. in social assistance, education, roads). The development of the welfare state and the leading role assumed by the State in the economy have consolidated this evolution (Bernard, 1968; Bourjol, 1975; Delorme and André, 1983). The constitution of the Fifth Republic of 5 October 1958 upholds the unitary, centralist and 'republican' tradition of government in proclaiming that '*La France est une république indivisible . . ., démocratique et sociale. Elle assure l'égalité devant la loi de tous les citoyens*' (Article 1).

Two waves of decentralization (1982–6 and 2003–04) have profoundly changed French intergovernmental structures (Kuhlmann, 2009b, pp. 82 ff.).

In 1982, 22 regions (*régions*, with Corsica becoming a *sui generis* local government in 1991) were introduced as a third, upper level of local self-government (*collectivités territoriales*). There was agreed from the outset that *régions* should be placed on the same legal footing as *départements* and *communes* without giving them any institutionally 'elevated' position, let alone any sort of federal status.

The *préfets* heading state administration at the level of the *département* have been deprived of their power of *a priori* supervision (*tutelle*) of local government bodies. In several steps, they have received full authority over subnational branches and offices of state administration (*services extérieurs*), which have lost in substance through several waves of personnel transfer to *départements* and *régions* and whose functions have been redesigned (see Hoffmann-Martinot, 2003, pp. 160 ff.).

A crucial component of the second decentralization reform has been the constitutional amendment of 2003 that explicitly recognized that the French Republic is 'decentrally organized',[5] a rather symbolic change considering the previous wording of article 72 of the constitution and constitutional jurisprudence before and after this amendment (Marcou, 2005).

Whereas the general competence clause had already been recognized at all local self-government levels (*commune*: 1884; *département*: 1926; *région*: 1986), the constitutional amendment of 2003 has also introduced a subsidiarity-like provision, according to which local governments are 'entitled to take all decisions on tasks that can be better performed at their level' (Art. 72, par. 3). This enables several local government units to take up a certain task not assigned to a specific authority at the same time and side by side. Following the same organizational logic, no local government level, including the *régions*, can exercise oversight over another level (*non-tutelle*).[6]

The amendment has provided a constitutional guarantee for the regulatory power (*pouvoir réglementaire*) of local government authorities to carry out their responsibilities. More controversial was the possibility given to local governments for regulatory experimentation, giving them the power to replace legislative provisions by local regulations. This could endanger the principle of the unity of the law and the principle of equality before the law. However, this possibility, which is in any case conditional on specific enabling legislation, has not been used except for government reform of the minimum income allowance, for example for measures applicable only temporarily to a beneficiary.

Notwithstanding the two rounds of decentralization (*Acte I* and *Acte II*), 51 per cent of public sector personnel are still state employees (see Table 2.2, line 2). The French state still appears to embrace the principle (and 'Napoleonic' legacy) of 'carrying out its policies directly on the local level' (Marcou, 2004, p. 239).

Régions

The 22 *régions métropolitaines* and 4 *régions outre-mer* (in France and overseas) with an average population of 2.4 million are responsible for regional economic development, secondary school (*lycée*) construction and upkeep, and regional public transport. Moreover, the regions play an important role in co-programming and co-financing local projects financed by EU structural funds and in partnership with the French state (*contrats de projets Etat-région*). Per capita expenditure amounts to an average €286 (as compared to €1211 by *communes*; see Table 2.4, line 1), most of it capital investment (see Dexia, 2008, p. 309). By the end of 2009, *région* personnel, quite limited until 2006, will on average have tripled with the transfer of about 43 000 from the ministry of education (Doligé, 2007; Kuhlmann, 2009a, p. 95).

Départements

In the wake of decentralization in 1982 (*Acte I*), the 96 *départements*, with an average population of 630 000, were the main addressees and beneficiaries of devolution. Primarily social service provision (*aide sociale légale*), previously in the charge of *département* state administration, was transferred to the departmental self-government level and council (*conseil général*) and council-elected *president*. When in 1988 the *Revenu Minimum d'Insértion* (RMI), a new social benefit scheme for the elderly, was introduced, the *départements* were put in charge of implementing the scheme; it was extended in 2004 to labour-market-related *insertion* activities (see also Bönker, Hill and Marzanati, Chapter 4 in this volume, for details, see also Wollmann, 2008a, pp. 428 ff.). Social policy has consequently become a prime responsibility of the *départements* (see also Table 2.3, line 2).[7]

While, thus, the *départements* have been assigned crucial and growing responsibilities in social policy, they have relatively little to do with health, with the exception of specific tasks such as mother and child health protection (see Table 2.3, line 4) due to the specificity of the French health system (see Chapter 6 in this volume). Public hospitals constitute a separate structure, employing 19 per cent of the public sector personnel (see Table 2.2, line 2).

While benefit and service entitlement is, in principle, regulated by national legislation, since 1983 the *départements* have regulatory powers (*pouvoir réglementaire*) of their own (see Kuhlmann, 2009b, p. 84) by virtue of which each *département*, through its elected council (*conseil général*), can modify the entitlement scheme to be applied on its territory; the *département*'s own regulation must not fall below national criteria, but may go beyond them (but not for RMI). As a result, noticeable differences and disparities in social assistance have emerged between *départements*. This has triggered a debate about the compatibility of decentralized decision-making by way of *département*-specific *règlements* with its potential for interregional disparities and the constitutional – and traditional 'republican' (*républicain*) – imperative of equality (*égalité*) (see Hassenteufel and Loncle-Moriceau, 2003).[8]

The devolution of social policy responsibilities from the state to the *département* self-government and the *conseils généraux* in 1982 unleashed a rapid expansion of administrative units and professional personnel, most of whom state employees from the state units in the *département* and people already employed for budgetary purposes by the council but integrated in state units. *Département* staff now amounts to 16.3 per cent of the entire local level personnel or some 5 per cent of total public sector personnel (see Table 2.2, line 2, last column).

While the *départements* have used their own staff to perform their new functions, including the provision of social services, they have also not only cooperated with the *communes* but, abandoning their anti-clerical and anti-associational stance,[9] begun to outsource service delivery to both non-profit (*non-lucratif*) providers, including church organizations, and for-profit providers (*associations*) (see Borgetto and Lafore, 2004, p. 137).

Communes

Despite the high degree of urbanization of the French population (over 80 per cent), the 35 569 *communes* have an average population of 1720 (see Table 2.1, line 2) – the vast majority (95 per cent) having fewer than 5000 inhabitants and only 0.1 per cent more than 100 000, including Paris (2 100 000), Marseilles (795 000) and Lyon (468 000). The boundaries of most municipalities date back to before the French Revolution, if not to medieval times, and have remained largely unchanged ever since.

When, in line with the zeitgeist, national legislation was adopted in 1971 to induce *communes* to embark on voluntary amalgamation, this initiative failed almost entirely – making France the epitome of extremely fragmented local government structures, categorized as the 'South European' pattern (see Norton, 1994, p. 43).

Intercommunalité

To remedy the problems caused by the small size of municipalities (*communes*) and their lack of administrative capacity, national legislation was introduced as early as 1890 to provide them with an institutional frame (*établissements publics de coopération intercommunale*, EPCI) for single-purpose, intermunicipal cooperation (*syndicats à vocation unique*, SIVU). In 1959 national legislation on multiple-purpose intermunicipal cooperation for the provision of public services followed (*syndicats à vocation multiple*, SIVOM). In 1966, central government, conspicuously deviating from the '*volontariat*' principle, decided to establish obligatory *communautés urbaines*, amalgamating big cities with neighbouring municipalities, in four metropolitan areas (Lyon, Marseilles, Lille, Strasbourg); other metropolitan areas followed suit on a voluntary basis (for details see Marcou, 2000). In order to simplify the maze of intermunicipal bodies (*intercommunalité*), the legislation of 1999 (*Loi Chevènement*) sought to encourage municipalities to regroup in three types of community (*communauté*), depending on size and settlement characteristics. To strengthen them functionally and make them more attractive to join, the *communautés* have been given the right to levy their own local taxes (*à fiscalité propre*).

Hailed by some as an 'intermunicipal revolution' (Borraz and LeGalès, 2005), the 1999 *Loi Chevènement* has been remarkably effective in inducing municipalities to regroup. By 1 January 2009, 2601 *communautés* (*à fiscalité propre*) comprising 16 *communautés urbaines* (the big cities and their metropolitan hinterland), 174 *communautés d'agglomération* (in urban agglomerations) and 2406 *communautés de communes* (in urbanized areas) had been established, covering 87.3 per cent of the entire population. The advent of the *communautés* pursuant to the *Loi Chevènement* has organizationally strengthened and territorially structured intermunicipal cooperation in a number of important local activities, in intermunicipal planning and public service provision. Some 10 per cent of local government personnel are now employed by intermunicipal bodies (ECPI) (see Table 2.2, line 2, last column, and Kuhlmann, 2009a, p. 95).

Reforming the Subnational Space

France's subnational space has always been characterized by functional overlap (*enchevêtrement*), cross-financing (*financement croisé*) and personnel duplication (*doublon*); although no precise estimate of the last is available – indeed it is difficult to evaluate beyond samples – it should not be overestimated. As a result, the French state resembles 'a loosely coupled network' (Thoenig, 2006, p. 43). Contracts (*contractualisation*) intended to achieve cooperation and coordination between horizontal and vertical actor networks have thus become a key feature and 'trademark' of France's subnational space and intergovernmental world (see Gaudin, 1999, 2004).

Against this background, the Comité Balladur was appointed by

President Nicolas Sarkozy (October 2008) to make recommendations on the reforming subnational self-government (*pour la réforme des collectivités locales*). The report that the Comité presented on 25 February 2009[10] identifies, among other crucial issues, the indiscriminate assignment of the general competence clause (*clause de competence générale*) to all three local government levels as a main reason for serious malfunctions (functional overlap, cross-financing, personnel duplication etc.). Consequently one of the key recommendations[11] proposes assigning general competence only to municipalities (*communes*) and specifying the competences given to *départements* and *régions*.

In another remarkable proposal,[12] the Comité Balladur suggests turning municipal agglomerations, beginning with existing *communautés urbaines* (note: by way of binding legislation, *par la loi*), into so-called 'metropolises' (*métropoles*) as the institutional point of departure for further innovations, such as creating new municipalities or reassigning *département* functions. This may point the way to generating integration through 'single-tier' local government on the lines of Germany's county-free cities. Furthermore, the Comité has suggested financial incentives to encourage, if not pressure, intermunicipal bodies to restructure territorially and organizationally to form 'new municipalities'[13] – and hence to achieve territorial reform.

Furthermore, in addressing the thorny issue of the democratic legitimacy of intermunicipal bodies, the Comité Balladur recommends that the councils of intermunicipal bodies (*communautés*) should be elected along with the councils of member municipalities, so that some councillors are members of both.

Finally, the Comité has tackled the problem that, 'after 25 years of decentralization', the number of people employed by the state, far from being reduced, has increased (see Table 2.3, line 2), and proposes that state field offices be abolished.[14]

It remains to be seen whether, when and to what degree these and other reform proposals will be put into practice. A framework bill is expected in September 2009 to implement most of them. The government has undertaken to reorganize its field administration, but it is highly unlikely that it will be abolished, depriving the state of major capacities for implementing national policy (Marcou, 2009).

Functions of Municipalities (*Communes*)

Rooted in the historical 'general competence clause' (*clause de competence générale*), municipalities (*communes*) have traditionally been responsible for matters of local relevance and 'closeness' (*proximité*), in particular 'voluntary' social assistance and social services (*aide sociale facultative*, which is meant to complement *aide sociale légale*) for which the *départements* have been responsible at the local level since 1982. In many places, *communes* have been involved in operating 'centres communaux d'action sociale (CCAS)', which are municipal public-law corporations for the provision of local social services.

Traditionally, the *communes* have also been responsible for providing public utilities ('public services of industrial and commercial character', *services publics industriels et commerciaux*, SPIC). Owing to the lack of operational resources, many municipalities have largely 'outsourced' (*gestion déléguée*) service provision since the nineteenth century (water, electricity etc.) (see Lorrain, 1995; and Chapter 10 in this volume).

Although some competent observers have described the *communes* as having been 'forgotten' (*territoires oubliés* – Borraz, 2004), international comparative data on per capita spending show that they have achieved a respectable functional profile (see Table 2.3). In 2005, French *communes* spent an average €1211 per head of population, less than their German counterparts (€1498) but more than Italian municipalities (€1040). It should also be noted that per capita spending by French municipalities is almost twice that of *départements* (€790), which have often been considered the prime beneficiaries of decentralization, playing a functional role similar to that of the *Landkreis* in Germany.

It should be taken into consideration that in some respects, especially socioeconomic, France is a country of 'two speeds' (*à deux vitesses*), with economically active and prosperous metropolitanized and urbanized zones in strong contrast to peripheral and rural areas. Average per capita spending in big and middle-sized cities, particularly in *communautés urbaines* and *communautés d'agglomération*, can plausibly be assumed to be much higher, whereas rural *communes* are often socioeconomically and administratively deficient, constituting an 'administrative wasteland' (*véritable friche administrative* – Jegouzo, 1993).

Personnel

The entire local government sector (*communes, départements, régions*, as well as the intermunicipal bodies) employs about 33 per cent of total public sector personnel (late 2006; see DGCL, 2008), while 51 per cent are still employed by the state (including teachers) and 19 per cent work in the public hospital sector (see Table 2.3). Within the local government sector, some 70 per cent are municipal employees, an indication of the functional importance of municipalities compared with *départements* (18 per cent). The proportion of public sector personnel employed by intermunicipal bodies (especially *communautés urbaines*) has risen to some 10 per cent.

Notwithstanding the decentralization of France's intergovernmental system, the percentage of state personnel has remained as high as 51 per cent (see Hoffmann-Martinot, 2003, pp. 159 ff.). This reflects the persistence of the 'Napoleonic' state tradition and 'dualism' (*dualisme*) under which central government continues to carry out 'its policies directly on the local level' (Marcou, 2004, p. 239).

While the other three countries under discussion have reduced public sector personnel at all levels of government over the past 15 years (particularly in Germany), the public sector workforce in France has grown by 13 per cent (see Table 2.5). Whereas decentralization can plausibly explain a 15 per cent increase in local government personnel, the 7 per cent increase in the state workforce is remarkably high.

ITALY

Central State Level

Following the collapse of the Fascist regime after the war and the abolition of the monarchy by general referendum, a democratic Italy was established by the constitution of 1948 in the 'Napoleonic' tradition of the unitary state, a 'one and indivisible' (*una e indivisible*) republic in obedience to the 'unitary' (*unitario*) principle that 'all citizens have equal social dignity and are equal before the law'[15] and committed to 'political, economic and social solidarity'.[16] On the other hand, formally abandoning the centralist tradition, the constitution of 1948 established a decentralized structure based on newly defined regions (*regioni*), provinces (*province*) and municipalities (*comuni*), of which the constitution undertook to 'recognize and promote the local autonomy'.[17]

Of the two types of regions (*regioni*) stipulated, the five 'special statute regions' (*regioni a statuto speciale*) and the 15 'ordinary statute regions' (*regioni a statuto ordinario*), only the former, based on cultural, geographical and ethnic particularities, were created at brief intervals,[18] whereas the step-by step-establishment of the latter took until well into the 1970s.

Italy embarked on real decentralization and regionalization only from the 1990s, when the collapse of the scandal-ridden political party system opened the door to profound political and institutional change that was finally engineered in the late 1990s under a centre–left coalition. The so-called Bassanini reform of 1997 (Law no. 59) prepared the ground for 'administrative decentralization' (*decentramento amministrativo*), the transfer of state functions to regions, provinces and municipalities. The constitutional breakthrough came with the constitutional reform of

2001, which declared that the republic consisted 'of the municipalities, the provinces, the regions and the State',[19] thus putting the three sub-national levels on a constitutionally equal footing with the state. The most important move and novelty of the 2001 constitutional reform was probably to have constitutionally elevated and upgraded the *regioni*, in particularly endowing them with legislative powers in their own right – in contrast to France, where the regions have retained 'ordinary' local government status. It is especially this regional administrative and legislative autonomy that has transformed Italy into what has been called 'a quasi-federal state' (Bobbio, 2005, p. 29). However, the 'unitary' nature of Italy's post-1947 governmental system has continued to be emphasized by certain influential authorities, not least the constitutional court (Corte Costituzionale).[20]

The Constitution (Article 117) distinguishes between 'exclusive' competences (*legislazione esclusiva*) vested in either central or regional government and 'concurrent' legislative powers (*legislazione concorrente*). Under concurrent powers in relation to matters enumerated by the constitution, the central government level may define the framework and the 'essential level' (*livello essenziale*) while regional legislation fills in the details (see Balboni, 2007; Balboni et al., 2007). This constitutional arrangement is fraught with tensions – typical of a federal, quasi-federal or regionalized system – between the 'unitary' (*unitario*) principle and correlations such as 'equality' (*uguglianza*) and differences and disparities as defined by regional legislation. Such tensions also arise between Italy's Napoleonic unitary tradition and the political will and competence of the regions to define matters for themselves. The frictions inherent in Italy's new and developing quasi-federal system have surfaced in a number of decisions by Italy's constitutional court, which, ruling on regional legislation containing regional differentiations and disparities, proved a staunch advocate and guardian of a unitary interpretation, declaring such regional legislation unconstitutional[21] (for a detailed account and analysis of this controversy see Groppi, 2008).

Regioni

The 22 regions (five special statute and 15 ordinary statute regions – the latter becoming 'operative' only in the late 1970s) differ substantially in size[22] and population,[23] with a deep economic divide running between them, especially between those in northern and southern Italy.[24]

In 2000, the direct election of regional presidents was introduced, lending political momentum to the regions in the intergovernmental setting. The constitutional reforms of the early 2000s, giving quasi-federal status to the regions, endowed them with important intergovernmental powers and responsibilities.

In particular, they have the right to fill in the framework legislation (such as *livello essenziale*) passed by central government. This has produced significant variance between regions as to whether and how each has made use of its legislative competence. Furthermore, the regions have come to play an important role in financing and coordinating policy in the subnational space. By contrast, the administrative tasks assigned directly to the regions are limited, as indicated by the fact that only about 4 per cent of public sector personnel are employed by the regions (see Table 2.2).

The functional profile of the *regioni* was greatly broadened in 1995 when they were assigned major financial, regulatory and coordinating responsibilities in running the national health service (Servizio Sanitario Nazionale, SSN).

Health care is a case in point. In 1978, the SSN, a major policy innovation, was introduced in the form of a tax-based ('Beveridgean') public health system, *tutela della salute* (see Chapter 6 in this volume). It is under the supervision of the national ministry of health and operates through 171 local public agencies (*aziende sanitarie locali*, ASL) and independent public hospitals, while the regions play a key role in regulating and also co-financing the system. While the central government defines the 'essential level' (*livello essenziale*) of health care provision,[25] detailed regulation is largely left to each region. In employing their regulatory discretion, the regions show significant interregional differences, which has evoked political and judicial controversy about the constitutional compatibility of such disparities.[26]

Operating the SSN is a major financial commitment for the regions, reflected by the average per capita spending of €2320 as compared with €1040 by *comuni* (see Table 2.4). Eighty-four per cent of *regioni* spending is current expenditure (see Dexia, 2008, p. 411), primarily – it can plausibly be assumed – on health care.

From the organizational and staffing point of view, the SSN is a self-standing structure, including local ASLs and independent hospitals employing some 20 per cent of public sector personnel, counted separately for statistical purposes from regional and local government (see Table 2.2, line 3).

While the regions have thus gained significant functional salience, particularly in connection with the SSN, many consider that they have largely failed to meet the great expectations set for them in the early 1990s as agents for revitalizing democracy and for renewal in the subnational space (see Balboni, 2007, p. 4).

Province

The 106 *province*, with an average population of 550 000, were established in 2000[27] as a new level of local self-government with an elected council and directly elected president, while continuing in the Napoleonic tradition to serve as the lower administrative level for deconcentrated state administration under the direction of the central-government-appointed prefect (*prefetto*). Employing 13 per cent of local government personnel, less than 2 per cent of the public sector workforce (see Table 2.2, line 3), and spending an average of only €200 per capita (see Table 2.3), the provinces (*province*) have remained 'the weakest link in the chain of local government in Italy, enjoying the scantest powers and feeblest popular support' (Balboni, 2007, p. 3).

Comuni

Italy counts 8101 municipalities (*comuni*) with an average population of 7270. Seventy-one per cent have fewer than 5000 inhabitants and only 1.8 per cent more than 50 000 (see Table 2.1). While fragmentation is enormous in northern Italy ('pulverized municipalities', *comuni-polvere*), municipalities in the South are much larger (see Dexia, 2008, p. 404).

In 1990, national legislation was introduced to encourage the voluntary amalgamation of municipalities and provinces. But the results were 'derisory [as] the number of municipalities has not decreased and the number of provinces has even increased' (Bobbio, 2005, p. 38).

In 1993 the direct election of mayors (*sindaci*) was introduced, which has all but 'revolutionized' local politics (see ibid., pp. 40 ff.).

Functions of Municipalities

The provision of social services is a responsibility of Italy's *comuni* that dates back to medieval times and was mostly met by local charitable organizations, primarily affiliated with the Catholic Church (for a recent excellent historical overview and analysis see Marzanati, 2009). This essentially charity-based scheme was confirmed by the *Legge Crispi* of 1890, which remained in force practically until the national legislation of 2000 (see Balboni, 2007; see also Bönker, Hill and Marzanati, Chapter 4 in this volume). As the latter has so far failed to define county-wide, binding 'essential levels' (*livelli essenziali*), it has largely remained up to the regions to adopt and apply schemes of their own. Again, this has produced considerable inequalities between regions and municipalities.[28]

Social services are delivered locally partly by local authorities themselves, particularly in the case of larger cities. For the most part, however, they continue to be delivered by non-profit (charitable) providers in line with the traditional pattern (see Bobbio, 2005, p. 43).

The provision of public utilities (water, sewage disposal, waste management, public transport, energy) has also been a time-honoured local government task in Italy. Traditionally, municipal corporations (*municipalizzate*) were established, often with a multi-utility profile, to provide public services (for details see Chapter 10 in this volume).

Whereas decentralization has significantly changed the intergovernmental position of regions since the early 2000s, raising them to quasi-federal status, the continuing fragmentation of municipalities and the 'the extreme discrepancy in scale between the large communes and the thousands of small rural communes' (noted by Norton, 1994, p. 203) has proved an obstacle to effective strengthening of the municipal level, leaving them in a territorially 'pulversized' (*polvere-comuni*) and functionally weak state.

The limited functional profile of municipalities is reflected in comparatively low per capita spending: €1040 compared with €1211 in France and €1498 in Germany (see Table 2.3).

Intermunicipal Bodies

Responding to the high degree of territorial fragmentation, particularly in northern Italy, the *comuni* have resorted to various forms of intermunicipal and inter-organizational cooperation to cope with tasks beyond the individual municipality's range and capacity.

Intermunicipal bodies (*consorzi*), both single-purpose and multi-purpose (comparable to France's *syndicats*) have become a familiar and much-used feature of intermunicipal cooperation in the subnational space (for details see Norton, 1994, pp. 205 ff.). Because municipalities in the North tend to be small, *consorzi* are much more numerous there than in the South, for example in Puglia, where municipalities are considerably larger.

Central government has encouraged intermunicipal cooperation by providing a legislative framework (141/1990 and the 267/2000)[29] (on the following see Dexia, 2008, p. 409).

Framework legislation proposes several forms of intermunicipal cooperation, including unions of municipalities (*unioni di comuni*) (somewhat similar to French *communautés*) and mountain communities (*comunità montana*).

Between 2000 and 2008, the number of voluntary *unioni di comuni* rose from 50 to 278, covering over 3.9 million inhabitants and 1240 member municipalities. *Comunità montane* are meant to promote the development of mountain areas by sharing management structures among several municipalities.

There are currently 356, covering 10.8 million inhabitants and 4201 municipalities. All these and similar organizations are financed by the contributions of member municipalities and fees collected for services provided.

In 1994, national legislation (*Legge Galli*) was adopted to overcome territorial and organizational fragmentation in water supply by creating so-called 'agencies of optimal territorial scope' (*autorità di ambiti territoriali ottimal*, ATO) (see Chapter 9 in this volume). The ATOs can be seen as a conceptually innovative variant of mandatory intermunicipal cooperation of the *consorzi* type designed to put water supply on a territorially, technically and economically optimum footing. As of 2006, 91 ATOs, generally covering *province*, have been put in place (see Chapter 9 in this volume). In 2006, the ATO scheme was extended to waste management (see Ianello, 2007; Citroni and Lippi, 2009; see also Chapter 7 in this volume).

By 2003, a total of 87 per cent of municipalities managed their services through a form of intermunicipal cooperation (see Dexia, 2008, p. 409).

Personnel

Although Italy has engaged in decentralization since the 1990s, the share of local government personnel (*comuni* and *province*) in total public sector personnel amounts only to 14 per cent, significantly less than in the other countries. At the same time, the share of central government in the public sector workforce is still 54 per cent (see Table 2.2, line 3), leaving aside the 20 per cent share of the health sector (SSN). This figure, higher even than in France (51 per cent), relates to the persistence of a Napoleonic and dualist governmental tradition, with subnational central and local government structures persisting side by side.

In recent years, the public sector workforce has been shrinking in Italy, probably in reaction to budgetary pressures. Cutbacks in local government personnel (minus 16 per cent) have been even higher than in central government employees (minus 11 per cent), suggesting that decentralization has not only been stagnating but even receding.

Cooperation in the Subnational Space

Since decentralization has, however, deprived central government of a great deal of clout, and networks of lower-level actors have expanded, coordination in the subnational arena has been an increasingly important issue in Italy, too. As in France, 'one of the most characteristic features of the decade was the development of contracts between public administration (local governments, regional governments, ministries and other public agencies) to put in place projects of joint interest' (Bobbio, 2005, p. 39).

Such agreements have been concluded between different levels and actors, such as central and regional governments (*intese istituzionali di programma*) or to establish 'territorial pacts' (*patti territoriali*) between municipalities, public authorities and private stakeholders (for details see Bobbio, 2005, p. 39; Norton, 1994, p. 161).

UK/ENGLAND

Central Government

The UK emerged over time in a series of territorial enlargements. England annexed Wales in 1536 and united with Scotland in 1707 to form what was called Great Britain. In 1801 Ireland was added to the other three parts to constitute the United Kingdom (UK). Throughout this development, the country was ruled by a unitary government embodied in 'Crown in Parliament' and based on parliamentary sovereignty – with the Crown presiding 'over a multi-national kingdom' with 'four nations under one Crown' (Rose, 1982, pp. 6 ff.). Scotland, in particular, has retained important differences from England since union in 1707, maintaining separate legal, educational and local government systems. This means that the description of the system of government in the UK as 'unitary' needs to be understood in relative terms. Eighty-five per cent of the UK population live in England, 9 per cent in Scotland, and 5 per cent in Wales.

Notwithstanding the underlying multinational scheme, the UK has shown a conspicuous 'anti-territorial bias' (Sharpe, 2000, p. 70) over the centuries when it came to establishing administrative functions at the regional level. Unlike most continental European countries that adopted the Napoleonic concepts of prefect and prefecture at the regional level, the British government refrained from creating such functionally comprehensive, territorial administrative units. Instead, (central) government departments were administratively responsible for the entire country. Government departments operated at the subnational level through a structure of regional offices differently defined for each department without any attempt at institutional or territorial coordination (see Chandler, 2001, p. 29).

'Quasi-federalization', Regionalization

It was only in 1997 that the newly elected New Labour government embarked upon a radical programme of 'devolution' for Scotland, Wales and Northern Ireland, the outcome of which has been described as having 'changed not just the content of the British constitution but its very nature: Britain is now effectively a quasi-federal state' (Wilson and Game, 2006, p. 81). The referendums that were to decide on the creation of 'regional parliaments' were held in September 1997, that in Wales succeeding 'by the very narrowest of majorities' (ibid., p. 84).

Following on from this devolution, the government was set to upgrade the political and functional status of the eight English regions. The aims was essentially to establish directly elected regional assemblies as the political precondition for substantive devolution. In line with the previous moves in Scotland and Wales, the decision to adopt this scheme was to be taken by referendum in each of the regions. When the first was held in the North East on 4 November 2004, it was rejected by an overwhelming majority of the regional electorate (see Wilson and Game, 2006, pp. 89 ff.). The government has since abandoned holding referenda in other regions for the foreseeable future.

Hence political decentralization in the UK has taken a strikingly asymmetrical course. While Scotland and Wales have obtained quasi-federal status, the eight English regions continue to be technical and administrative entities that essentially serve to implement central government policy (on planning, infrastructure etc.) in the subnational space (see Table 2.1, line 4).

Executive Agencies

Following the 'Next Steps' Report of 1988, the Conservative Thatcher government introduced 'executive agencies'. Basically devolving individual executive functions from Whitehall to self-standing administrative units, the agencies operate under powers delegated by ministers and government departments. They vary considerably, but all follow the standard model of an administrative unit headed by a chief executive personally accountable for performance against targets in a framework of delegated responsibility (see James, 2001, p. 17). Most agencies are funded by their parent department and, although required to publish separate accounts to be submitted to Parliament, these accounts are an integral part of the parent department's accounts.

Local Government System

Dating back to the Municipal Corporation Act 1835, England's modern local government system underwent massive territorial reforms in 1888 and 1894, which, creating a two-tier (county/district) structure, laid the territorial and institutional groundwork for the Victorian model of local self-government with its broad, multifunctional profile. While based on the 'ultra-vires' principle, reflecting the basic principle of parliamentary sovereignty (see Stewart, 2000, p. 37) and according to which a local authority may exercise only those responsibilities explicitly assigned to it by parliamentary legislation, local authorities have come to be endowed with a wide range of local tasks, including social services (following in the 'poor-law' tradition), primary and secondary health care, education and public utilities (energy, water supply, waste management etc.) (see Hill, 2003; see also Chapter 4 in this volume).

Functions were distributed between central and government relations to constitute a 'dual polity' (Bulpitt, 1983), with central government responsible for 'high politics' (foreign policy, trade policy, legislation) and local authorities in charge of 'low politics', an array of local responsibilities in accordance with parliamentary legislation. Local authorities enjoyed a significant degree of autonomy not least because they had had the right since 1835 to levy local taxes (the legendary 'rates') to cover expenditure.

This Victorian phase ('golden age'; Norton, 1994, p. 352) of English local government, so admired by other European countries, lasted well into the 1930s. Since then the traditional local government system has undergone fundamental changes in both functional and intergovernmental status.

The first major shift came after 1945 when the functional model was largely redefined in developing the national welfare state. Local government lost some historical responsibilities, which were 'nationalized', that is, transferred to state agencies.

- Health care was taken over by the National Health Service (NHS), established in 1948 (and reorganized in 1974) as a autonomous public agency, leaving local authorities with responsibility only for environmental health.
- In 1948, responsibility for social assistance (social benefits) was transferred to the new National Assistance.
- In 1947, local power plants and private energy companies were transferred to a single nationalized industry. In 1957, a unified public system for the generation and transmission of electricity across the UK was created.
- In 1974, water supply – another traditional local government task – was transferred to new, regional water authorities.

On the other hand, local responsibilities have been greatly expanded in education, social services and social housing. From being an active producer of public utilities (electricity, gas, water etc.), British local governments now became primarily social service providers, supporting and implementing central government policy on social services (Chandler, 2001, p. 53) and education.

The next radical change took place after 1979 under the Conservative Thatcher government, but also after 1997 under the New Labour government, a combination and sequence of central government measures that cannot be dealt with in detail at this point (see Wilson and Game, 2006, pp. 353 ff.; Wollmann, 2008b, pp. 131 ff.). They included:

- Curtailment of traditional local authority budgetary autonomy.
- Reduction of local government responsibilities and the influence of local government by outsourcing service delivery (compulsory competitive tendering) and 'quangoization' – creation of quasi-non-governmental organizations ('quangos') to carry out public tasks outside local government proper (see Skelcher, 1998, 2005). Some 5000 such organizations were established at the local level (for an account see Wilson and Game, 2006, pp. 143 f.).
- Strengthening direct central government intervention and control over local government operations, for instance in local planning (see Wollmann, 2008b, pp. 227 ff. for an account).
- The introduction under New Labour of a central-government-defined and-controlled performance management regime ('best value' etc.) to monitor local government operations (see Wilson and Game, 2006, pp. 361 ff.).

In short, England has been transformed 'from a unitary de-centralised into a unitary highly centralised country' (Jones, 1991, p. 20).

Territorial Reform

In response to rampant industrialization and urbanization, England embarked, as early as 1838 and 1894, on large-scale territorial and organizational reform of local government without parallel in contemporary Europe. While in England an entirely new two-tier structure (counties/districts) of elected local councils was created and the traditional parishes practically eclipsed, other European countries retained the small-scale format of towns and parishes within centuries-old boundaries. This 'separated developments in England from much of Europe where the commune remained the basic unit of local government' (Stewart, 2000, p. 31).

In 1974, a further major round of local government territorial and organizational reform raised the average population of districts/boroughs to 130000 and of counties to 700000 (see Norton, 1994, p. 40). This was again in strong contrast to other 'North European' countries, which had also introduced territorial reforms during the 1960s and 1970s, such as Sweden (where the average population of municipalities rose to 31 000) and in some German *Länder* (see above), let alone to 'South European' countries like France and Italy, where, in the absence of territorial reforms, small local government entities were retained. In subsequent territorial and organizational reforms, the 36 single-tier metropolitan councils/districts (comprising most big cities) were restored in 1986 and a growing number of unitary authorities was created from the 1990s, combining county and borough functions and covering most of urbanized England (for details see Wilson and Game, 2006, pp. 64 ff.; Wollmann, 2008b, pp. 64 ff.; see also Table 2.1, line 4).

The demographic and territorial format of local government in England as it has developed notably since 1976 has been criticized for 'sizeism' (Stewart, 2000, p. 66), for demographic 'oversize' which, in the judgement of many observers, has a great deal to do with the participatory and democratic shortcomings of English local government, for instance low identification of local citizens with their locality and low voter turnout.

The local government system comprises (see Table 2.1, line 4):

- 34 (two-tier) counties
- 36 (single-tier) metropolitan counties/districts
- 46 (single-tier) unitary authorities
- 238 shire districts/boroughs (within two-tier counties)
- 33 London boroughs (within the two-tier Greater London Authority)
- The (two-tier) Greater London Authority.

Functions

Notwithstanding functional curtailment after 1979 (outsourcing, quangoization etc.), local government 'still is very big business' (Wilson and Game, 2006, p. 118).

This is evidenced by comparative data on local government expenditure (see Table 2.4, column 4). Measured by local government per capita expenditure (€3930) and by share of local expenditure in total public sector spending (29.5 per cent), English local authorities have a much higher functional profile than French, Italian and German authorities (in Italy and Germany excluding *regioni* and *Länder*). Expenditure (see Table 2.3, column 4) is highest on education (30 per cent) and social security (29 per cent).

Personnel

Only 16.8 per cent of public sector personnel are employed by central government as compared to 56 per cent by local government. Twenty-six per cent work in the National Health Service (see Table 2.2, line 4). Hence, notwithstanding functional losses, local government is still 'very big business' (Wilson and Game, 2006, p. 118).

Counties have the largest share (with 36), followed by metropolitan councils (comprising big cities) with 25.6 per cent, and unitary authorities (in urbanized areas) with 19 per cent.

Over the past decade or so, there have been major cutbacks in public sector employment – with central government taking a conspicuous lead, with a reduction of 36 per cent between 1990 and 2003, followed by local authorities with a 5 per cent cut. The NHS, in contrast, saw a steep, 16 per cent increase in personnel (see Table 2.5, line 4).

NOTES

1. '. . . ist ein demokratischer und sozialer Bundesstaat'.
2. With the important exception of the Federal Agency for Labour.
3. The comparative ranking looks different if the two local government tiers in the individual countries are counted together. Then the UK local government levels come first, followed by Italy, France and Germany. The picture and ranking change again if one adds up the subnational levels. In this perspective Germany tops the list (with the *Länder* looming large) and France trails the field (see the data in Table 2.4).
4. In interpreting these at first sight strikingly high reduction rates, it should also be taken into account that, as a result of 'corporatization' (see Chapter 10 in this volume), a significant share of local government functions have in the meantime been transferred to organizationally self-standing (still municipally owned) corporations whose personnel are, in statistical terms, not counted as local employees proper.
5. '*La République . . . son organisation est décentralisée*', article 1, as amended by the constitutional law of 28 March 2003.
6. Article 72, section 5, constitution 2003: '*Aucune collectivité territoriale ne peut exercer une tutelle sur une autre.*'
   ⁹ Article 72, section 3: '*Dans les conditions prévues par la loi, ces collectivités s'administrent librement par des conseils élus et disposent d'un pouvoir réglementaire pour l'exercice de leurs compétences.*'
7. In Table 2.3 the expenditure data pertain to the 'subnational levels', that is, in the French case, to all three levels. The spending on 'social protection' essentially relates to the *départements*.
8. The Conseil Constitutionnel, which was called upon to decide on the constitutionality of the amended RMI legislation of 2003 (on the grounds that it violated the principle of nationwide equality, *égalité*) ruled on 18 December 2003 that it did not recognize any incompatibility between the constitutional imperative of *égalité* and the constitutional principle of 'self-government/administration' (*libre administration*).
9. For an intriguing historical analysis of the origin and persistence of the traditional 'anti-associational' and 'anti-clerical' bias social policy which amounted to a 'principle of inverse subsidiarity' (*principe de subsidiarité inversée*) see Archambault (1996), p. 17.

10. See Comité Balladur (2009), Comité pour la réforme des collectivités locales, www.reformedescollectiviteslocales.fr/propup/?mode=news&id=75.
11. See proposition no. 11.
12. See proposition no. 8.
13. See proposition no. 9: '*permettre aux intercommunalités de se transformer en communes nouvelles en redéployant, en leur faveur, les aides à l'intégration des communes*'.
14. Proposition no. 13: '*Plus d'un quart de siècle après les grandes lois de décentralisation l'Etat n'en a pas encore tiré les conséquences en termes d'organisation de ses services déconcentrés.*'
15. '*Tutti i cittadini hanno pari dignità sociale e sono eguali davanti alla legge.*'
16. '. . . *politica, economica e sociale solidarietà*'.
17. '. . . *riconosce e promuove le autonomie autonomie locali*'.
18. Sicilia, Valle Aosta, Friuli–Venezia, Trentino–Alto Adige/Südtirol.
19. '*La Repubblica è costituita dai Communi, dalle Province . . ., dalle Regioni e dallo Stato.*'
20. See Schefold (2007), p. 27. Notwithstanding the broad legislative competences assigned to the regions (*regioni*), the Constitutional Court, in a ruling of 20 April 2002, has typically refused to call the regional assemblies 'parliaments' as this term is reserved for the national parliament of an, in the Court's view, essentially 'unitary' (*unitario*) state. See also the following note.
21. See, for instance, the ruling handing down by the Constitutional Court in 2007 (sentenza n. 365 del 2007): 'It is well known that the debate in the Constituent Assembly was absolutely firm in ruling out concepts that might be related to models of the federalistic type or even federal type' ('*E ben noto che il dibattito costituente . . . fu assolutamente fermo nell' escludere concezioni che potessero anche solo apparire latamente riconducibili a modelli di tipo federalistico o addirittura di tipo confederale*' (quoted from Groppi, 2008, p. 1, n. 1).
22. Between 3300 km^2 in Valle Aosta and 25 800 km^2 in Sicily.
23. Between 124 000 in Valle Aosta and 9.5 million in Lombardia.
24. In 2004, per capita GDP in the richest regions was 65 per cent higher than in the eight poorest regions in the Mezzogiorno (see Dexia, 2008, p. 404).
25. The current definition of essential-level assistance in health was issued by Decree of the President of the Council of Ministers of 29 November 2001 (see Balboni, 2007, p. 8).
26. See above, note 22.
27. *Testo unico delle leggi sull'ordinamento deglio enti locali, Tuel.*
28. In 2003, in social service provision, the per capita expenditure was, on average, €91.3: it amounted in the richest region (Autonomous Province of Bolzano) to €417.4 and in the poorest (Calabria) to €26.9 (see Balboni, 2007, p. 7).
29. *Testo unico delle leggi sull'ordinamento deglio enti locali, Tuel.*

REFERENCES

Archambaut, Edith (1996), *Le secteur sans but lucratif. Associations et fondations en France*, Paris: Economica.
Balboni, Enzo (2007), 'The political and institutional framework regarding social services in Italy: the intergovernmental pattern', paper presented to Villa Vigoni, Italy.
Balboni, E., B. Baroni, A. Mattioni and G. Pastori (2007), *Il sistema integrato dei servizi sociali*, 2nd edn, Milan: Giuffrè.
Benz, Arthur (2005), 'Verwaltung als Mehrebenensystem', in B. Blanke, S. von Bandemer, F. Nullmeier and G. Wewer (eds), *Handbuch zur Verwaltungsreform*, 3rd edn, Wiesbaden, Germany: VS Verlag, pp. 18 ff.

Bernard, Paul (1968), *Le grand tournant des communes de France*, Paris: Armand Colin.
Bobbio, Luigi (2005), 'Italy after the storm', in B. Denters and L.E. Rose (eds), *Comparing Local Governance*, New York: Palgrave Macmillan.
Bönker, Frank and Hellmut Wollmann (2006), 'Public sector reforms and local government in Germany: the case of local social policy', in Vincent Hoffmann-Martinot and Hellmut Wollmann (eds), *State and Local Government Reforms in France and Germany. Convergence and Divergence*, Wiesbaden, Germany: VS Verlag, pp. 190–206.
Bönker, Frank and Hellmut Wollmann (2008), 'Réformer l'aide sociale en Allemagne, en Suède et au Royaume Uni: une analyse comparative des évolutions récentes', in Michael Borgetto (ed.), *Qui gouverne le social?*, Paris: Dalloz.
Borgetto, Michel and Robert Lafore (2004), *Droit de l'aide et de l'action sociale*, 5th edn, Paris: Montchrestien.
Borraz, Olivier (2004), 'Les territoires oubliés de la décentralisation', in G. Marcou and H. Wollmann (eds), *Annuaire 2004 des collectivités locales*, Paris: CNRS, pp. 193–201.
Borraz, Olivier and Patrick LeGalès (2005), 'France: the intermunicipal revolution', in Bas Denters and Lawrence E. Rose (eds), *Comparing Local Governance. Trends and Developments*, Basingstoke: Palgrave Macmillan, pp. 12–28.
Bourjol, Maurice (1975), *La réforme municipale*, Paris: Berger-Levrault.
Bulpitt, James (1983), *Territory and Power in the United Kingdom*, Manchester: Manchester University Press.
Chandler, J.A. (2001), *Local Government Today*, 3th edn, Manchester: Manchester University Press.
Citroni, Guilio and Andrea Lippi (2009), 'Pubblico e private nella governace dei rifiuti in Italia', *Revista Italiana di Politiche Pubbliche*, **1**, 71–108.
Comité Ballâdur 2009, Comité pour la réforme des collectivités locales, Il est temps de décider, Paris.
Delorme, R. and C. André (1983), *L'Etat et l'économie, un essai d'explication de l'évolution des dépenses publiques en France 1870–1980*, Paris: Le Seuil.
Dexia (2006), *Local Government Employment in the 25 Countries of the European Union*, Paris: Dexia.
Dexia (2008), *Sub-National Governments in the European Union. Organisation, Responsibilities and Finance*, Paris: Dexia.
Direction Générale des Collectivités Locales – Ministère de l'Intérieur (2008), 'La fonction publique territoriale représente un tiers des emplois publics', *Bulletin d'Informations Statistiques de la DGCL*, **63**, September.
Doligé, Eric (2007), *Rapport d'information au nom de l'Observatoire de la décentralisation sur le transfert des personnels techniciens, ouvriers et de service de l'Education nationale et celui des personnels des directions départementales de l'équipement*, Sénat, session ordinaire 2006–2007, no. 62.
Gaudin, Jean-Pierre (1999), *Gouverner par contrat*, Paris: Presses de Sciences Politiques.
Gaudin, Jean Pierre (2004), 'La contractualisation des rapports entre l'Etat et les collectivités locales', in Gérard Marcou and Hellmut Wollmann (eds), *Annuaire 2004 des Collectivités Locales*, Paris: CNRS, pp. 215–234.
Groppi, Tania (2008), 'L'evoluzione della forma di Stato in Italia. Uno stato regionale senz'anima?', unpublished paper.

Hassenteufel, Patrick and Peul Loncle-Moriceau (2003), 'Territorialisation n'est pas décentralisation', *Pouvoirs Locaux*, **58** (3), 49–54.
Hesse, Konrad (1967), *Grundzüge des Verfassungsrechts der Bundesrepublik Deutschland*, München: Beck.
Hill, Michal (2003), *Understanding Social Policy*, 7th edn, Oxford: Blackwell.
Hoffmann-Martinot, Vincent (2003), 'The French Republic: one but divisible?', in Norbert Kersting and Angelika Vetter (eds), *Reforming Local Government in Europe*, Wiesbaden, Germany: VS Verlag, pp. 157–82.
Iannello, Carlo (2007), 'L'emergenza dei rifiuti in Campania: i paradossi delle gestioni commisariali', *Rassegna di Diritto Pubblico Europeo*, **2**, 137–78.
James, Oliver (2001), 'New Public Management in the UK: enduring legacy or fatal remedy?', *International Review of Public Administration*, **6** (2), 15–26.
Jegouzo, Yves (1993), 'Communes rurales, décentralisation et intercommunalité', in G. Gilbert and A. Delcamp (eds), *La décentralisation dix ans après*, Paris: Librairie générale de droit et de jurisprudence, pp. 183 ff.
Jones, George (1991), 'Local government in Great Britain', in J.J. Hesse (ed.), *Local Government and Urban Affairs in International Perspective*, Baden-Baden, Germany: Nomos.
Kuhlmann, Sabine (2009a), *Politik- und Verwaltungsreform in Kontinentaleuropa. Subnationale Institutionenpolitik im deutsch-französischen Vergleich*, Baden-Baden, Germany: Nomos.
Kuhlmann, Sabine (2009b), 'Une convergence des modèles administratifs locaux? Etude comparée de la décentralisation en France et en Allemagne', *Pouvoirs Locaux*, **81**, 81–5.
Kuhlmann, Sabine and Manfred Röber (2006), 'Civil Service in Germany: between cutback management and modernization', in Vincent Hoffmann-Martinot and Hellmut Wollmann (eds), *State and Local Government Reforms in France and Germany*, Wiesbaden, Germany: VS Verlag, pp. 89–102.
Lorenz, Sabine and Hellmut Wollmann (1999), 'Kommunales Dienstrecht und Personal', in Hellmut Wollmann and Roland Roth (eds), *Kommunalpolitik*, 2nd edn, Wiesbaden, Germany: VS Verlag, pp. 490–512.
Lorrain, Dominique (1995), 'France: le changement silencieux', in D. Lorrain and G. Stoker (eds), *La privatisation des services urbains en Europe*, Paris: La Découverte.
Marcou, Gérard (2000), 'La réforme de l'intercommunalité', in GRALE, *Annuaire 2000 des Collectivités Locales*, Paris: CNRS, pp. 3–10.
Marcou, Gérard (2004), 'Décentralisation – quelle théorie de l'Etat?', in G. Marcou and H. Wollmann (eds), *Annuaire 2004 des Collectivités Locales*, Paris: CNRS, pp. 235–52.
Marcou, Gérard (2005), 'La France est une République indivisible . . . son organisation est décentralisée', in F. de la Morena (ed.), *Actualité de l'article 1er de la Constitution de 1958*, Toulouse, France: Presses de l'Université des sciences sociales de Toulouse, pp. 13–52.
Marcou, Gérard (2008), 'Le bilan en demi-teinte de l'Acte II: décentraliser plus ou décentraliser mieux?', *RFDA*, **2**, 295–315.
Marcou, Gérard (2009), 'Le rapport du Comité Ballâdur: les bonnes pistes et les fausses pistes', *Revue Lamy des collectivités territoriales*, **44**, 70–98.
Marzanati, Anna (2009), 'L'assistenza sociale in Italia: il ruolo del governo locale' (in French translation) in G. Marcou and H. Wollmann (eds), *Annuaire 2009 de Collectivités Locales*, Paris: CNRS (forthcoming).

Norton, Allan (1994), *International Handbook of Local and Regional Government*, Aldershot, UK and Brookfield, USA: Edward Elgar.
Rose, Richard (1982), *Understanding the United Kingdom*, London: Longman.
Scharpf, Fritz, Bernd Reissert and Fritz Schnabel (1976), *Politikverflechtung. Theorie und Empirie des kooperativen Föderalismus in der Bundesrepublik*, Kronberg, Germany: Scriptor.
Sharpe, Lawrence J. (2000), 'Regionalism in the United Kingdom. The role of social federalism', in Hellmut Wollmann and Eckhard Schröter (eds), *Comparing Public Sector Reform in Britain and Germany*, Aldershot: Ashgate, pp. 67–84.
Schefold, Dian (2007), 'Verfassungs- und Verwaltungsrecht', in S. Grundmann and A. Zaccaria (eds), *Einführung in das italienische Recht*, Frankfurt, Germany: Verlag Recht und Wirtschaft, pp. 22–118.
Skelcher, Chris (1998), *The Appointed State*, Buckingham: Open University Press.
Skelcher, Chris (2005), 'The new governance of communities', in Gary Stoker and David Wilson (eds), *British Local Government into the 21st Century*, Basingstoke: Palgrave Macmillan.
Stewart, John (2000), *The Nature of British Local Government*, Basingstoke: Macmillan.
Thoenig, Jean-Claude (2006), 'Sub-national government and the centralized state: a French paradox', in Vincent Hoffmann-Martinot and Hellmut Wollmann (eds), *Comparing Public Sector Reforms in France and Germany*, Wiesbaden, Germany: VS Verlag, pp. 39–58.
Wachendorfer-Schmidt, Ute (2004), 'Aspects politiques de la réforme du fédéralisme. Le cas allemand', in Gérard Marcou and Hellmut Wollmann (eds), *Annuaire 2004 des Collectivités Locales*, Paris: CNRS, pp. 257–91.
Wilson, David and Chris Game (2006), *Local Government in the United Kingdom*, 4th edn, Basingstoke: Palgrave Macmillan.
Wollmann, Hellmut (2003), 'Is the traditional model of municipal self-government in Germany becoming defunct?', *German Journal of Urban Research*, **1**, 24–49.
Wollmann, Hellmut (2004), 'The two waves of territorial reform of local government in Germany', in John Meligrana (ed.), *Redrawing Local Government Boundaries*, Vancouver: BC: UBC Press, pp. 106–29.
Wollmann, Hellmut (2008a), *Reformen in Kommunalpolitik und -verwaltung. England, Schweden, Frankreich und Deutschland im Vergleich*, Wiesbaden, Germany: VS Verlag.
Wollmann, Hellmut (2008b), *Comparing local government reforms in England, Sweden, France and Germany, Between continuity and change*, accessed at www.wuestenrot-stiftung.de/download/local-government.
Wollmann, Hellmut (2010), 'Territorial local level reforms in the East German regional states Länder: phases, patterns, and dynamics', *Local Government Studies*, **36** (2), 249–59.
Wollmann H. and G. Bouckaert (2006), 'State organisation in France and Germany: between "territoriality" and "functionality"', in V. Hoffmann-Martinot and H. Wollmann (eds), *State and Local Government Reforms in France and Germany. Convergence and Divergence*, Wiesbaden, Germany: VS Verlag, pp. 11–37.

3. New public management in continental Europe: local government modernization in Germany, France and Italy from a comparative perspective

Sabine Kuhlmann and Paolo Fedele

1. INTRODUCTION

This chapter examines new public management (NPM) reforms at the local level in Germany, France and Italy. Continental Europe is often regarded as a 'maintainer' or 'latecomer' in terms of NPM-inspired reforms, whereas the Anglo-Saxon countries are seen as 'forerunners', 'marketizers' and 'minimizers' (see Pollitt and Bouckaert, 2004). With the increasing budgetary and economic problems at the beginning of the 1990s, the NPM debate was, however, able to gain a foothold in continental Europe, although some of its elements had long been well known and practised at the local level. Local actors in continental Europe often did not explicitly refer to the 'NPM agenda' or even – particularly in France – purposely avoided this term because of its unpopular connotations in the national context. However, many of the strategic NPM elements were in practice taken up by local governments. Against this background, the purpose of this contribution is twofold. On the one hand, we wish to show to what extent and with what effects the NPM agenda has been adopted at the local level in continental Europe.[1] On the other hand, the chapter, taking a longitudinal, comparative perspective, investigates whether these reforms have brought greater convergence or divergence between the three countries.

In order to assess the outcomes of reform and identify patterns of convergence/divergence, we make an analytical distinction between two dimensions of NPM reforms (external and internal). On the one hand, the NPM approach proposes a redistribution of tasks between the state and the market, largely favouring market-type mechanisms, outsourcing and an institutional 'autonomization' of public services (external dimension). There are at least three discernible forms of 'externalization' (see also Grossi, Marcou and Reichard, Chapter 10 in this volume): (1) 'functional privatization' aimed at delegating service provision via contracts to private or non-profit actors, leaving ultimate responsibility with the local authority; (2) 'organizational privatization', the introduction of private-law municipal companies and/or the inclusion of private shareholders in municipal corporations; (3) 'corporatization', in the course of which administrative units of the municipal core administration are spun off while remaining part of the municipal organization and are transformed into institutionally separate municipal 'corporations' or service entities. On the other hand, the concept of NPM includes the internal reorganization of administrative structures, changes in financial management (output- instead of input-orientation in budgeting), controlling systems (e.g. performance measurement, new accounting systems), and human resource management as well as a clear separation between politics and administration (internal dimension). Here we predominantly address the introduction of performance management systems and output-oriented steering.

After introducing our theoretical framework (Section 2), we analyse the two reform dimensions in separate 'country reports' (Sections 3 and 4). These sections are followed by a cross-country comparison (Section 5) and some concluding remarks (Section 6).

2. THEORETICAL BACKGROUND AND EXPLANATORY SCHEME

This chapter proceeds from the hypothesis that similar reform discourses and trends can produce quite distinct institutional outcomes and effects in different countries. Instead of general institutional convergence resulting from the adoption of NPM as an international paradigm of public sector modernization (see Kettl, 2000), we expect that the traditional institutional features of the three systems under consideration[2] will shape the corridors and outcomes of reform. From this viewpoint, convergent and divergent patterns of institutional evolution are likely to occur simultaneously in different fields and with respect to different dimensions of reform (see Pollitt, 2001) depending on the specific national/local 'starting conditions' and past institutional choices.

Theoretically, we draw on the historical and sociological approaches of new institutionalism; both approaches suggest that the functioning and performance of institutions are historically and culturally 'embedded'. Historical institutionalism stresses path-dependencies, which are assumed to predetermine further institutional development (see Steinmo et al., 1992; Immergut, 1992). From this theoretical perspective, policy choices appear to be conditioned by 'policy legacies' springing from, and ingrained in, the past. According to this approach, institutional structures sculpt historical landscapes and thus act as a determinant in guiding historical development along a set of 'paths'. The sociological approach to new institutionalism puts greater emphasis on cultural imprints, cognitive scripts and moral templates that provide 'frames of meaning' guiding human action. According to sociological institutionalism, this underlying cultural authority and 'embeddedness' of institutional arrangements is not bound to result from the introduction of new formal rules. Instead, there can be misfit between new institutional structures and cultural legacies springing from the past. Stressing the limited scope of reforms and pointing to cultural frames, both historical and sociological institutionalism suggest more incremental than large-scale institutional change.

Against this background, we expect the following developments in convergence and divergence:

1. We assume that NPM reforms affecting the internal structures and procedures of German, French and Italian local government will turn out to be rather limited in scope and outcome because the new managerial rules will largely contrast with the deeply embedded 'rule-of-law' tradition and legalistic institutional practices in the three countries (Pollitt and Bouckaert, 2004; König, 2006). The administrative regime of legalism will hinder NPM-driven reform measures, such as performance management, output-steering and contractual arrangements (see Capano, 2003; Borgonovi, 2005).
2. With regard to the external dimension of NPM reforms, we assume that there will be less convergence and even some divergence between the three countries due to their different traditions of local service production. We expect more resistance to change in Germany and Italy than in France. Sticking to the institutionally inherited systems of municipal 'in-house production' (see contributions by Grossi, Marcou, Reichard, Chapter 10, and Citroni, Chapter 9, in this volume), Germany and Italy will oppose marketization and liberalization, whereas in France the NPM-inspired demand for market competition and outsourcing matches the historic tradition of *délégation* at the local level well (see Lorrain, 1995).

3. EXTERNAL NPM REFORMS: PRIVATIZATION AND OUTSOURCING

Germany

The privatization and 'corporatization' of local public services have particularly affected the public utility sector in Germany. Not so much a result of the NPM debate but as a result of EU liberalization and the federal legislation (1998 Energy Act – *Energiewirtschaftsgesetz*), the traditionally protected markets in the utility sector have opened up to market competition. According to a survey conducted by the German Institute of Urban Studies, only 30 per cent of municipal energy companies are still entirely the property of cities; more than 70 per cent have external shareholders.[3] In the big German cities, local governments have minority holdings in roughly 20 per cent of energy companies. Although the time-honoured *Stadtwerke* have not yet disappeared from the local landscape, energy supply in Germany is increasingly being monopolized by private companies. Furthermore, since the 1990s the quasi-monopoly of non-statutory welfare associations (*freie Wohlfahrtsverbände*) in social services has, at least in some sectors of service delivery, been replaced by private actors operating as contractual partners of local governments. Mobile services for the elderly (*ambulante Pflegedienste*), for instance, are predominantly rendered by commercial firms (see Table 3.1), whereas local authorities hardly play any role as service providers in this field.

Hitherto, there has been little empirical evidence on the quality of privatized or 'corporatized' local public services. Surveys[4] have shown that, in municipalities where services have been privatized, only a minority of German staff council leaders (20 per cent) and heads of youth welfare boards (40 per cent) assert that privatization has improved quality, while about 80 per cent of the former and 60 per cent of the latter took an opposing view. German mayors seem to react favourably to both quality improvements and budgetary relief. Privatization directly reduces fiscal stress and is accordingly encouraged by mayors, who take the initiative in privatizing services to this end (see Figure 3.1).

In the meantime, privatization and corporatization in German local government have had a number of awkward (unintended) consequences. By privatizing profitable services, for instance electricity supply, municipalities have lost important sources of local income, which had been widely used to cross-finance other, less lucrative sectors of activity (e.g. public transport). Hence, selling profitable companies in one sector imposes fare increases when cross-financing ceases. There are also precarious effects on steering and horizontal coordination. The traditionally

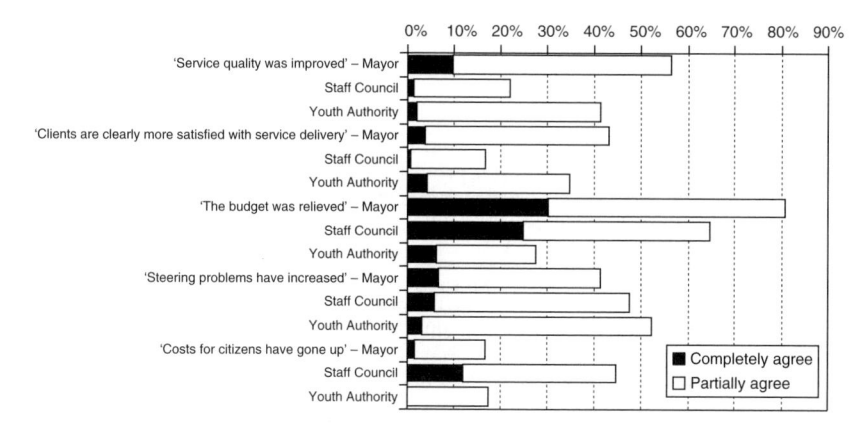

Note: Mayor *n* = 460, Staff Council *n* = 270, Youth Authority *n* = 87.

Source: Survey Research Project, '10 Years New Steering Model in Germany'. Adapted from Bogumil et al. (2007), p. 75.

Figure 3.1 Effects of privatization and contracting out in German local government

broad, multi-purpose model of German local self-administration was cut back (Wollmann, 2002), conspicuously weakening the guiding principle of territoriality and cross-policy coordination. As local governments progressively restrict themselves to an 'enabling function', surrounding themselves with a multitude of quasi-autonomous, single-purpose 'satellites', institutional fragmentation of the local landscape increases markedly. This development, which some observers have called 'atomization of the city' (Dieckmann, 1996, p. 341), is reinforced by a tendency for subsidiary municipal companies (*Tochterunternehmen*) to outsource further to secondary subsidiaries, so-called 'grandchild companies' (*Enkelunternehmen*). Corporatization and privatization have also reduced local government capacity for political steering, amounting to what could be called self-deprivation of local council political powers and thus deprivation of citizens' influence. Against this background, some observers are already predicting the 'end of local self-administration' in Germany (Wohlfahrt and Zühlke, 2005).

France

In France, public services have been subject to contracting out and outsourcing (*délégation*) since the nineteenth century. In the utility sector,

Table 3.1   Modes of local service delivery in the French water sector, 2000

Mode of service provision	% of the municipalities	% of the population
Water provision		
Direct service provision (local government)	48	21
Delegation (to private companies)	52	79
Sewage		
Direct service provision (local government)	62	48
Delegation (external provider)	38	53

Source: Hansen and Herbke (2004), p. 300.

municipal suppliers are in a minority position almost everywhere. One example is the water supply sector, where 60 per cent of the population was served by private suppliers in 1983 (Lorrain, 1995, p. 108) and 80 per cent in 2000 (Table 3.1; see also Citroni, Chapter 9 in this volume). Similar developments have occurred in other sectors, such as sewage and waste disposal, road cleaning and public transport (Huron and Spindler, 1998, p. 57). Typically, nearly all the firms with which French municipalities collaborate are contracted by the same big companies (*grands groupes*) operating at the national if not international level.

The provision of social services, too, is similarly being increasingly delegated to external, non-public actors. This development is due not least to the devolution of state tasks in this policy sector to the subnational level (Kuhlmann, 2008a). It has already been mentioned that the most important package of *Acte II* was the complete transfer of the Minimum Social Protection and Integration Scheme (*Revenue Minimum d'Insertion* – RMI) to the *départements* in January 2004. The transfer of RMI has imposed a serious financial burden on *départements*, which was met with strong criticism from local actors. The RMI has had this impact because central government compensation is not planned to increase progressively with the numbers of recipients but to remain stable at the 2004 level. Since dependence on RMI is growing in most *départements*, there will be an increasing gap between financial transfers from the state and RMI payments by the *départements*. Leaving aside the general councils' demand that they and not the central government should have full responsibility for determining the level of RMI, the *départements* and *communes* have pursued at least two strategies to cope with their new RMI competencies. First, they have reduced non-mandatory functions to gain sufficient resources to finance the additional mandatory tasks. There are fears that these developments will transform general councils from fully fledged local governments *(collectivités locales de plain excercice)* into 'big social assistance boards' (Portier, 2003, p. 64), depriving them of political and policy-making powers in favour of tasks imposed by the central government. Second, the *départements* and the *communes* (*centres communaux d'action sociale* – CCAS) to which RMI service provision is often delegated have reacted by outsourcing service provision to private and non-profit providers (*associations*). In the Département Alpes-Maritimes, for instance, RMI services are predominantly rendered by *associations* (73 per cent of all providers; Kuhlmann, 2009, p. 157).

For France, too, there is limited empirical evidence on the effects of functional privatization and *délégation* on performance. Concerning public utilities, there are some empirical findings on prices and fares. In general, water prices in France are about 20 per cent higher under private management than under municipal management (Finger and Allouche, 2002, p. 196). In Nîmes, for instance, water prices soared from 5.88 francs per cubic metre in 1983 under municipal management to 17.38 francs per cubic metre in 1995 under private management by SAUR (an outsourced water and sanitation services manager) – a total increase of nearly 200 per cent (Maury, 1997, p. 152). Private or 'associative' suppliers often have a record of unreliable service delivery and have failed to meet public demand. In Le Havre, where school canteens have been 'delegated' to an association, parents were not willing to accept higher prices accompanied by lower service quality. As a result, school canteens in Le Havre have recently been 'remunicipalized', not least in order to prevent serious losses of local electorate support (Kuhlmann, 2009). Thus there seems to be a 'remunicipalization' trend in some French cities, departing to some extent from the traditional model of *délégation* (also see the famous example of Grenoble).

Besides the widespread practice of concession-granting and *délégation*, there is an increasing trend towards 'satellization'. A growing number of quasi-(non)-governmental and semi-public actors have come to surround local governments like 'satellites', providing various local services on a contract basis (Huron and Spindler, 1998). These manifold semi-public and mixed economy 'satellites' have developed into an over-complex, almost unmanageable, system of governance. Municipalities are consequently less and less able to control and steer all these single-purpose service providers in orbit around them (Lachaume, 1996). This is seen as detrimental to overall institutional efficiency and local political steering. Privatization and the contracting out of local public services have also caused a loss of political control in some areas, as evidenced by the election defeat of conservative mayors (e.g. in Nîmes; see Maury, 1997). Such outcomes of elections are often prompted by corruption in the 'entrepreneurial' cities.

Italy

As in Germany, the Italian model of local service delivery was traditionally based on direct delivery by local authorities and a limited set of decentralized delivery options (see Grossi, Marcou and Reichard, Chapter 10 and Citroni, Chapter 9 in this volume). With the introduction of statutory local government autonomy in the early 1990s, municipalities and provinces enjoyed greater organizational flexibility. This allowed them to adopt different delivery options depending on the basic features of the service provided. The reform provided for different types of quango, two types of local public enterprise and some forms of contracting-out mechanism.

The result has been not only the spread of autonomization, corporatization and formal privatization at the local level, with a preference for the joint stock company (*società per azioni*), bringing about what has been called a 'radical change from municipality to local public group of companies' tending to extend its activities beyond the municipal territory (Elefanti, 2003; Grossi, 1999, p. 6). Material privatization, too, has proceeded apace (see Lippi, 2003, p. 163), and municipal corporations have been partially or completely sold to private actors (especially in the energy sector), thus 'operating beyond "their" old municipal boundaries' (Bobbio, 2005, p. 43). In the case of limited companies (*società a responsabilità limitata – srl*), for instance, there is a growing percentage (40 per cent) in which private shareholders have a majority interest. Functional privatization by means of concessions and service contracts has also gained in importance, since local governments are increasingly prone to externalize (*esternalizzare*) service provision.

There is some evidence that these developments have brought about improvements. The institutional option of spinning off local entities tends to relieve municipal budgets by lowering local authority payroll costs. In this regard, outsourcing in its various forms has been successful (Lippi, 2003, p. 163). As far as corporatization is concerned, it has brought greater professionalism to top management in municipal corporations comparable to the private sector (Longo and Plamper, 2004, p. 332). Reporting, performance monitoring and accounting for externalized entities and corporations have been improved and adapted to private sector standards (Grossi and Mussari, 2008, pp. 30–32).[5]

Corporatization, outsourcing and privatization have, however, had certain negative consequences in connection with upgrading the position of the mayor. It has been noted that the relationship between managers of local corporations and mayors has become increasingly personalized and opaque (Longo and Plamper, 2004, pp. 332–3). Their interactions have turned out to be based more on confidence than on evidence. Furthermore, in many Italian cities, the boards of directors of corporatized municipal entities consist partly of local politicians, who lack the management techniques and knowledge to adequately steer and control municipal entities (ibid., p. 331; Grossi and Mussari, 2008, p. 31). While the Italian NPM legislation instigated a shift to a municipal contract model with clear performance guidelines and targets, the general upgrading of local executives together with corporatization and only partially implemented performance management have reinforced the model of 'political confidence' (*rapporto politico-fiduciario*). Although the majority of local governments had formally concluded long-term concession contracts with their corporations, as provided by the *Testo Unico Enti Locali* (Decree 267/2000),[6] in reality it is not these contracts that guide and constrain interactions between mayors and top managers of municipal companies. The main mode of steering and control is 'mutual-confidence-building' (Del Vecchio, 2001, p. 163).

The reforms have also negatively affected social service delivery, where massive delegation to the private social sector has increased the risk of fragmenting social policy, weakening its egalitarian and universalistic scope and preparing the triumph of 'privatism' (Bobbio, 2005, p. 43). In general, corporatization and privatization have enhanced institutional fragmentation and reduced horizontal cross-sectoral steering capacities in Italian local government. The diversification of delivery options has produced 'networked' local government, transforming its traditional role as service provider to that of a manager of contractual or quasi-contractual relations (Meneguzzo, 1997). Although reforms have been accompanied by stronger instruments for mayors to fulfil their executive function as local leaders, they are still considered insufficient in human and technical respects. There is still doubt that they will provide mayors with the full support they need in managing increasingly complex partnerships with local and non-local business (Magnier, 2003, p. 193).

4. INTERNAL NPM REFORMS: PERFORMANCE MANAGEMENT AND OUTPUT-ORIENTED STEERING

Germany

In the 1990s, the new steering model (NSM) became the predominant reference model of performance-oriented administrative modernization in

Table 3.2 *Modernizing local service provision: implemented NSM elements in German local governments**

NSM Core Elements	Entirely implemented	Partly implemented
New result-oriented department structures	43.6% (379)	9.3% (81)
Strategic steering units	25.9% (225)	12.4% (108)
Decentralized/operative controlling	10.9% (95)	13.6% (118)
Replacing central resource management units by internal service centres	23.9% (208)	24.7% (215)
Abolition of levels of hierarchy	34.5% (300)	25.4% (221)
Decentralized management of resources	33.1% (288)	26.2% (228)
New budgeting procedures	33.1% (288)	34.4% (291)
Output analyses (definition of 'products')	29.0% (252)	9.9% (86)
New accounting systems (cost and activity accounting)	12.7% (108)	33.0% (287)
Reporting	22.1% (192)	20.7% (180)
	Implemented	
Contracts between politics and administration	14.8% (129)	**
Contracts between top management and services	24.3% (211)	**

Notes:
*   Empirical basis: responses of 870 mayors.
** Item not applicable.

Source: Adapted from Bogumil et al. (2007), p. 40.

German local government (Bogumil et al., 2007; Kuhlmann et al., 2008). The NSM was largely inspired by the international debate on new public management, particularly in the Netherlands (the Dutch city of Tilburg; see Banner, 1991) and fostered by the KGSt.[7] According to the survey mentioned above (see note 4), virtually every German local authority with more than 10 000 inhabitants (92 per cent) has pursued modernization since the 1990s, 80 per cent of which was guided by the NSM concept. Despite the unquestionable conceptual and discursive predominance of NSM, the actual implementation of reform presents a quite different if not disappointing picture. Although NSM protagonists have repeatedly pointed to the need for holistic, NSM-guided reform, more than 66 per cent of municipalities have adopted only selected elements of the concept, and local authorities intent on full NSM implementation are a small minority (15 per cent). After more than ten years of NSM modernization in Germany, no single element of the NSM has been implemented by a majority of German local governments. Only 22 local authorities (2 per cent) can be considered 'NSM hardliners', claiming to have implemented seven core NSM elements throughout their entire administrative structures. Measured against the normative call for holistic and comprehensive NSM reform, there is quite obviously an implementation gap.

NPM/NSM reforms in German local government have undoubtedly had a number of positive effects, judging not only from the encouraging self-assessment of mayors but also from actual service and performance improvements, particularly in sectors with direct and frequent contact to customers. Nearly 60 per cent of German municipalities with more than 10 000 inhabitants have created one-stop agencies (*Bürgerbüros*) and about 70 per cent have extended their office hours. Half of the mayors report reductions in the time necessary for administrative procedures in local government. A vast majority of respondents report greater customer focus in their authorities (95 per cent), improved service quality (95 per cent), better citizens' advice services (85 per cent), shorter waiting times (90 per cent) and reductions in processing time (50 per cent). To this extent, there is undoubtedly a link between NSM reform and the output improvements achieved.

As far as the fiscal problems facing German local authorities are concerned, one of the most attractive reform instruments has, unsurprisingly, been the introduction of new budgeting procedures, which were to trigger a transition from traditional cash accounting to a resource-based accruals accounting system (for details see Reichard and Bals, 2002). The survey results show that new budgeting systems have been introduced in 33.1 per cent of municipalities; in a further 34.4 per cent they have been implemented in certain service units. However, in most cases, a pure input-oriented method of budgeting has been pursued and only in 15.7 per cent of cases have measurable objectives and performance targets been defined.

NSM reform has caused problems for some cities in their endeavours to decentralize resource competencies, abolish levels of hierarchy, and strengthen service units acting as quasi-autonomous 'result centres' without establishing appropriate controlling systems and central steering mechanisms. The (at least partial) abolition of hierarchical subordination and levels of hierarchy has produced a sort of 'management vacuum' (*Führungsvakuum*), with awkward consequences for steering and decision-making (see Bogumil et al., 2007, pp. 151–3). In reaction to the unintended consequences of NSM modernization, local authorities have already reversed significant elements of the reform, pointing to a 're-Weberianization' of German local government after ten years of NSM experimentation. Furthermore, knowledge utilization is inadequate in

German local government (Kuhlmann, 2007). Comprehensive 'catalogues of products' have been elaborated as new tools of output steering. Yet they are rarely used in decision-making. Instead, a new 'product bureaucracy' has been established in the place of a potentially more flexible system of performance management. As a consequence, a substantial proportion of municipalities (between 33 per cent and 66 per cent) that have defined such 'products' use them neither to determine nor to negotiate budgets, nor to reorganize administrative processes. Even more strikingly, 14.2 per cent of the local governments that have elaborated 'catalogues of products' do not use them for any purpose at all.

France

In the case of France, it should be recalled that some management elements usually considered part of the NPM concept have had a long tradition. 'Contracts' (*contrats/conventions*), for instance, had been employed even before the decentralization of *Acte I* (Marcou et al., 1997; Gaudin, 2004; Wollmann, Balboni and Gaudin, Chapter 2 in this volume). Yet such contracts were not conceptually linked with the NPM approach but were designed to cope with the growing problems of coordinating the administrative system, which is increasingly fragmented by the proliferation of institutional actors and bureaucratic levels since decentralization. Controlling mechanisms (*contrôle de gestion*), too, had already been established in French local government in the first wave of decentralization in the 1980s (Kuhlmann, 2008b). Hence some general councils and municipalities have more than 20 years of experience with *contrôle de gestion*. In contrast to Germany, there has never been a holistic and overarching concept of local public management reform in France (see Rouban, 2008). Performance and quality management (*démarches de performance/de qualité*) has been introduced in a more pragmatic and incremental manner, although some specific legal prescriptions with nationwide relevance have helped accelerate the municipal modernization process. This applies particularly to new local accounting systems and the budgetary reforms introduced in French municipalities as long ago as the early 1990s.[8] The Financial Reform Act of 2001 (*loi organique relative aux lois de finances* – LOLF), too, can partly be interpreted as driving performance-oriented reforms. In making performance management, evaluation and output-oriented budgeting compulsory for the deconcentrated state authorities, the LOLF has had an at least indirect impact at the local level, prompting a debate on its possible extension to local authorities (see Richard, 2006, p. 127; Fievet and Laurent, 2006). Yet French local governments have resisted such generalization and standardization, pointing out that performance-oriented steering methods were already practised at the local level long before the LOLF (Richard, 2006, p. 7).

Notwithstanding these reforms, more comprehensive modernization projects have been limited to big cities and the *départements*, whereas the vast majority of French municipalities do not participate because they lack the size and administrative resources to do so. Focusing on the more viable local governments, one crucial element of NPM-related administrative reforms is the 'performance tables' (*tableaux de bord*), which measure and monitor selected performance indicators of various administrative services. According to a survey conducted in 82 French *communes* with populations of over 5000 (see Meyssonnier, 1993), about 30 per cent had introduced controlling instruments, such as performance tables (*tableaux de bord*), as long ago as 1993. Fifty-five per cent had adopted new accounting procedures (*comptabilité analytique*) and 15 per cent had employed controllers (*conseiller/analyste de gestion*). In the 1990s, performance measurement, controlling (*contrôle de gestion*) and quality assessments (*démarches de qualité*) in local service delivery continued to gain in importance. A survey by the French Association for Public Sector Quality (France Qualité Publique) revealed that all local government members of this association (53) have meanwhile appointed 'quality managers' (*directeur qualité, responsable qualité, ingénieur qualité, référent qualité* etc.). Quality management is often combined with other elements of performance management, most frequently performance tables (72 per cent). Finally, but importantly, French local governments increasingly use self-evaluation tools, for instance in social service delivery (see the example of the Conseil Général du Territoire de Belfort) or in the public utility sector (see the example of water provision and sewage in Lille; Kuhlmann, 2009). According to a survey conducted in 2002, roughly 60 per cent of cities with more than 50 000 inhabitants introduced internal self-evaluation procedures, 30 per cent having done so more than five years previously.[9] Interestingly, controlling units have in many cases been set up to enhance the overall cross-policy steering capacities of city governments. Unlike in Germany, organizational reforms of municipal administration are not primarily designed to strengthen decentralized service units. Their aim is rather to reintegrate local administration and to overcome policy egoisms. The predominant rationale of this reorganization process is '*transversalité*' and not, as in Germany and Italy, the decentralization of management capacities.

As for the effects of these reforms, there can be no doubt that local government performance has become more transparent and administrative action more output-oriented. In *communes* and *départements*, where controlling (*contrôle de gestion*), performance tables (*tableaux de bord*) and policy evaluations have been introduced, local managers and councillors are clearly better informed on performance evolution and (at least sometimes) on the costs of local service delivery. Set-up costs for performance management were also quite moderate in sectors (e.g. child care) where reporting (e.g. to state authorities) had long been practised and local actors were able to apply existing methods of self-evaluation and monitoring. There are examples, like Le Havre (see Kuhlmann, 2009), where comprehensive performance tables have proved an appropriate instrument of top management and even of political steering. Since the tables show the core indicators of performance to be policy relevant, local councillors (*adjoints*) show a conspicuous interest in these tools. It is none the less striking that performance and quality measurement is based largely on quite simple, measurable indicators and 'countable' routine administrative actions, whereas more complex, 'non-countable', qualitative data are often not displayed in the *tableaux de bord*. Furthermore, the cultural embeddedness of performance management is still rather limited, even in advanced municipalities. The density of performance supervision has increased, particularly in service units where performance can easily be measured and single actions by employees can be (electronically) counted (e.g. telephone calls, consulting time, waiting duration etc.). In these sectors involving more or less routine tasks, performance measurement tends to make the employee feel closely supervised, to the detriment of motivation. This makes quality improvements (e.g. citizens' advice) more unlikely.

In general, there seems to be no immediate causal link between NPM-oriented reforms by French local governments and actual output improvements in service production. Instead, quality and service improvements have resulted from more conventional, policy-related modernization in the context of so-called *projets de service* (service projects) tailored to the specific demands of a policy field. In contrast to controlling and performance management as more general approaches in administrative reform, the *projets de service* are customized to fit specific local services and adapted to particular sectors of activity. With this 'policy sensitivity', the French *projets de service* have brought visible innovations and considerable service improvements for the public (see Kuhlmann, 2009).

Italy

During the 1990s, when the entire Italian political system was going through a period of severe crisis, local governments underwent a cycle of reforms largely inspired by the NPM doctrine (Valotti, 2000). Strikingly, unlike both Germany and France, the NPM reforms at the local level in Italy were imposed mainly by national legislation (Lippi, 2003, pp.

159–60; Capano, 2003, p. 787). However, this strategy of 'statutory' NPM has proved only partly, if at all, successful.

The budgetary reforms of 1995 (Decree 77/1995) and 1997 (Bassanini II) as well as the major reform act (Law 142/1990) that required local governments to introduce new forms of management control (confirmed by Law 29/1993) are key moves towards reforming output-oriented steering in performance management. One core element of the 1995 reform act was the introduction of the so-called *piano esecutivo di gestione* – PEG ('management plan') to promote the diffusion of new controlling practices (*controllo di gestione*) in assigning targets to local managers, programming performance objectives, and recording indicators of efficiency (Del Vecchio, 2001; Anessi-Pessina, 2000; Garlatti, and Pezzani, 2000). The PEG also provided for clearer separation between the executive leaders (*guinta*) and administrative directors (*dirigenti*) on the basis of target contracts and output-related resource allocation to each of the administrative departments. Besides this, accrual accounting was made compulsory for all Italian local governments (Decree 77/1995), including the monitoring of costs and activities and their evaluation against previously defined management targets. Together with the reform of the internal controls system in 1999 (Decree 286; see Dente and Azzone, 1999),[10] these legislative steps sought to enhance performance orientation and management capacities at the local level. Furthermore, with the statutory introduction of *carta dei servizi* (Mussari, 2001) (citizens' charter), the measurement of quality indicators and consumer satisfaction was statutorily imposed on Italian local governments (Laws 241/1990 and 59/1997).

Local government implementation of these statutory (although not generally mandatory) reforms is regarded as 'patchy' (see Ongaro and Valotti, 2008, pp. 183–6). Important differences stem from regional administrative cultures (see Magnier, 2003, pp. 189 f.). The NPM process appears to be led by municipalities in Emilia-Romagna, Tuscany, Umbria, and the North East (Lippi, 2003). On the other hand the wide disparities in the pace of adaption, which tend to create an evident cleavage between those 'who are "in step" and those who are "latecomers"' (Lippi, 2003, p. 163), is also due to local actor constellations and reform strategies. Whereas in some municipalities political leaders and senior managers have been favourable to the reforms or knowledgeable about the innovations required, in others they have opposed them, bringing implementation of NPM to a halt (ibid., p. 161).[11] It is none the less worth noting that local governments had adopted planning and results assessment as long ago as 1993. This included financial autonomy for up to 60 per cent of resources and expanded managerial strategies in public services (ibid., p. 152). In 2001, 93 per cent of Italian municipalities had already set up an independent unit providing managerial accounting services, and 50 per cent had adopted innovative accounting methods (Capano, 2003, p. 794). At the time of publication, almost all municipalities and provinces had formally set financial targets (making managers accountable for financial inflows and outflows) and introduced management control systems.

Notwithstanding these remarkable achievements by Italian local governments, NPM reforms have only partly been finalized. In practice, the predominant budgetary method within the newly established PEG remains input-oriented, with information on outputs or outcomes rarely being included (Longo and Plamper, 2004, p. 328; Ongaro and Valotti, 2008, p. 184). According to a survey conducted in 1999 (see Promberger et al., 2000, pp. 96 f.), only about one quarter of Italian municipalities had defined performance indicators within the PEG for measuring efficiency and effectiveness. Likewise, only few local governments had set performance targets that included non-financial issues. At the end of the 1990s, five years after *controllo di gestione* became obligatory, more than half the municipalities with a population of over 20 000 had not yet introduced reforms (Magnier, 2003, p. 188). The legal provision of the *carta dei servizi* has prompted very few cities to conduct quality analyses or service comparisons.[12]

So far, changes in performance have been only indirectly connected with the formal introduction of controlling systems and new budgetary procedures. Some scholars (see Longo and Plamper, 2004; Lippi, 2003) attribute local performance improvements to the redefinition of roles and competencies in the local arena. The strengthening of the executive branch and the mayor with the introduction of a city manager (*direttore generale*; Decree 127/1997) and the general upgrading of local organizational autonomy are the most common improvements. However, NPM modernization has also contributed to these changes in partly transforming local decision-making and administrative cultures. Transparency on outputs, efficiency, costs and quality has increased significantly with the introduction of PEG and performance reviews, although this information is not adequately used for budgeting, fixing performance pay, or contract management, and calculations are mostly not based on predefined performance targets. Nevertheless, the instruments that have so far been implemented have obliged local executives 'to look at real processes instead of simply paper shuffling, to measure performance and output instead of hiding behind conformity to regulations' (Bobbio, 2005, p. 42). Furthermore, heads of administrative departments (*dirigenti*) enjoy greater autonomy *vis-à-vis* the cabinet (*giunta*), so that no more than 20 per cent of all business now passes through the *giunta* compared to about 80 per cent before the reforms (Longo and Plamper, 2004, p. 327). The managerial autonomy of the *dirigenti* and their budgetary responsibilities have thus been noticeably enlarged. However, these changes have also had negative consequences. Centrifugal forces and institutional fragmentation within local administration have increased, and the unity of the community has tended to erode, while intra-organizational disparities within local governments and between administrative departments have grown (ibid., p. 328).

Considering the degree of NPM implementation against the ambitious reform objectives of national and regional legislation, there is – not surprisingly – an obvious 'implementation gap' (Capano, 2003, p. 794). The actual use of information on performance is in fact rather limited, with the sole exception of financial indicators, the application of which has deep roots in the Italian system (traditional control system of the court of accounts). Furthermore, the majority of local administrations have not complied with the formal requirement to establish their own *carta dei servizi* and, where it has been established, it has become a 'ritual, symbolic expression of good intent, and not a manual of fair conduct for organizations with respect to their own clients' (ibid.). Notwithstanding this critical assessment, local governments must be acknowledged as pioneers of NPM in Italy. They exemplify the most advanced public sector reform in Italy (Lippi, 2003, p. 152), since they have been much more willing than national ministries to tackle modernization and to restructure (Bobbio, 2005, p. 43). Local authorities have undertaken a profound transformation of operational procedures and their achievements have largely inspired reform at other levels of government and in other sectors.

5. COMPARISON ACROSS COUNTRIES: CONVERGENCE OR DIVERGENCE?

This section turns from the initial question of the effects of institutional reform on convergence in local government systems to considering the debate on cross-country convergence or divergence (e.g. Pollitt, 2001; Hoffmann-Martinot and Wollmann, 2006; Wollmann, 2008; Kuhlmann, 2008a).

Patterns of Convergence

German and Italian local governments have converged considerably with the French model of local service delivery in terms of contracting out, corporatization and 'satellization'. In France, the euphoria about liberalization and privatization, which seized some (conservative) mayors in the 1980s, has meanwhile calmed down (Maury, 1997; Thoenig, 2005). German and Italian local authorities, by contrast, are increasingly predisposed towards such strategies. Hence, recent developments in Germany and Italy make for an institutional rapprochement with the French system where public services are traditionally contracted out to private firms, and local authorities have numerous (single-purpose) 'satellites'. In Germany and Italy, too, the number of actors in local service delivery and decision-making has tended to grow, with similar effects on local steering and coordination. In both countries, organizational diversification and institutional fragmentation at the local level has been increasingly guided by similar concepts of the 'enabling authority' (Libbe et al., 2004) and networking administration. The scope for comprehensive cross-policies and the political influence of the local councils are weakened; in Italy, but also in North Germany, this marks a real break with traditional institutional practices and cultures in parliamentary democracy and party competition. The institutional landscape and the steering practice of German and Italian local government have increasingly come to resemble their French counterparts.

As far as the external dimension of NPM reform is concerned, we can thus conclude that historical path dependencies and institutional traditions have greater explanatory power in France than in Germany and Italy. In Germany and Italy, the functionally strong system of local service production and delivery inherited from the nineteenth and twentieth centuries has increasingly come under pressure and has changed significantly. Historically ingrained institutional structures of service delivery have been transformed into a new system of 'local governance', replacing the old model of 'unitary local government'. French local governments, by contrast, have not abandoned the traditional path of institutional development – at least in terms of service provision – inherited from the nineteenth century. Whereas the hypothesis of historical path dependencies thus appears to be confirmed by these findings, the assumption of divergence of the German and Italian systems from the French model must be rejected.

Furthermore, convergence is apparent with regard to the internal dimension of NPM (see also Kuhlmann, 2008a). In all three countries such measures were implemented at the local level, contributing to more transparency and better output performance. Germany and Italy both suffer from what has been referred to in both countries as an 'implementation gap' (Kuhlmann et al., 2008; Capano, 2003), measured in Germany from a normative perspective against the NSM and in Italy against the copious NPM reforms imposed on local government by national legislation, which have only partly or 'apparently' been implemented and applied ('apparent implementation') (Gherardi and Mortara, 1988; Lippi, 2003, p. 161). Due to the extensive formal regulation of NPM reform in Italy, this 'gap' between legal rules, local implementation and actual outcomes is most striking from a transnational perspective, although actual modernization at the local level can be considered fairly advanced. France has produced neither a holistic local reform model nor national legislation comparable to Italy but a 'silent' modernization without a 'vision' (see Rouban, 2008). The three legalistic countries, Germany, France and Italy, show striking convergence: all three have increasingly combined traditional, bureaucratic steering instruments with new elements of managerial reform (see Bouckaert, 2006; Capano, 2003; Lippi 2003; Kuhlmann et al., 2008). This new mixture of classical Weberian elements and new NPM features might prove to be a typical continental European version of NPM reform. Yet we have shown here that the organizational features in this mix are only partly compatible and often contradictory, which has had a number of unintended consequences.

Patterns of Divergence and Persistence

German, French and Italian local authorities also show some divergence and, more remarkably, strong patterns of persistence. Whereas NSM implementation in German and Italian local government produced a more decentralized organizational structure, French authorities put much greater emphasis on reintegrating the local administrative system by reinforcing cross-sectoral steering capacities. In Germany and Italy, by stark contrast, public management reform was primarily directed at further decentralizing and unbundling local government units. Hence intra-organizational decentralization in German and Italian municipalities conspicuously contrasts with what is called '*transversalité*' in France, which – in this respect – mirrors the divergence between the two countries. This assessment thus contradicts the hypothesis of general convergence in internal governmental NPM reforms between the three countries.

In the 'new steering model', German local authorities have a relatively uniform, comprehensive reference model that was one of the most important driving factors in the astonishingly fast diffusion of reforms, managed by a locally steered think tank (KGSt). In Italy, by contrast, the legislative steering and top-down attempts to introduce NPM reforms by law is one of the most striking peculiarities. This approach to introducing NPM meant that reforms were imposed on local government. French local governments, by contrast, could not draw on any kind of comprehensive, widely accepted model of administrative reform, owing not least to the persisting fragmented territorial structure of the French subnational system. Apart from certain limited legal provisions, there was also no noteworthy national legislation prescribing local NPM measures in France, since French municipal executives have always successfully resisted centrally imposed standardization. In France, the intensity of NPM reform differs considerably between the majority of tiny rural *communes* and the functionally strong municipalities of major cities, reflecting what is called '*France à deux vitesses*'. In Germany and Italy, differences in the implementation of NPM can be attributed to regional cleavages: in Germany a gap between East and West (see Kuhlmann et al., 2008) and between North and South in Italy (see Lippi, 2003; Magnier, 2003).

As far as the classical continental European 'rule-of-law' culture is concerned, there are noticeable patterns of persistence over time, once again in keeping with historical institutionalism theory. Although there has been a considerable move towards new managerial instruments and techniques of performance measurement, none of the three local government systems has witnessed a paradigm shift to a 'local managerial state'. The adoption of new evidence-based and performance-oriented instruments notwithstanding, the systems under analysis have retained their rule-of-law culture under which legalistic, rule-bound mechanisms of steering prevail. Even more remarkably, attempts to replace the Weberian bureaucracy undertaken by some cities have meanwhile been reversed to an extent that could be considered at least partial 're-Weberianization'.

6. CONCLUSION: TOWARDS A NEO-WEBERIAN ADMINISTRATION?

Measured against the normative vision of NPM, the reforms examined here have only partly succeeded. Considering that the administrative sciences have repeatedly emphasized public authorities' institutional inertia and their successful resistance to change and reform (see Jann, 2001, p. 329), local governments in continental Europe provide evidence for a quite different conclusion. In contrast to upper levels of government, they have proved capable of modernizing their administration and adapting to new institutional challenges, although – in all three countries – in a more incremental and pragmatic than comprehensive and strategic manner. As a result, local governments in the countries under study undoubtedly have greater citizen and customer focus and are better informed on performance and outputs, even though, or perhaps precisely because, they have implemented NPM only incompletely or selectively. Hence no transformation of the traditional rule-of-law culture has taken place in legalistic countries. Instead, a somewhat ambiguous mix of new managerial instruments and traditional legalistic practices that could be called 'neo-Weberian' has developed (Bouckaert, 2006). Hopes that this model would combine the advantages of the bureaucratic model with those of NPM have yet to be realized. Quite frequently, the 'old' methods of steering (legal rules and hierarchy) have been weakened before the 'new' managerial approaches come to bear (economic incentives and decentralized management). Instead of the efficient 'neo-Weberian' model proclaimed by some scholars, local governments are now, in the post-NPM phase, witnessing a re-emergence of bureaucratic Weberian administration (see Drechsler, 2005), particularly in cities where reforms were most advanced.

Furthermore, the partial failure of NPM and the implementation gap have a great deal to do with the theoretical shortcomings of the reform concept itself. Hence the failure or non-implementation of some reform elements can be understood as a rational answer by local governments to these conceptual deficiencies or, as it were, 'false theory' (see Pressman and Wildavsky, 1984). Political scientists and practitioners have pointed to these problems of the NPM concept from the very beginning. Today, it is generally undisputed that NPM, with its schematic dualism of politics and administration, is conceptually misleading and stands in stark contrast to the reality of political decision-making. Likewise, the model does not take into account the political rationale of the public sector, preventing political actors from defining measurable objectives, from closing binding contracts and from assessing political goal attainment. Since there is little interest on the part of either political or administrative actors to be restricted to an exclusively strategic or managerial role, it is not surprising that, particularly in Germany and Italy, where this approach has been debated, most of the political reform elements have barely functioned.

To sum up, there can be no doubt that the NPM doctrine has left its mark on the continental European administrative landscape and that some of its ideas will survive in the 'institutional memory' of local governments. Yet there has been no shift to a managerial administration and the NPM has lost most of its initial attraction. Whether the 'neo-Weberian' marriage between legalistic and managerial principles will provide a happily-ever-after ending to local government reform remains to be seen.

NOTES

1. The chapter does not assess NPM from a normative point of view. However, in the concluding section we offer some critical remarks concerning the (partly false) 'NPM theory'. For a detailed introduction to NPM as a reform concept see Pollitt and Bouckaert (2004).
2. For a detailed introduction to the three local government systems, see the contribution by Wollmann, Balboni and Gaudin, Chapter 2 in this volume; for Germany and France see Kuhlmann (2008a); Wollmann (2008).
3. Empirical basis: analysis of 3034 corporations of 36 big German cities. The study

4. Data basis: a nationwide survey of a total of 1565 German local governments, which was undertaken from the end of January to June 2005, including all municipalities with more than 20 000 inhabitants, three-quarters of municipalities with between 10 000 and 20 000 inhabitants (without regional bias) as well as two-thirds of the German counties. The survey was part of a research project financed by the Hans Boeckler Foundation (Germany). The response rate after two follow-ups was between 42 and 55 per cent. For details see Bogumil et al. (2007); Kuhlmann et al. (2008).
5. One example is the city of Pisa in Tuscany (90 000 inhabitants), where consolidated annual accounts were introduced in order to allow the municipality to 'assume the role of director of the controlled companies . . . verifying that the results effectively correspond with prearranged objectives' (Mayor of Pisa, quoted in Grossi and Mussari, 2008, p. 31).
6. Moreover, until 2003, most of the local governments in Italy had not yet passed the legally prescribed annual contract (*contratto annuale di servizio*) which were supposed to include information on the amount and quality of services to be delivered as well as on target groups, payment procedures and exact timing (see Longo and Plamper, 2004, p. 332).
7. The KGSt is a non-profit organization, mainly funded by municipalities, with a long and excellent record in consulting particularly local authorities in administrative and organizational matters.
8. In this context, the circular M14 is particularly worth mentioning as it introduced in 1994 (and generalized in 1997) a new system of municipal accounting that marked a rapprochement to private sector accrual accounting that applied to all municipalities. The M14 rule was at the time, however, strongly criticized for its complexity, particularly because it retained a double accounting system (*une double comptabilité*) of traditional cash-based 'administrative accounting' (*comptabilité administrative*) on the part of the municipality on the one hand and resource-based accrual accounting using double-entry book-keeping (*comptabilité financière*) on the part of the state-appointed Comptable du Trésor on the other.
9. The survey was conducted by Maurice Basle in 118 French cities with more than 50 000 inhabitants, 48 of which responded (see Basle, 2003).
10. The new internal control system complemented the traditional modes of 'compliance control' by three new performance-oriented forms: (1) management control; (2) strategic control; (3) evaluation of personnel (see Del Vecchio, 2001; Lippi, 2003, pp. 154–8).
11. Furthermore, the size of the municipalities has turned out to be a determinant of NPM modernization with the medium-sized entities (towns or smaller provinces) benefiting the most and the metropolitan cities, larger provinces and tiny municipalities being the less active and flexible in reform matters (Lippi, 2003, p. 161).
12. One example is the city of Florence (see Longo and Plamper, 2004, p. 336), another is the *municipalizzate* of Brescia (see Promberger et al., 2000, p. 90), where various elements of quality management had already been introduced during the 1980s, hence long before these measures were formally adopted by national legislation.

REFERENCES

Anessi Pessina, Eugenio (2000), *La contabilità delle aziende pubbliche*, Milan: Egea.
Banner, Gerhard (1991), 'Von der Behörde zum Dienstleistungsunternehmen – ein neues Steuerungsmodell für die Kommunen', *VOP*, **13** (4), 3–7.

Basle, Maurice (2003), 'Les pratiques évaluatives des villes de plus de 50 000 habitants', *Pouvoirs Locaux*, **2** (57), 42–4.
Bobbio, Luigi (2005), 'Italy: after the storm', in Bas Denters and Lawrence E. Rose (eds), *Comparing Local Governance. Trends and Developments*, Basingstoke and New York: Palgrave Macmillan, pp. 29–46.
Bogumil, Jörg, S. Grohs, S. Kuhlmann and A. Ohm (2007), *Zehn Jahre Neues Steuerungsmodell. Eine Bilanz kommunaler Verwaltungsmodernisierung*, Berlin: Sigma.
Borgonovi, Elio (2005), *Principi e sistemi aziendali per le amministrazioni pubbliche*, Milan, Italy: Egea.
Bouckaert, Geert (2006), 'Auf dem Weg zu einer Neo-Weberianischen Verwaltung. New Public Management im internationalen Vergleich', in J. Bogumil, W. Jann and F. Nullmeier (eds), *Politik und Verwaltung. PVS Sonderheft*, **37**, 354–72.
Capano, Giliberto (2003), 'Administrative traditions and policy change: when policy paradigms matter. The case of Italian administrative reform during the 1990s', *Public Administration*, **81** (4), 781–801.
Del Vecchio, Mario (2001), *Dirigere e Governare le amministrazioni pubbliche: Economicità, controllo e valutazione dei risultati*, Milan, Italy: Egea.
Dente, B. and G. Azzone (1999), *Valutare per governare*, Milan, Italy: Egea.
Dieckmann, Jochen (1996), 'Konzern Kommunalverwaltung. Zwischen Diversifizierung und Einheit der Verwaltung', *Verwaltung und Management*, **2**, 340–43.
Drechsler, Wolfgang (2005), 'The re-emergence of "Weberian" public administration after the fall of New Public Management: the Central and Eastern European perspective', *Halduskultuur Journal*, **6**, 94–108.
Elefanti, Marco (2003), *La liberalizzazione dei servizi pubblicli locali*, Milan, Italy: Egea.
Fievet, F. and P. Laurent (2006), 'Faut-il une LOLF pour les collectivités locales?', *Revue Française de Finances Publiques*, **95**, 129–45.
Finger, M. and J. Allouche (2002), *Water Privatisation. Trans-national Corporations and the Re-regulation of the Water Industry*, London and New York: SPON Press, Taylor & Francis Group.
Garlatti, A. and F. Pezzani (2000), *I sistemi di programmazione e controllo negli enti locali*, Milan, Italy: Egea.
Gaudin, Jean-Pierre (2004), 'La contractualisation des rapports entre l'Etat et les collectivités territoriales', in G. Marcou and H. Wollmann (eds), *Réforme de la décentralisation, réforme de l'Etat, régions et villes en Europe. Annuaire 2004 des collectivités locales*, Paris: Litec, pp. 215–34.
Gherardi, S. and V. Mortara (1988), 'Può il concetto di cultura organizzativa contribuire allo studio della Pubblica amministrazione?', *Rivista Trimestrale di Scienza dell'Amministrazione*, **1**, 39–58.
Grossi, Giuseppe (1999), 'The phenomenon of group in the Italian municipalities: the experience of Rome', Sienna participation series no. 54, presentation to seminar at the Institute of Local Government Studies, Stockholm. University School of Business, 26 February, Stockholm.
Grossi, G. and R. Mussari (2008), 'Effects of outsourcing on performance measurement and reporting: the experience of Italian local governments', *Public Budgeting & Finance*, **28** (1), 22–38.
Hansen, W. and N. Herbke (2004), 'Länderstudie Frankreich', in W. Schönbäck, G. Oppolzer, A. Kraemer, W. Hansen and N. Herbke (eds), *Internationaler*

Vergleich der Siedlungswasserwirtschaft, **153** (3), Informationen zur Umweltpolitik, Vienna: Österreichischer Städtebund/Bundesarbeitskammer.
Hoffmann-Martinot, V. and H. Wollmann (eds) (2006), *State and Local Government Reforms in France and Germany. Divergence and Convergence*, Wiesbaden, Germany: VS Verlag.
Huron, D. and J. Spindler (1998), *Le management public local*, Paris: LGDJ.
Immergut, Ellen (1992), *Health Care Policies: Ideas and Institutions in Western Europe*, Cambridge: Cambridge University Press.
Jann, Werner (2001), 'Verwaltungsreform und Verwaltungspolitik: Verwaltungsmodernisierung und Policy-Forschung', in E. Schröter (eds), *Empirische Policy- und Verwaltungsforschung. Lokale, nationale und internationale Perspektiven*, Opladen, Germany: Leske + Budrich, pp. 321–44.
Kettl, Donald F. (2000), *The Global Public Management Revolution: A Report on the Transformation of Governance*, Washington, DC: Brookings Institution Press.
König, Klaus (2006), 'Öffentliches Management in einer legalistischen Verwaltungskultur', in W. Jann, M. Röber and H. Wollmann (eds), *Public Management. Grundlagen, Wirkungen, Kritik*, Wiesbaden, Germany: VS Verlag, pp. 23–34.
Kuhlmann, Sabine (2007), 'Leistungsmessung und evidenz-basierte Politik im internationalen Vergleich: was können die deutschen Kommunen lernen?', in J. Bogumil, L. Holtkamp, L. Kißler, S. Kuhlmann, C. Reichard, K. Schneider and H. Wollmann (eds), *Perspektiven lokaler Verwaltungsmodernisierung*, Berlin: Sigma, pp. 75–84.
Kuhlmann, Sabine (2008a), 'Reforming local public services: trends and effects in Germany and France', *Public Management Review*, **10** (5), 573–96.
Kuhlmann, Sabine (2008b), 'Dezentralisierung in Frankreich: ende der unteilbaren Republik?', *Der moderne Staat*, **1** (1), 201–20.
Kuhlmann, Sabine (2009), *Politik- und Verwaltungsreform in Kontinentaleuropa. Subnationaler Institutionenwandel im deutsch-französischen Vergleich*, Baden-Baden, Germany: Nomos.
Kuhlmann, S., J. Bogumil and S. Grohs (2008), 'Evaluating administrative modernization in German local governments: success or failure of the "New Steering Model"?', *Public Administration Review*, **68** (5), 851–63.
Lachaume, Jean-François (1996), 'Les modes de gestion des services publics', *Les Notices de la Documentation Française*, notice 11, 63–9.
Libbe, J., J.H. Trapp and S. Tomerius (2004), *Gemeinwohlsicherung als Herausforderung – umweltpolitisches Handeln in der Gewährleistungskommune*, networking papers – pamphlet 8, Berlin: Deutsches Institut für Urbanistik – DIFU.
Lippi, Andrea (2003), 'As a voluntary choice or as a legal obligation? Assessing New Public Management policy in Italy', in Hellmut Wollmann (ed.), *Evaluation in Public Sector Reform. Concepts and Practice in International Perspective*, Cheltenham, UK and Northampton, MA, USA: Edward Elgar, pp. 140–68.
Longo, F. and H. Plamper (2004), 'Italiens Staats- und Managementreformen am Beispiel der Controllingsysteme und der Leistungsvergleiche', in S. Kuhlmann, J. Bogumil and H. Wollmann (eds), *Leistungsmessung und -vergleich in Politik und Verwaltung*, Wiesbaden, Germany: VS Verlag, pp. 323–40.
Lorrain, Dominique (1995), 'France: le changement silencieux', in D. Lorrain and G. Stoker (eds), *La privatisation des services urbains en Europe*, Paris: La Découverte, pp. 105–29.

Magnier, Annick (2003), 'Subsidiarity: fall or premise of "local government reforms"'. The Italian case', in N. Kersting and A. Vetter (eds), *Reforming Local Government in Europe*, Opladen, Germany: VS Verlag, pp. 183–96.
Marcou, G., F. Rangeon and J.L. Thiébault (1997), *La coopération contractuelle et le gouvernement des villes*, Paris: L'Harmattan.
Maury, Yves (1997), 'Les contradictions du néo-libéralisme gestionnaire: l'exemple du système municipal Nîmois 1983–1995', *Revue Politiques et Management Public*, **15** (40), 145–69.
Meneguzzo, Marco (1997), 'Ripensare la modernizzazione amministrativa e il NPM. L'esperienza italiana: innovazione dal basso e sviluppo della governance locale', *Azienda Pubblica*, **10** (6), 587–606.
Meyssonnier, François (1993), 'Quelques enseignements de l'étude du contrôle de gestion dans les collectivités locales', *Revue Politiques et Management Public*, **11** (1), 129–45.
Mussari, Riccarco (2001), 'Carta die Servizi ed autonomia degli enti locali: un'armonia da ricercare', *Azienda Pubblica*, **14** (5), 515–40.
Ongaro, E. and G. Valotti (2008), 'Public management reform in Italy: explaining the implementation gap', *International Journal of Public Sector Management*, **21** (2), 174–204.
Pollitt, Christopher (2001), 'Clarifying convergence: striking similarities and durable differences in public management reform', *Public Management Review*, **4** (1), 471–92.
Pollitt, C. and G. Bouckaert (2004), *Public Management Reform. A Comparative Analysis*, 2nd edn, Oxford: Oxford University Press.
Portier, Nicolas (2003), 'Les "gagnants" et les "perdants" de "l'Acte II"', *Pouvoirs Locaux*, **4** (52), 62–8.
Pressman, J.L. and A.B. Wildavsky (1984), *Implementation*, 3rd edn, Berkeley, CA: University of California Press.
Promberger, K., J. Bernhart, G. Früh and R. Niederkofler (2000), *New Public Management in Italien*, Bozen, Italy: European Academy Bolzano (EURAC).
Reichard, C. and H. Bals (2002), 'Resource-based accounting and output budgeting as common patterns of public sector management reforms', in D. Bräunig and P. Eichhorn (eds), *Evaluation and Accounting Standards in Public Management*, Baden-Baden, Germany: Nomos, pp. 137–51.
Richard, P. (2006), 'Solidarité et Performance. Les enjeux de la maîtrise des dépenses publiques locales. Rapport publié le 11/12/2006', accessed 5 March 2007 at www.interieur.gouv.fr.
Rouban, Luc (2008), 'Reform without doctrine: public management in France', *International Journal of Public Sector Management*, **21** (2), 133–49.
Steinmo, S., K. Thelen and F. Longstreth (eds) (1992), *Structuring Politics: Historical Institutionalism in Comparative Analysis*, Cambridge: Cambridge University Press.
Thoenig, Jean-Claude (2005), 'Territorial administration and political control: decentralization in France', *Public Administration*, **83** (3), 685–708.
Valotti, Giovanni (2000), *La Riforma delle Autonomie Locali: dal Sistema all'Azienda*, Milan, Italy: EGEA.
Wohlfahrt, N. and W. Zühlke (2005), *Ende der kommunalen Selbstverwaltung. Zur politischen Steuerung im 'Konzern Stadt'*, Hamburg, Germany: VSA Verlag.

Wollmann, Hellmut (2002), 'Die traditionelle deutsche kommunale Selbstverwaltung – ein Auslaufmodell?', *Deutsche Zeitschrift für Kommunalwissenschaften*, **1**, 24–51.
Wollmann, Hellmut (2008), *Reformen in Kommunalpolitik und -verwaltung. England, Schweden, Deutschland und Frankreich im Vergleich*, Wiesbaden, Germany: VS Verlag.

4. The local government role in pre-school child care policy in France, Germany, Italy and the UK

Michael Hill, Martine Long, Anna Marzanati and Frank Bönker

INTRODUCTION

Child care policy for pre-school children may be seen as including:

- care that will supplement (or even exceptionally replace) the care provided by parents;
- care for children who are exceptionally vulnerable because of their own health problems or disabilities;
- educational activities for children that will prepare them for the compulsory education system;
- care to facilitate labour market participation on the part of the parents.

There is evidence that these distinctions are valid across the four countries, particularly because widespread attention is being paid to the issues of both early years education and parental labour market participation. But, naturally, modern provisions emerge within systems established earlier, when the first two concerns were more dominant, so it is often difficult to separate later services from the more limited earlier forms. These earlier forms are important inasmuch as they determined the roles of local authorities and other providers in each country.

While in all these cases there are likely to be reasons for provisions to be located close to families and homes, there is scope for very varied roles for local government. These may be seen as involving both regulatory roles and provider roles, but their exact manifestations will be affected by:

- roles adopted by religious and voluntary organizations as protectors of families and children, and as education providers;

- the institutional locations of closely related services, in particular: mainstream education, health care and services to support labour market participation;
- alternative views of the extent to which these activities should under normal circumstances be the responsibility of parents – making their own provisions or purchasing services in the market.

TRADITIONS

France

In France the Roussel Law of 23 December 1874 created a system of medical inspection of children. In 1889, legislation enabled neglected children to be made wards of the state, and in 1898 administration was eased by a law giving judges the power to confer guardianship of children on the public authority (Assistance Publique) or on a third party (Pedersen, 1993, p. 69). A law of 27 June 1904 created the départemental service of assistance to children, facilitating the taking of children into the state's care.

The first reception centres in France were developed in the late nineteenth century. They offered places of protection to the children of workers to protect them from the dangers of the street. They were at first called rooms of asylum or 'hospitality'. But after 1881 they were called nursery schools.

Germany

Voluntary child care activities were also widespread in late nineteenth-century Germany (Evers and Sachße, 2003, p. 62). Alongside municipal poor relief, there was a wide variety of private charities and civil associations that offered services for mothers and orphans as well as for neglected and deviant children. These activities were complemented by state and national legislation. In the last quarter of the nineteenth century, most German states adopted legislation on corrective education and child care and on the registration and control of foster parents. Regulations at the national level were largely confined to the 1903 Child Protection Act (*Kinderschutzgesetz*), which tightened the limits to child labour and provisions on the curtailment or removal of parental responsibility in the new German Civil Code, which became effective in 1900.

Child care activities included day care for children (Evers and Sachße, 2003, p. 64). As testified by the international diffusion of the term, the very idea of kindergarten was originally born in Germany in the late eighteenth and early nineteenth centuries (Wollons, 2000). But kindergartens did not become widespread until the end of the nineteenth century. By 1910, they accounted for 13 per cent of children aged three to six. This development was more pronounced in the south than the north of Germany, and providers of kindergartens were predominantly private. States and municipalities largely refrained from subsidizing, let alone running, child care facilities, but encouraged their establishment.

After the First World War, a national framework for child protection and child care was created. The 1922 Imperial Youth Welfare Act (*Reichsjugendwohlfahrtsgesetz*) codified a right to education for all children, obliged all states and municipalities to establish youth offices in charge of child protection, and enshrined the strong role of non-profit organizations, the so-called welfare associations (*Wohlfahrtsverbände*), in the formulation of policies and the provision of services (Bönker and Wollmann, 2000).

In the early years of the Weimar Republic, child care places declined. It took until 1928 for the pre-war level to be reached again. The increasing involvement of municipalities in the provision of child care led to a growing proportion of public child care, which stood at about 30 per cent of all places in the late 1920s (Evers and Sachße, 2003, p. 66; Konrad, 2004, pp. 150–51).

Under the Nazis, the child care sector was largely dominated by a party welfare organization, the Nationalsozialistische Volkswohlfahrt (Konrad, 2004, ch. 7; Evers and Sachße, 2003, p. 68). The latter took over the facilities of Left and non-confessional providers and became the main partner of the municipalities. Only the facilities run by church-related welfare associations maintained some autonomy. While the Nazis were committed to a traditional notion of motherhood, they expanded child care services.

Italy

In Italy, a national welfare service began to develop in the first years of the seventeenth century, under the influence of the Catholic Church by means of congregations dedicated to fundraising and management of poorhouses. At the turn of the eighteenth century, also an educational aim began to develop beside that of protection: this change helped to increase bequests of money in favour of *opere pie* (charitable institutions) as the organizations in charge of welfare service.

These were the reasons why, before the unification of Italy, welfare assistance was conceived as a kind of charity more for ethical and religious purposes than as an assistance service to the poor. For the poor, the Catholic Church was the appointed institution to organize and manage family and childhood protection, and provide charity funds. After the unification of Italy, the historical tie between the Church and charity was severed.

The very first attempt to impose rules and regulations upon the welfare system was represented by three important acts: a statute dated 1862 that was followed by the Crispi Act in 1890. The first was issued by a strongly liberal-oriented parliament and aimed to give self-governing power to *opere pie*; the deliberate goal of the law was to remove *opere pie* from any Catholic or political influence. The 1890 Crispi Act set out 'Rules on public welfare and charity organizations'. It provided a strong definition of the state role and activities in respect of welfare service: the idea was to change the structure of assistance and charity organizations by eliminating the aim of Catholic redemption in favour of tangible help for the needy. From a structural point of view, the Crispi Act converted the *opere pie* into a beneficent institute, denominated Ipab (*Istituzioni pubbliche di assistenza e beneficenza*), and supported it with charity and assistance boards, called Eca (*ente comunale di assistenza*).

In the Fascist era there were considerable increases in public assistance. Between 1925 and 1929, the regime created two distinct institutes for children and orphans (ONMI – National Organization for Maternity and Childhood (abrogated in 1975) and ONOG – National Organization for War Orphans). In 1934 a consolidation act was approved for protection and assistance to childhood and maternity; in the same year juvenile courts were created. However, the only surviving legislation after the Fascist era was the Crispi Law of 1890 – a unique organic body of law on welfare service in Italy in force until the year 2000.

The UK

In the UK a voluntary organization, Doctor Barnardo's, founded in 1869, together with religious-denomination-based children's societies, pioneered the development of institutional care for children. But perhaps more important in the long run was the role the National Society for the Prevention of Cruelty to Children (NSPCC) began to play in 1884 as a pioneer of interventions to prevent the ill-treatment of children. The NSPCC secured the passing of various child protection legislation around the turn of the century and played an important role in its enforcement (Hendrick, 1994). Whilst legislation was important for this voluntary activity, there was however very little public funding.

In the UK, at the beginning of the twentieth century, official concerns about why so many volunteers to fight in the Boer War had been found unfit to do so led to measures concerned with child health and development.

A school medical service was established, meals were provided within the public education system, and there were measures to protect the health of mothers and infants. Local authorities were made responsible for the implementation of these measures.

The First World War saw the setting up of day nurseries in the UK to facilitate female labour market participation. The 1918 Maternity and Child Welfare Act brought these under the jurisdiction of local authorities. In the same year an education act gave local education authorities the power to establish nursery schools and classes. Yet most day nurseries were disbanded after the war and nursery school development was minimal.

CONSOLIDATION AFTER 1945

France

In France a 1912 law that created a court for children and the possibility of establishing surveillance and education measures to avoid the need to take children into institutional care was consolidated by an ordinance in 1945. This set up a system of children's judges and established powers to investigate social situations. The law set up a two-tier system of child welfare: administrative protection provided by state services in the form of the *départementale* direction of sanitary and social affairs, and judicial protection. This law recognizes two categories of children in need of care: children in danger and delinquent children.

The decentralization laws of 7 January and of 22 July 1983 transferred social security responsibilities in respect of protection of children to the *départements*. They now handle the administrative protection of children in danger or at risk of danger. The law of 10 July 1989 redefines the roles and rights of relatives in respect of the service.

In France the development of pre-school education in the postwar period was much more dramatic than in the UK and Germany. By 1981, 90.2 per cent of three-year-olds and 34.8 per cent of two-year-olds were in pre-school education. By 1988 these figures amounted to 97.4 per cent and 36 per cent respectively (Ambler, 1991, p. 24).

Germany

In Germany, the Weimar legal framework for child protection and child care was largely restored after the Second World War (Bönker and Wollmann, 2000, p. 337). More comprehensive legal reform became effective only in the 1990s. The 1990 Act on Child and Youth Support (*Kinder- und Jugendhilfegesetz* – KJHG) drew a distinction between children and young people, and tried to eliminate the paternalistic remnants of the 1961 legislation. It introduced a right to support (*Hilfe zur Erziehung*) for all parents who feel that they cannot cope with their children and favoured a more preventive approach (Baistow and Wilford, 2000). It aimed to replace the removal of children from their homes with better support for children and their parents. At the same time, however, the new law did not affect the strong position of the welfare associations and left the responsibility for child care with the youth offices.

With regard to child protection, the KJHG was complemented in 1998 by the first major reform of parent and child law (*Kindschaftsrecht*) since 1896. This changed the procedure of curtailment and removal of parental responsibility. Most importantly, it brought a new actor to the proceedings in the family courts – the *Verfahrenspfleger*, in charge of representing the child's interests, particularly if the interests of child and parents seem to diverge.

While Germany was the home of the kindergarten, it became a laggard with regard to child care provision after the Second World War. The growth in child care facilities since the mid-1960s has been weaker than in most other EU countries, and most child care places have been part-time only. A number of factors have worked against a stronger expansion of child care (Aust and Bönker, 2004, p. 32; Hagemann, 2006): First, (West) Germany has long been a stronghold of the male breadwinner model and a traditional model of motherhood (Vinken, 2001). Second, the experience of fascism in the past and state socialism in the former GDR has added to reservations against public child care. Third, the institutional setting has been unfavourable. The competencies of the federal government in the field have been limited to funding; most legislation and provision rests with the states, the municipalities and non-profit organizations. This institutional fragmentation has been inimical to an expansion of services by increasing the need for cooperation and provoking conflicts over competencies. Moreover, states and local governments have often lacked the resources to finance child care facilities, enjoying little autonomy in levying taxes and burdened by unfunded mandates imposed on them by the higher tiers of government.

The expansion of child care facilities received a push in 1992 with an amendment to the KJHG, which established a legal entitlement to a kindergarten place for every child aged three to six (Bönker and Wollmann, 1996, p. 453). Due to pressure from local governments, which complained about a lack of resources, in November 1995 the full enactment of the entitlement was delayed until 1999.

While the 1992 entitlement contributed to an increase in kindergarten places for children aged three to six, it did little to create new facilities for younger children and to introduce more full-day places. These issues were addressed only in the new millennium (Aust and Bönker, 2004, pp. 39–40). In the run-up to the 2002 parliamentary elections, the sitting Red–Green government launched a campaign for an expansion of public child care that contributed to the surprising re-election of the government. After the 2005 parliamentary elections, the conservative CDU/CSU joined the bandwagon. The new inter-party consensus on an expansion of child care documents the gradual erosion of the traditionally strong reservations against public child care in Germany. This erosion has been favoured by rising female labour market participation as well as by concerns about declining birth rates and about shortcomings of the German education system, most notably a high social selectivity and a weak integration of migrants.

Building on the new consensus and in line with earlier announcements by the Red–Green government, the government has strongly committed itself to an expansion of child care. It has departed from earlier practice and has injected federal money into the system. The currently debated Child Support Act (*Kinderförderungsgesetz*) promises federal subsidies worth €4 billion for the expansion of child care from 2009 to 2013. Moreover, the federal government wants to extend the existing legal entitlements by adding a right to a nursery (*Krippen* – see below) place for all children aged 1–3 with effect from 2013.

Italy

With the Republican Constitution, dated 1948, the welfare system for family and childhood was given formal legal shape by the 31 article, which recognized it as a general aim for the Italian Republic. In 1949 a new association was founded: the National Board for the Protection of Motherhood and Childhood (ENPMF).

More detailed law and procedures arrived some years later, between 1960 and 1970. The many changes in the cultural, social and economic national life of Italy led Parliament to start to regulate public protection policies. In this respect, the following acts are important: Law 898 (1 December 1970) reformed the family law system; Law 194 (22 May 1978) contained rules for the working mother's protection; and Law 903 (9 December 1977) imposed legal measures for the effective equality of rights between men and women.

In particular, regarding early childhood care and education, Law 444 (18 December 1968) provided national funds for pre-primary schools, and this led to the development of a state-run *scuola materna* system, but also formalized the tripartite nature of pre-school sector (state, or municipal, or private/church); while Law 1044 (6 December 1971) and Law 405 (29 July 1975) respectively declared the provision of *asili nido* for 0- to 3-year-olds a social service of public interest and increased the number of public nursery schools and family guidance centres.

In 1977, Decree 616 delegated functions of public assistance to municipal districts from the former corporate bodies, leaving the promotion of an integrated social and health assistance programme to regions. This increased the variety in the availability of child care services provided in the different parts of the country. However, the concrete realization of constitutional expectations arrived only recently, with Law 285 (28 August 1997) and Law 328 (8 November 2000) which have established an organic welfare service.

The UK

In the UK there are differences in administrative arrangements across the four component countries. While the systems are very similar, the following discussion relates explicitly to England. The Children Act of 1948 established a system for child protection, giving a central role to local government. This act consolidated the existing child care legislation, and created departments in which professional social work practice would develop in child care and, in due course, in work with families. The key point of this legislation was to give local authorities power to seek authority from the courts to remove children from their family of origin if they were deemed to be seriously at risk of ill-treatment. Local authorities were required to set up specialist 'children departments' under the supervision of the Home Office, and the act set up a specialized inspectorate to monitor the quality of local government work. Legislation in the 1970s integrated these departments with adult social care departments, and shifted the supervisory responsibilities to the ministry concerned with health and social care.

Other measures to support children at risk and vulnerable families emerged in legislation in the 1950s and 1960s. Development of the system seems to have been stimulated by concerns about juvenile crime (Packman, 1975) and by 'scandals' that put weaknesses in the regulatory system on the political agenda (Butler and Drakeford, 2003).

With the development of the child protection system in the UK came the power to offer free day nursery or subsidized day nursery places. As far as general day nursery provision was concerned, the First World War story of the wartime growth and then peacetime retrenchment was repeated after the Second World War (Ginsburg, 1992, p. 172).

In practice, until the 1990s, the development of pre-school education was very slow. The most significant stimulus came from reviews of educational under-attainment in the 1960s (Plowden Report, 1967) urging the development of this form of education, particularly in socially deprived areas. Yet the Conservative governments of the early 1970s and the 1980s rejected this approach, so little change occurred.

Significantly, however, against a background of government neglect, private forms of both nursery education and child care (in day nurseries and most importantly in private 'childminding' arrangements) developed rapidly in the 1980s. Liu quotes figures for rates of change between 1980 and 1990 showing a continuing slight decline in public day nursery places, and a 20 per cent decline in full-time places in public nursery schools offset against a 26 per cent increase in part-time places, but increases of over 100 per cent in the numbers of childminders and private day nurseries and substantial increases in private nursery schools.

Then, in the 1990s, the government began to encourage the development of nursery classes in state schools and introduced a voucher system enabling parents of children over four years of age to get state subsidies for places in private nursery schools. By 1996–7, 58 per cent of children aged three or four were – at least part time – in nursery schools. The incoming Labour government in 1997 abolished the voucher system but continued to expand public provision and then accepted the case for subsidizing private provision too.

SYSTEMS TODAY

The account of the development of child care policy suggests the existence of three threads:

1. Child protection with a focus on intervention into family life in exceptional circumstances.
2. Early-years child care, largely for children of three or under, whose development as a public activity was linked to child protection concerns but can in modern times also be seen as a response to increases in female labour market participation.
3. Pre-school education, where there are now high child participation rates after the age of three across all four countries.

These three topics will now be explored separately.

Child Protection

In France, the relevant 'social service' responsibilities for child protection are concentrated at *département* level. Here a specialist section, Aide

Sociale à l'enfance, investigates cases where intervention to protect children at risk of ill-treatment may be appropriate, and a formally designated *inspecteur* decides whether action is necessary. That may well depend upon a legal order made by a children's judge.

In emergencies, referral to the judges need not necessarily come through the *département* social services. Appropriate services to support children where preventive action has been taken may be provided by voluntary agencies offering residential care, fostering services and social work under contract to the *département* social services. Following investigations of administrative problems, a law of 2007 reformed the child welfare system, introducing more regulation of the process of referral to a court and aiming at better coordination between the administrative protection service and the judicial protection role. The social security service (*service de l'aide sociale*) can contribute to child protection through home help to families, grants and placements in the interest of the child.

In Germany, the main actors involved in child protection are the family courts (*Familiengerichte*, until 1998 *Vormundschaftsgerichte*), the local youth offices and non-profit organizations running services for children and families. The family courts decide on the curtailment or removal of parental responsibility. The local youth offices have to be heard by the courts, bring most cases to the courts and are in charge of guaranteeing the provision of services for children and parents. The set-up of the youth offices and the infrastructure of services can differ between different states and municipalities. As with social services in general, a substantial part of services is provided by the welfare associations, which thus play an important role in child protection.

In Germany, as in the other countries, the legal framework aims at reducing public interventions into family life. The KJHG, with its emphasis on prevention, has brought an expansion of various kinds of counselling for families (Statistisches Bundesamt, 2008). The KJHG also reformed cooperation between the youth offices and the family courts, with a view to shifting the youth offices' focus from supporting the courts to supporting families. While the new law left the traditional role of the youth offices as guardians of children's interests (*Wächteramt*) and the resulting possibility of taking social workers to court for not protecting children untouched, it weakened the legal obligation for the youth offices to bring cases to the family courts and created some uncertainties.

In recent years, a number of spectacular cases in which children were mistreated and abandoned by their parents have led to a debate about how to improve child protection. Critics have argued that the youth offices are understaffed and tend to shy away excessively from assignments to homes or foster parents. In 2005, the KJHG was amended to clarify the legal situation and encourage cooperation between the youth offices, the police, kindergartens and other local actors. Along with a greater public awareness of the issue of child mistreatment and extended training of social workers, these amendments have contributed to a spectacular rise in the number of cases in which parental responsibility was restricted or removed, by about a quarter from 2005 to 2007 (Berth, 2008).

In Italy, child care services are located in local government, within municipalities and *comuni*, in departments in which they are linked with local health services. But initial help in cases where there are children with problems may also be provided by schools and by voluntary agencies.

In Italy, formal interventions depend upon a decision by a youth court. Local 'procurators', rather than staff of social services departments, initiate action. Voluntary organizations are heavily involved in the provision of services for children. The law is explicit about avoiding the removal of a child from its environment wherever possible, and there are strict safeguards involving the courts around the subject of adoption. Fostering is a service provided by private individuals who act in partnership with public agencies (generally municipalities). The latter are responsible for the functions of planning, monitoring, surveillance and support. The fostering procedure is activated by the staff of local social services departments, who identify an appropriate foster provider in consultation with the birth family. If the family approves the decision, foster care is brought into effect by a decree of the judge in charge of guardianship (*giudice tutelare*). If the birth family opposes the decision, the local social service department must obtain a fostering order from the Juvenile Court. Fostering ceases with a cessation order issued by the same authority that made the decision in favour of fostering.

The UK system is similar to that in Italy. Here the key agency is a department of the county council, metropolitan borough, London borough or unitary district, until recently called the 'social services department' but now generally the service is integrated with education (and separated from adult social services) in a department whose name may vary but is commonly a 'department of education and children's services'. Hence all the services discussed in this chapter are now integrated in the UK in the same department.

Investigatory and consequent preventive work is undertaken by social workers employed by these departments. Juvenile court approval is necessary if parental rights are to be removed or suspended, although a considerable amount of intervention occurs without recourse to this formal step. But unlike the situation in Italy, once this has happened the local authority can determine the best arrangements for the care of the child. The only exception to this is that they have to go back to the courts if proposing adoption.

In the UK, access to the courts has to be by way of the local authority, but other actors (health care workers, schools, police, relatives and voluntary organizations) may play a role in drawing attention to problems. As in France, these activities may be contracted to voluntary and private agencies. This particularly applies to the use of adoption and fostering services.

The system established in England and Wales under the Children Act of 1989 tries to ensure that children are protected while at the same time recognizing that public interventions in family life should be kept as low as possible. It supports a long-standing concern to minimize the likelihood of the removal of children from their family of origin. The legislation identifies a wide range of ways in which authorities may spend money to try to avoid taking children into direct care. Social workers in the child care authorities have a crucial role to play in situations in which evidence comes to light that children may be at risk of ill-treatment, abuse or neglect. Their authorities are required to maintain 'child protection registers' of children 'at risk' and develop 'child protection plans' to offer appropriate supportive services to these children and their families. Only a small proportion of children at risk are taken away from their families, over two-thirds are then placed with foster parents. Only about 11 per cent are in some kind of institutionalized care. As in Italy and Germany, foster parents are paid by the local authorities, who supervise their work.

We thus have similarities across the four countries in the way the issues of child protection are tackled. There are variations, affected by differences in local government systems. All four systems involve, where necessary, specialist courts, but only in the UK is that access to those courts specifically channelled through the local authorities.

In all systems voluntary organizations are involved. These seem more important in Germany and Italy than in France and the UK, but there are no data to enable this difference to be quantified. In the UK and in Italy foster care under the supervision of local government is important.

Early-years Child Care

In the four countries different arrangements apply as between pre-school education and implementation of child care policy.

In France – with an explicit focus on those under three – two different ministries, the Ministère des Affaires Sociales, du Travail et de la Solidarité and the Ministère de la Santé, de la Famille et des Personnes handicapées, are responsible for regulation governing the provision of child care policy. They work closely with the family allowance fund (Caisses Nationale des Allocations Familiales) to develop local services in partnership with the *communes*, independent non-profit organizations and sometimes the *départements*. The services include crèches and more individualized forms of day care. The latter are principally licensed *assistantes maternelles*, who take in small numbers of children for care. It may be noted here that while this formal licensing is a characteristic of the French system (and a related phenomenon will be noted in respect of the UK), in Italy and Germany this applies only when the use of public funds is involved. The French approach to this topic is particularly interesting because a new law (27 June 2005) aims to further professionalize childminding, providing training and improving payment levels.

A 2007 report indicates that in France, among children under the age of three, a total of 43 per cent are in some form of child care outside the family: 29 per cent with registered childminders, 11 per cent in collective reception arrangements (day nurseries) and 3 per cent in *crèches familiales*. In 2005, 81 per cent of the day nurseries and 85 per cent of the crèches were managed by local authorities (mainly towns, but in some cases *départements*).

The OECD report *Starting Strong* (2006, p. 329) describes the funding of this part of the French child care system as 'relatively complex', involving 'a number of different actors, direct and indirect grants to settings, as well as family subsidies and tax benefits. It is calculated that in centre-based care, families pay approximately 27 per cent of costs, or about 12 per cent of monthly income'. The family allowance system is an important source of subsidies.

As far as the monitoring of the French system is concerned, there are *départemental* organizations, Protection Maternelle and Infantile, that have responsibility for licensing and monitoring.

In Germany, a system of day centres, *Krippen*, exists. In most cases, *Krippen* and kindergarten places are offered by a single provider. Provision for children aged 0–3 by way of this system varies. There are lower rates of provision in the former West Germany than in the East. As with pre-school education, it is the *Länder* rather than the federal government that have the main responsibility for policy. At the state level, the responsibility has traditionally rested with the ministries of youth and family affairs, but, as with pre-school child care, the education ministries have been increasingly involved. Policies to secure the provision of *Krippen* are then the responsibility of municipalities. Provision is largely public in the East, but largely by way of voluntary and private organizations in the West. It is estimated that about 70 per cent of the costs of these provisions are met out of the public purse, other contributions being about 10 per cent from voluntary organizations and the rest recovered from parents (23 per cent in the West, 20 per cent in the East) (Evers et al., 2005, p. 200).

The system is expanding very rapidly, from provisions for around 6.3 per cent of relevant children in 1994 (Evers and Sachße, 2003) to over double that at the time of writing. According to official estimates, the implementation of the announced legal entitlement to early-years child care requires facilities for about one-third of all children aged 0–3.

The promotion of early-years child care also includes measures to promote care by private childminders (*Kindertagespflege*). The federal government regards the latter as a functional equivalent and stresses the advantages that the more personal atmosphere of child care by private childminders might have. To promote this type of child care, some tax and health insurance privileges have been introduced for childminders. The local youth offices have started to promote subsidized child care by private childminders. In order to get money from the youth offices, child-minders, who normally take up to five children for care in their homes, have to be accredited with them. They do not need formal qualifications, but have to take part in certain courses. Rooms have to meet specific standards. Parents essentially pay the rates they would have to for a *Krippen* place. The number of children aged below three taken care of by publicly subsidized childminders has risen dramatically. Following an increase of almost 30 per cent from 2006 to 2007, the figure now stands at more than one-seventh of all children in *Krippen*. The new Child Support Act expects the share of child care by private childminders to reach 30 per cent.

There have been attempts to professionalize early-years child care, including child care by private childminders. Federal and state legislation has been changed accordingly, and the Federal Ministry for Family Affairs has requested the German Youth Institute (DJI) to revise and refine the 2002 DJI curriculum on qualifications in child day care.

The Italian system, like the French, makes a fairly clear division between the pre-school education system and the child care system. Again, separate ministries are responsible. In the case of child care, the Ministry of Health, Labour and Social Affairs is responsible. An important modern framework law (328/2000) aims to improve social services for children and adults, giving particular attention to support measures for children from underprivileged backgrounds or suffering from neglect, as well as measures designed to harmonize working timetables with the task of looking after a family and measures to support women in difficulties.

While throughout much of the system very different arrangements apply to the *nidi d'infanzia* (child care centres) than to the *scuola dell'infanzia*, there are integrated systems in some places. *Nidi d'infanzia* are centres for children from three months to three years offering places for about 10 per cent of all the children in this age group. Regions and municipalities are responsible for this aspect of child care policy. Distribution of *nidi d'infanzia* across the country is very varied (with more in the north than in the south). Providers are diverse, but most are municipality owned. Public funding is available, but parents normally have to pay a proportion of the costs. Fees vary widely. The 2007 budget law has dedicated €100 million per year for the three-year period 2007–9 to the development of *nidi d'infanzia*. Regions fund their own plans and supplement municipality budgets.

While Italian provisions for children under three are generally rather low, there has been considerable growth in the recent past. A survey conducted by the Istituto degli Innocenti (2006) on the development of the child care system over the past decade outlined some of the characteristic developments of the system during the 1990s: growth in the number of day nurseries for 0–3-year-olds (from 2180 in 1992 to 3008 in 2000, an increase of roughly 38 per cent) and growth in the range of supply (from 5.8 per cent in 1992 to 7.4 per cent in 2000, to 10 per cent in 2007); a growing presence of private day nurseries for 0–3-year-olds; a substantial development of integrative services, which figure in the survey as services such as play areas, child care or family centres or in-home services; a close correlation between the level of presence of services and the extent of demand, with longer waiting lists in areas with a greater number of services; and, finally, a marked lack of homogeneity of levels achieved in different parts of the country.

While the coverage of day nurseries for 0–3-year-olds is around 10 per cent in Italy as a whole, there are significant geographical variations. In Southern Italy there are relatively few services, these offer a limited number of hours of care, often with a lower level of quality in terms of educational approach and facilities.

Overall in Italy there is, as shown above, considerable awareness of the need for increased provision of day nurseries for 0–3-year-olds, partly in compliance with the objectives set by the 2000 European Council of Lisbon but also influenced by the aim of reaching 60 per cent female labour market participation.

In England, responsibility for all aspects of child care has been brought under the control of the education ministry. Earlier there was a division rather like the French one between the education ministry's responsibility for pre-school education and the health ministry's responsibility for other aspects of child care. The change to education system control is reflected in a similar reorganization at local level in which the child care responsibilities of the social services departments has been shifted to departments combining education and child care responsibilities. This change has no impact on the division of tasks between the different tiers of local government.

In the UK, about 20 per cent of children aged 0–3 have 'access to licensed services' (OECD, 2006, p. 416); this involves a mix of services for the children of working parents: 'private childminders, play groups and day nurseries, constituting the highest proportion of private "child care" in Europe' (ibid., p. 417). There is a very small amount of public provision; this is used by local authorities as a resource for the child protection system. UK official statistics are confusing, as they quote child care places for children under eight. Nevertheless, the figures from 2001 illustrate the dominance of private facilities. In England there were 7800 day nurseries providing 285 100 places. But within that total there were only 460 local-authority-provided nurseries (just under 6 per cent of the total) providing 18 200 places (just over 6 per cent). There were also 72 300 registered childminders, providing 304 600 places (note that this amounts to an average of only four places per childminder). Local authorities provided (meaning in this case they would be paying for) 860 (1 per cent) of the childminders and 3300 (1 per cent) of the places.

Local authorities subsidize the places in the day nurseries they own, while they may impose charges. In practice, the resources of the vulnerable families who are being supported in this way will be low and charges are unlikely. Otherwise the only public subsidy for child care (as opposed to pre-school education) comes as part of a tax credit, introduced in 1998.

Reference has been made above to the registration of childminders. In the UK, all childminders and day nurseries must be registered by the local authority, which has a duty to approve arrangements and inspect from time to time. Undoubtedly there are some childminding arrangements that have not been registered, but there is now a well-established local authority role which – given the numbers quoted – will be a not inconsiderable task. The costs of this activity and the costs of the limited number of local authority places in nurseries and childminding arrangements fall upon the normal budgets of local authorities.

Looking across the four countries, we see day care for under-threes as in general much less widely provided than pre-school education, with no uniform system across any of the countries. It is interesting to note the official registration of all private facilities including childminding in France and the UK, but only where public subsidy is involved in the other two countries. Nevertheless early-years child care is everywhere a private activity in receipt of limited public subsidy.

We find – across the four countries – efforts to expand child care provisions. We comment above on German and Italian awareness of the issue, connected to the increase in female labour market participation. Evers et al. write of such policy as being seen in Germany as 'necessary above all for economic reasons . . . to make use of mothers' human capital and to address the problem of the low German birth rate' (2005, p. 196) and in the UK as part of 'the recasting of work/welfare relationships . . . to facilitate an adult worker model family' (ibid.). However, as far as the role of local government is concerned, these developments can be seen as driven by central government. Whilst traditionally local authorities have been key actors (with varying degrees of collaboration with the voluntary sector), modern developments are often passing them by.

Pre-school Education

All four countries now have high levels of participation in education by children beyond the age of three in systems under the supervision of a central ministry of education (except inasmuch as it is a *Länder* responsibility in Germany). All, with France very much in the lead, nowadays see the education dimension of activities for 4–6-year-olds as important. But there are interesting differences.

France stands out as having a particularly unified system. The *écoles maternelles* are available to all children between the ages of two and six, with a legal right to places applying from the age of three. These places are fully funded. The system is organized by the state. Central government determines how the system should operate – curriculum, opening hours etc. – and recruits, trains and remunerates the teaching staff. The local *commune* has the responsibility to provide the physical infrastructure and teaching materials. There are also some church-based facilities, working under contract to the state.

Italy comes closest to the French model, with universal access to the pre-school education system (the *scuola dell'infanzia*) at least from the age of five; this is free in the public sector (excluding meal costs). A central education ministry is responsible for the system overall, but there is a mixed system of provision. Local authorities run only 13 per cent of these schools, private organizations 33 per cent (these include religious bodies, which account for about 20 per cent), while the rest are the direct responsibility of the Ministry of Education (54 per cent). By comparison with the French system, those schools that are outside the control of the central state have quite high levels of autonomy.

The funding situation in Italy is complex. Municipalities are expected to meet the physical infrastructure costs of all public schools, both those they run and those the state runs. Where the municipality runs the schools, it has to finance teachers' salaries. But then there are state subsidies both to municipalities and to the religious and private school providers. Attendance at publicly provided schools is free. 'Fees in church pre-primary schools are also generally modest; but high fees can be charged by private (schools)' (OECD, 2001a, p. 18).

Germany stands out on a number of counts:

- It has rather lower levels of overall child participation in the pre-school education system. Furthermore, a significant proportion of the places provided are for less than full-time attendance.
- Places are not generally free. It is reported that parents pay on average 14 per cent of the costs but there are substantial variations between both states and municipalities. Children from low-income families may be able to pay lower fees, but there is nevertheless evidence that participation from this group tends to be lower.
- Child care facilities are still seen as an element of child and youth support. Formal competencies thus rest largely with the local youth offices and the state ministries of family affairs. The role of the federal government has risen, but is still limited. The main operational legislation is at the state level, with each of the states having a separate law on child care determining the size of groups, funding rules etc. The federal government has only recently started to inject money and has little control over its use.

The German system is dominated by the voluntary sector, and there are only a few commercial providers. They can be subsidized by the states and municipalities, but normally receive less funding. A recent proposal by the Federal Ministry of Family Affairs to put the funding on an equal footing has triggered fierce controversies and has been opposed by the SPD (Social Democratic Party).

The education dimension of child care has been discovered only recently, not least because of Germany's poor showing in the OECD PISA study (OECD, 2001b). Compared to the other countries, pre-school education in Germany has been much less professionalized. Kindergarten teachers (*Erzieher*) have traditionally been seen as a kind of 'public mothers' and have not been treated like (school) teachers (*Lehrer*). They do not have university degrees and are paid much less. Following the 'PISA shock', state ministries for youth and family affairs, traditionally responsible for child care, and state education ministries in most states have agreed on new curricula that aim at professionalizing pre-school education and at smoothing the transition from kindergarten to school.

The new interest in kindergartens in Germany has also prompted a debate about child care fees. Calls for eliminating the fees have grown louder, and some states and municipalities have started to abolish fees for the last kindergarten year. Critics have argued that the existing fees tend to prevent parents from sending their children to kindergartens and have pointed to the unsocial effects of demanding fees for child care, but (until recently) not for university education.

In the UK, all education in state schools is free. But levels of provision of full-time state pre-school education have historically been low. Since 1998, all four-year-olds have been entitled to a publicly funded early education place and since 2004 this entitlement has been extended to 3-year-olds. Compulsory education starts at five. A funded place guarantees only a minimum of 12.5 hours per week for 33 weeks a year; not all parents take it up. These funded places may be in state or independent schools.

In England in 2006, 98 per cent of children aged three and four were receiving some free pre-school education. This figure is made up of 59 per cent in state schools and 39 per cent in independent schools. It does not seem possible to secure data for attendance beyond the state-supported minimum.

Regulation and inspection of the whole system is by the state. The funding is distributed by local government. But there is a formula-based earmarked grant from central to local government, implying a requirement to pass on a fixed sum to the education provider. As far as public provision is concerned, the local authority may provide additional resources out of local taxation. The private providers secure a fixed sum, which may not equate with their unit costs or with the fee levels set for provision outside the guaranteed hours. There has been some controversy about this, with private providers alleging that they are, in practice, forced to cross-subsidize the free hours.

To summarize, although all countries show tendencies towards universal provision by the state, it is strongest in the French case and weakest in the German case. Responsibility is almost entirely in the hands of the *Länder* in Germany but shared between central and local government in the UK. It is difficult to be sure about the data on the devolution of provision to the independent sector (using that expression to include religious bodies), but this seems to be strong in all countries except France. More difficult still is to determine to what extent this devolution involves shared funding, either with local authorities or with the private sector, but that seems considerable in respect of infrastructure provision in all countries.

Devolution of costs to parents is largely absent in France, quite explicit in Germany, and seems to take a number of rather complex and ambiguous forms in Italy and the UK.

CONCLUSIONS

This chapter has dealt with an area of policy where there are strong similarities across the four countries:

- Similar approaches to child protection, with involvement of the courts and key roles for public agencies.
- Low-level provisions for child care in the early years, with quite strong independent sectors.
- A strong emphasis upon pre-school education systems, with the main institutional provisions linked to the regular education system except in Germany.

In many respects, differences flow from differences in local government systems and/or the relationship between central and local government:

- Relatively uniform systems across the board in France and the UK, with perhaps a stronger central role in the former (although this is debatable in the light of very strong central controls over local government in the UK).
- Variations between *Länder* and municipalities in Germany.
- Greater autonomy at regional and local levels is a source of diversity in Italy.

It is quite hard to be specific about variations between the countries in respect of independent sector roles given the lack of quantitative data. This is most readily available in the case of pre-school education, where the data seem to suggest high independent sector involvement in the UK, low involvement in France, and the other two countries somewhere in between (although it is harder to be specific about these two).

Finally, a UK development to unify all three areas of policy within the ambit of one central government department, and its related local government departments, is not found in the other countries. This measure implies separation of child care from adult care, reversing a change made in the 1970s, and is a change in the opposite direction to current efforts to integrate social care in Italy.

Had this study been done 20 years ago, greater variation between countries would have been found. The strong central policy drive towards the development of pre-school education and towards child care to facilitate parental labour force participation is tending to cause some convergence. In this respect we may particularly note developments in Italy, the UK and Germany that may be reducing the differences between their systems and that of France:

- The slow attack on the extent to which the Italian system is diverse in practice (despite central legislation).
- The increased central control over local authorities in the UK.
- Increasing concerns about family policy and education in Germany leading to federal intervention.

REFERENCES

Ambler, J.S. (ed.) (1991), *The French Welfare State*, New York: New York University Press.
Aust, A. and F. Bönker (2004), 'New social risks in a conservative welfare state: the case of Germany', in P. Taylor-Gooby (ed.), *New Risks, New Welfare: The Transformation of the European Welfare State*, Oxford: Oxford University Press, pp. 29–53.
Baistow, K. and G. Wilford (2000), 'Helping parents protecting children: ideas from Germany', *Children and Society*, **14** (5), 343–54.
Berth, F. (2008), 'Immer mehr Eltern wird das Sorgerecht entzogen', *Süddeutsche Zeitung*, **167**, 19/20 July, 1.
Bönker, F. and H. Wollmann (1996), 'Incrementalism and reform waves: the case of social service reform in the Federal Republic of Germany', *Journal of European Public Policy*, **3** (3), 441–60.
Bönker, F. and H. Wollmann (2000), 'The rise and fall of a social service regime: marketisation of German social services in historical perspective', in H. Wollmann and E. Schröter (eds), *Comparing Public Sector Reform in Britain and Germany: Key Traditions and Trends of Modernisation*, Aldershot: Ashgate, pp. 327–50.
Butler, I. and M. Drakeford (2003), *Social Policy, Social Welfare and Scandal*, Basingstoke: Palgrave Macmillan.
Evers, A., J. Lewis and B. Riedel (2005), 'Developing child-care provision in England and Germany', *Journal of European Social Policy*, **15** (3), 195–209.
Evers A. and C. Sachße (2003), 'Social care services for children and older people in Germany: distinct and separate histories', in A. Anttonen, J. Baldock and J. Sipilä (eds), *The Young, the Old and the State: Social Care Systems in Five Industrial Nations*, Cheltenham, UK and Northampton, MA, USA: Edward Elgar, pp. 55–80.
Ginsburg, N. (1992), *Divisions of Welfare*, London: Sage.
Hagemann, K. (2006), 'Between ideology and economy: the "time politics" of child care and public education in the two Germanys', *Social Politics*, **13** (1), 217–60.
Hendrick, H. (1994), *Child Welfare: England 1872–1989*, London: Routledge.

Istituto degli Innocenti (2006), 'I nidi e gli altri servizi educativi integrativi per la prima infanzia', paper no 36 of the Centro Nazionale di Documentazione e Analisi per l'infanzia e l'Adolescenza, Istituto degli Innocenti, Florence, Italy.

Konrad, F.M. (2004), *Der Kindergarten: Seine Geschichte von den Anfängen bis in die Gegenwart*, Freiburg, Germany: Lambertus.

Liu, S. (2001), *The Autonomous State of Child Care*, Aldershot: Ashgate.

OECD (Organisation for Economic Co-operation and Development) (2001a), *Early Childhood Education and Care Policy in Italy*, Paris: OECD.

OECD (2001b), *Knowledge and Skills for Life: First Results from the OECD Programme for International Student Assessment (PISA) 2000*, Paris, OECD.

OECD (2006), *Starting Strong*, Paris: OECD.

Packman, J. (1975), *The Child's Generation*, Oxford: Blackwell.

Pedersen, S. (1993), *Family, Dependence and the Origins of the Welfare State*, Cambridge: Cambridge University Press.

Plowden Report (1967), *Children and their Primary Schools*, report of the Central Advisory Council for Education, London: HMSO.

Statistisches Bundesamt (2008), *16 Jahre Kinder- und Jugendhilfegesetz in Deutschland: Ergebnisse der Kinder- und Jugendhilfestatistiken Erzieherische Hilfen 1991 bis 2006*, Wiesbaden.

Vinken, B. (2001), *Die deutsche Mutter: Der lange Schatten eines Mythos*, Munich, Germany: Piper.

Wollons, R. (ed.) (2000), *Kindergartens and Cultures: The Global Diffusion of an Idea*, New Haven, CT: Yale University Press.

5. Towards marketization and centralization? The changing role of local government in long-term care in England, France, Germany and Italy

Frank Bönker, Michael Hill and Anna Marzanati[1]

INTRODUCTION

Long-term care emerged as a major policy issue in most OECD countries in the 1980s.[2] A number of socioeconomic 'megatrends' have helped put the problem on the agenda and keep it there: the ageing of the population has increased the relative number of frail elderly people; rising female labour market participation and the weakening of family ties through less and less stable marriages, and the decline in multi-generation households have eroded the potential for informal care; the desperate attempts at cost containment in health care have increased the pressure to take care of frail people outside the health care system. Finally, personal social services have been widely perceived as one of the major expanding segments of the labour market, offering the prospect of employment growth, especially for less skilled people.

Since the beginning of the 1990s, most OECD countries have seen major reforms and changes in the field of long-term care. This also applies to the countries covered in this volume. In the UK, the 1990 National Health Service and Community Care Act put the provision of services for the elderly on a new footing and substantially changed the welfare mix. Germany and France introduced comprehensive new benefit schemes for the frail elderly in the mid-1990s. In Italy, a much-awaited law on social services was adopted in 2000 that aimed at establishing a uniform framework for services and reducing regional and local disparities in service provision. Moreover, the spread of 'grey' care markets has transformed the Italian care market 'from below'.

This chapter reconstructs key developments in long-term care in England,[3] France, Germany and Italy since the beginning of the 1990s, with a view to identifying changes in the horizontal and vertical governance of services, that is, the role of public, commercial and non-profit organizations in service provision and the distribution of competencies among the different tiers of government. In line with the overall focus of this volume, special attention is paid to the changing role of local government. Long-term care is particularly suited for such a focus. Whereas in other fields of social policy such as pensions, health care or labour market policy, central government stepped in at an early stage, the responsibility for providing and financing services for the frail elderly was until recently largely left with local governments in most OECD countries.

The structure of the chapter is as follows. The first section describes the basic features of long-term care in the four countries under analysis before the watershed of the 1990s. In outlining commonalities and differences in institutional arrangements, policies and reform pressure, it aims at identifying the points of departure for subsequent changes and their historical background. The second section charts changes that have taken place in each of the four countries since the early 1990s, and analyses the extent to which the role of local government has been transformed by marketization and centralization. The third and concluding section summarizes findings, providing a comparative reading of the four cases. It argues that, in the field of long-term care, substantial differences in policy reform have coincided with a strong common tendency to centralize and marketize services and consequently to reduce the role of local government.

LONG-TERM CARE UNTIL THE 1990s: COMMONALITIES AND DIFFERENCES

Until the 1990s, long-term care was a secondary policy issue. Except in France, the role of central government in the field was limited. In none of the countries was there a special benefit scheme for frail people. Services were still largely provided by local governments and non-profit organizations. Upon closer inspection, however, the national structures of service provision differed, and so did the levels of services (Table 5.1), regional and local disparities in service provision, and the pressure for reform.

England

In England, the overall position of local governments in long-term care at the end of the 1980s was arguably the strongest in the sample. Local

Table 5.1   The situation of elderly people in about 1990

	% of population aged 65+	% of 65+ living alone	% of 65+ in institutions	% of 65+ receiving home help
France	20.9	28.0	4.5	8.0
Germany	22.3	41.0	5.9	4.0
Italy	20.1	31.0	2.3	1.0
UK	23.0	36.0	5.0	9.0
Sweden	27.3	41.0	10.0	16.0

Source: Baldock and Ely (1996), Table 7.1.

governments enjoyed far-reaching competencies and delivered most of the services directly. The role of central government in long-term care was largely confined to financing disability benefits and, in the 1980s, reimbursing the board and lodging of frail people in private homes within the framework of the social assistance scheme. Non-profit organizations lost their traditionally strong role in service delivery in the 1960s and 1970s, and the market share of commercial providers, although increasing in the 1980s, was low.

The overhaul of the welfare state after the Second World War brought the nationalization of health care and social assistance. In exchange, local governments were vested with additional competencies in social housing, education and social services for the elderly (Wollmann, 2008, p. 122; Hill, 2000, pp. 311–12). The 1948 National Assistance Act split the cash and the service side of the old poor-law institutions. While putting central government in charge of regulating, financing and administering social assistance, it gave local governments the right to provide residential and domiciliary care.[4] Subsequent legislation gradually clarified and extended these rights. In 1968, local governments obtained a 'general power to promote the welfare for the elderly' (Hill, 2000, p. 312).

The role of central government was limited not only by the lack of competencies in the social services. Moreover, the national social assistance scheme did not reimburse the costs of care for most of the postwar period. Unlike in France and Germany, frail people without sufficient financial resources did not have to apply for social assistance but were eligible for in-kind services from local governments. It was not until November 1980 that the national social assistance scheme began to reimburse the board and lodging expenses of frail people in private homes. Apart from social assistance, the role of central government in long-term care was largely confined to financing and administering the Attendance Allowance, a small, non-means-tested disability benefit introduced in 1971 for people requiring significant amounts of personal assistance.

While the role of central government was limited right from the late 1940s, local governments only gradually emerged as the main service providers in the postwar period. Initially, high dependence on the – historically strong – non-profit sector persisted. In the 1960s and 1970s, however, local governments expanded their role in service provision and relegated non-profit organizations to the sidelines. Social services for the elderly emerged as 'the largest of the activities of local authority social services departments' (Hill, 2000, p. 317; Means and Smith, 1998). The crowding out of non-profit organizations reflected the widespread acceptance of the idea of a 'self-sufficient' public sector (Stewart, 2000, p. 51) according to which state services were the most effective and acceptable response to social problems. With non-profit organizations being widely perceived as niche providers, few attempts at formalizing the relationship between local government and non-profit organizations were made. Moreover, fears loomed large that any incorporation of the non-profit sector in decision-making would undermine its traditional independence.

In the 1980s, the public–private mix began to change again (Hill, 2000, pp. 317–18). This was brought about not by any direct attacks on the public provision of social services by the new Thatcher government, but by the changes in social assistance in 1980 mentioned above. The new possibility for social assistance to finance board and lodging expenses in private homes increased the demand for places in private facilities, most of them commercial. Local governments did not oppose this development. The injection of central government money and the rise of the private sector made it easier for them to deal with the increasing number of frail people.

Service levels in England were broadly similar to those in France, but higher than in Germany and Italy (Table 5.1). In the 1960s and 1970s, the extension of local government competencies went hand in hand with expansion of services for the elderly. Despite some 'aspirations to universality' (Land and Lewis, 1998, p. 61), however, residential care continued to be regarded as a last resort for poor people unable to make alternative arrangements for themselves. Moreover, local governments were reluctant to expand services because they feared that this might lead the NHS to reduce the number of geriatric beds and leave them to foot the bill (Means and Smith, 1998; Lewis, 2001, pp. 346–7). In the 1980s, the massive injection of social assistance funds helped allay these fears and contributed to a further acceleration of service growth. While the overall level of services was broadly similar to that in France, regional disparities in service provision were higher. The traditionally high level of municipal discretion, the lack of centralized welfare associations and strong general disparities between regions translated into substantial regional and local differences in service levels and modalities. For instance, there were no clear rules on financing domiciliary care: some municipalities delivered it free of charge, some imposed limited, standard charges, and others used means-testing (Hill, 2000, p. 312). The 1980 changes in social assistance further increased geographical disparities, because private homes were more widespread in the South of England than in other parts of the country.

Given the institutional arrangements described, the pressure for long-term care reform in England in the late 1980s was felt most strongly by central government. The 1980 changes in social assistance not only exacerbated geographical disparities and created a problematical bias in favour of residential care; they also produced a spectacular surge in spending (Wanless, 2006, p. 13, Fig. 1). From 1979 to 1988, social assistance spending on people in independent care homes exploded from less than £20 million to £850 million. This increase made central government the main advocate of reform.

France

France stands out in the sample as the country where central government and social insurance funds have played the strongest role in long-term care in the postwar period. From the Second World War to the decentralization of the early 1980s, major competencies in social services for the elderly rested with central government. Moreover, the old-age insurance funds, which were reformed after the Second World War as well, continued to play a major role even after decentralization. Thus, while local governments were never completely crowded out and played a more important part in the 1980s, they featured less prominently than in the three other countries.

In France, the reforms after the Second World War also affected long-term care. The post-1945 nationalization of *aide sociale légale* included social assistance and social services for the elderly (*assistance aux viellards*), which came to be handled by the state administration (Wollmann, 2008, p. 136). Although the administration of services was partly delegated to the *communes* and the latter also used their scope for 'voluntary' social assistance (*action sociale facultative*), the role of local government in long-term care thus remained limited until the decentralization of 1982/83. This brought France back into line by bringing the bulk of *aide sociale légale*, including social assistance and social services for the elderly, under the control of the *conseils généraux*, that is, local self-government at the *département* level. However, central government retained the power to regulate social assistance as well as the *allocation compensatoire pour tierce personne* (ACTP), a disability benefit originally introduced in 1975, which gradually emerged as the main 'substitute benefit' for frail people receiving domiciliary services.

A second French peculiarity has been the strong involvement of old-age insurance funds in financing social services for the elderly (Köstler, 1999, pp. 111–12). These funds have borne a proportion of investment costs for homes for the elderly, financed part of domiciliary services, and granted care allowances for some of the frail. In 1989, the old-age insurance funds shouldered more than half the total costs of domiciliary services. The involvement of social insurance funds was favoured by the traditionally strong role of central government in long-term care and the limited independence of the funds. It also reflects a particular interpretation of these funds as institutions of social solidarity rather than mere devices for guaranteeing individual pension claims.

In France, the non-profit sector was traditionally weak. For a long time, French etatism manifested itself in 'a reverse subsidiarity principle: the non-profit sector, whether religious or secular, dealt with public concerns that the state neglected, outside the scope of State supervision' (Archambault, 2001, p. 206). In the eighteenth century, the famous 1791 *Loi Le Chapelier* limited the scope for charitable activities. Legislation in 1901 made it easier to establish non-profit organizations and enabled church-related organizations to participate in the provision of welfare, provided that republican values were respected. However, not least because of the long-standing war between State and Church, the French Catholic Church did not develop welfare organizations on a scale similar to Germany or Italy. In the 1960s, the non-profit sector began to grow. The 'association boom' (Archambault 2001, p. 206) gained further momentum after decentralization, when many municipalities and *départements* delegated economic or social activities to associations or shared their new responsibilities with the non-profit sector. By the end of the 1980s, non-profit organizations thus played a substantial role in providing services for the frail, especially domiciliary services (Häusler, 1996, p. 45; Köstler, 1999, pp. 69–70). However, the non-profit sector was less centralized and the relationship between non-profit organizations and local governments was less formalized than in Germany.

The level of services in France was broadly similar to that in England (Table 5.1). In the late 1960s, the famous *Plan Laroque* led to an expansion of domiciliary services. Until the 1980s, the strong role of central government limited regional and local disparities. Decentralization changed the scene by aggravating fiscal differences between *départements* and by increasing the scope for local discretion.

As in England, the increasing fiscal costs of care were an important reform driver. Because of their financial responsibility for social assistance for the elderly and for ACTP, the *départements* felt these costs most strongly. Their total spending on frail elderly people increased from FF9.5 billion in 1989 to FF12.7 billion in 1994 (Köstler, 1999, p. 113, Table 19), making them a major advocate for reform.

Germany

In Germany, the provision of social services was traditionally characterized by close and highly institutionalized cooperation between local governments and strongly organized and centralized non-profit organizations, so-called welfare associations (*Wohlfahrtsverbände*) (Bönker and Wollmann, 2000). Whereas local governments were engaged in regulating and financing social services for the elderly, as well as in financing and administering social assistance, welfare associations provided the bulk of services. Moreover, they were also formally incorporated in local and state policy-making in the social services through membership in committees. Because of the centralized organization of welfare associations and their incorporation in decision-making, the German system has often been dubbed 'corporatist'.

Historically, welfare associations have grown out of the numerous charities and self-help organizations that mushroomed at the local level in the late nineteenth century. Their strong role in both service provision and policy-making dates back to the 1920s (Bönker and Wollmann, 2000, pp. 329–31; Evers and Sachße, 2003, pp. 61–71). It reflects the religious heterogeneity of Germany and conservative and liberal fears of the 'socialization' of services, as well as the strength of corporatist traditions and the strong influence of Catholic social thinking on German social policy. The latter found expression in the official endorsement of the famous principle of subsidiarity according to which social services ought to be provided by public authorities only if families and non-profit organizations cannot cope. In line with this principle, the 1961 Federal Social Assistance Act gave welfare associations clear priority in service provision and obliged local authorities to support and cooperate with them.

Unlike in France, social insurance funds have not been involved in financing long-term care. Health insurance funds have always drawn a strict line between illness and frailty, as well as between health care and long-term care;[5] and old-age insurance funds have confined themselves to paying pensions. Central government's role was largely limited to regulating social assistance. The overhaul of social assistance in the 1960s introduced a special allowance for frail people within the means-tested social assistance scheme (*Hilfe zur Pflege*). However, the financing and the administration of the scheme were left to local government.

In comparative terms, Germany was characterized by a medium level of services, that is, lower than in France and England, but higher than in Italy (Table 5.1). The main barriers to a further expansion of social services included relatively high wages in social services, the low fiscal autonomy of local governments, the strong role of Catholic social thinking in German social policy, and the relative weakness of the Left. Moreover, welfare associations may have lacked both the bureaucratic interest in expansion and the political incentive to cater to popular demands for additional services (Alber, 1995). The medium level of services coincided with rather weak regional and local disparities in service provision. For one thing, German federalism has been strongly committed to ensuring territorial equality through territorial reform and fiscal equalization. For another, the centralized organization of welfare associations favoured the far-reaching standardization of services.

In Germany, as in France, local government emerged as the main reform advocate in the 1980s (Bönker and Wollmann, 2006, p. 191; Morel, 2006). In the absence of any special benefit for frail people, the rising number of the frail and the rising costs of care, especially residential care, resulted in a strong increase in social assistance spending for frail people. Given the design of German social assistance, this increase was primarily felt by local governments. Between 1973 and 1993, real spending on social assistance for people in need of care increased by 370 per cent, eventually accounting for more than one-third of overall local spending on social assistance. This fiscal pressure made local governments – and the states (*Länder*), which represent local governments in formal terms – a major advocate for improving long-term care by introducing a new social benefit for frail people (Campbell and Morgan, 2005).

Italy

Italy differs from the other countries in the sample in the rather low aggregate level of services and extreme regional and local disparities in service provision. The low service level reflects the traditionally strong reliance of the Italian welfare state on the family and monetary transfers. Regional and local disparities stemmed from strong differences in regional and local traditions and administrative capacities. They were aggravated by the weak role of central government in the regulation and financing of personal social services. The national framework legislation for social assistance called for by the 1948 Constitution did not materialize until 2000, so that central government's role in the field was thus largely confined to paying a relatively generous universal disability benefit (*indennità di accompagnamento*), introduced in 1980, which a substantial number of frail elderly people managed to receive. In addition, central government provided some funding to regions and municipalities on a discretionary basis in the annual budget appropriations.

The failure of central government to define a legal framework for social services meant that the regulation, provision and financing of personal social services was largely left to local governments and, from the 1970s, the regions. The regionalization of the 1970s vested regions with the power to plan and to coordinate personal social services. The regions were granted the right to determine the zones of service provision and to force the – often very small – municipalities to cooperate. At the same time, they were required to provide municipalities with the necessary financial resources. Moreover, municipalities were put in charge of actually delivering services.

The regionalization of the 1970s contributed to the expansion of personal social services (Trifiletti, 1998, pp. 183–4; Fargion, 1997, pp. 139–48). Especially in northern and central Italy, municipalities and regions, notably those leaning to the Left, started to establish a broad range of domiciliary services. Southern regions and municipalities, in contrast, largely retained the traditional pattern with its emphasis on the family and monetary transfers. Local attempts at expanding social services often relied on the strong position of local governments within the National Health Service (Servizio Sanitario Nazionale, SSN) created in 1978. Local governments tried to use the resources of the health care system to provide social services. These attempts favoured the integration of health and long-term care, but were not always well designed and soon led central government to put stronger restrictions on the use of health care funds. In the 1980s, the expansion of services fell victim to tightening fiscal constraints (Fargion, 2000, p. 76).

As in France and Germany, the actual provision of services has largely rested with non-profit organizations (Caperchione and Gudera, 1995). Compared to France, the Catholic Church has been more deeply involved in charitable activities. The 1890 Crispi Law sought to limit its influence by placing the huge number of existing non-profit organizations, most of them Catholic (*opere pie*), under public law, but did not remove their autonomy. The 1948 Constitution kept the legal status of the so-called IPABs (*istituzione pubblica di assistenza e beneficenza*), but allowed for the creation of other forms of non-profit organization. Notwithstanding temporary attempts by leftist regions and municipalities in the 1970s and 1980s to expand the direct municipal provision of public services along Scandinavian lines, non-profit organizations kept their dominant role in service provision (Fargion, 1997, pp. 142–3; 2000, pp. 76–7). Relations between local governments and non-profit organizations were characterized by 'clientelistic ties and partisan links' (Fargion, 2000, p. 77).

In Italy, the pressure to reform was more dispersed than in the three other countries. Borne by central government, regions and municipalities alike, the fiscal costs of long-term care were weakly concentrated. Moreover, unlike in France and Germany, municipalities and regions were too heterogeneous to agree on the direction of reform and to exert strong pressure on national politics.

CHANGES AND REFORMS SINCE THE EARLY 1990s

In the late 1980s and early 1990s, the debate on long-term care intensified in all countries under analysis. Since then, major reforms have been adopted in all countries. These reforms, along with a number of changes 'from below', have transformed institutional arrangements.

England

Unlike France and Germany, England has not seen the introduction of a new benefit scheme for the frail. However, far-reaching reforms have put existing benefits and services on a new footing and have brought substantial changes to the welfare mix and the role of local government in long-term care. Under the Thatcher government, the imposition of a purchaser–provider split ended local governments' near monopoly in service delivery. Under the Blair government, the resulting privatization and marketization of services was complemented by an increase in central government control over municipalities, new initiatives towards a better integration of health and social care and, more recently, first steps towards expanding direct payments and personal budgets (Balloch, 2007).

The Thatcher government reacted to the rising costs of residential care by strengthening domiciliary care ('care in the community') and radically marketizing service delivery. In line with its overall market-liberal philosophy, the 1990 National Health Service and Community Care Act reduced the role of local governments in the delivery of services by forcing local governments to draw a clear line between the purchase and the provision of social services and inducing them to contract out services (Hill, 2000, pp. 317–19). At the same time, central government stopped the reimbursement of board and lodging expenses in private homes by social assistance. This left the Attendance Allowance as central government's main direct contribution to the financing of long-term care.

The Blair government refrained from reversing the changes initiated by its Conservative predecessor. It did not follow the recommendations of the 1999 Royal Commission on Long Term Care, which it had installed upon coming to office, to provide personal care free of charge and to drastically increase the income limits for living and housing costs. Instead, the Blair government's policies towards long-term care focused on increasing the quality of care through stronger central controls, measures to support carers and, more recently, on the promotion of direct payments and personal budgets.

The Blair government increased central government control over local governments by using a combination of instruments. In the field of long-term care, the standard system of local performance control established by the 1999 Local Government Act was complemented by establishing some national minimum standards and expanding inspections. The latter culminated in the creation of the Commission for Social Care Inspection (CSCI) in 2004. Reporting to both central government and Parliament, the CSCI, absorbed into the Commission for Health Care Audit and Inspection in 2008, registers and inspects all adult social care services in England and gives a star rating to local councils and, from 2008, a quality rating to care services. Finally, central government has tightened its control over local governments by basing the calculation of intergovernmental grants more strongly on spending norms. In calculating grants to local government and in scrutinizing any local government's taxation plans, central government now uses a complex computer formula that indicates for each service what it thinks each local government needs to perform its functions.

The Blair government sought to extend direct payments into a personal budget scheme, a reform element that featured prominently in the recent 2005 Green Paper on adult social care (Department of Health, 2005). The option of direct payments, which had been introduced in 1997 for adults of working age, was extended to people aged 65 and over in 2000. Since April 2003, local councils have been obliged to make direct payments when frail people so wish and are able to manage them, and the use of direct payments is already included as a performance indicator for the assessment of local governments. Due to a lack of information about the new options and reluctant support from local government, however, the take-up of direct payments has so far been limited (Balloch, 2007, pp. 29–30; Glendinning, 2008, p. 453).

As a result of the reforms adopted, the public–private mix in service provision has changed drastically since the early 1990s (Balloch, 2007, p. 22). Following the 1990 act, the 'market shares' of local governments dwindled in a short space of time. By 2002, 86 per cent of all local-authority-supported adult care home places and 63 per cent of home care hours were provided by commercial providers or voluntary sector organizations. In 2005, 88 per cent of residents paid for by their local authority were in independent sector homes compared to 82 per cent in 2000 and 20 per cent in 1993. Among independent providers, commercial enterprises dominate (ibid., pp. 30–31). Especially under the Thatcher government, there was little emphasis on strengthening the non-profit sector. In addition, the fragmented nature of the non-profit sector in England has limited its political clout as well as its capacity to reap economies of scale.

In England, centralization and marketization have thus gone hand in hand, hollowing out the role of local government, which has diminished relative to central government and service providers. However, the weakening of the local government role should not be exaggerated. For one thing, the lack of uniform assessment criteria for frailty gives local governments, who are in charge of the process, substantial discretion in assessing the degree of frailty and in determining care packages. For another, as progress with the expansion of direct payments and personal budgets has been slow, changes have so far left the strong role of local governments in commissioning services largely intact (Bode, 2007). Unlike in France, Germany and Italy, deals with service providers are still largely concluded by local governments rather than by the frail themselves or their relatives. This means that local governments enjoy strong market power as the main – and in some areas, only – purchasers of care services.

France

Unlike England, France saw the creation of a new benefit scheme for frail elderly people in the 1990s. The introduction of the new scheme – a tax-financed assistance scheme administered by the *départements* which has been amended several times – was complemented by generous tax deductions for various kinds of home services, a reform of internal and external assessments of service quality, and massive investment in the modernization of care infrastructure.

The new benefit was introduced after the 1995 presidential elections. The *prestation spécifique dépendence* (PSD) was a means-tested benefit for frail people over the age of 60. The level of the benefit depended both on income and on the degree of frailty. It could be used to purchase formal care services only, be they provided by local governments, non-profit organizations or by independent care workers.[6] However, the *départements* were left a high degree of discretion in determining the exact level of benefits and were only partly compensated for the new expenses. As a result, wide territorial disparities between rich and the poor *départements* emerged.

These disparities, along with strict means-testing and the unpopular principle of recouping costs from a deceased person's estate, kept take-up of the new benefit low and reduced its popularity. In 2001, the socialist government thus replaced the PSD with the *allocation personnalisée d'autonomie* (APA), a more generous assistance benefit to be administered by the *départements*. The new benefit came with much stronger constraints on local discretion. Moreover, central government increased its share in financing the benefit and the allocations to poor *départements*.

The costs of the new benefits were much higher than expected. Two years later, the new conservative government thus cut back on benefits and dramatically reduced the threshold for co-payments. In 2005, the government created a new source for financing the APA, as well as other age- and dependency-related expenditures, the Caisse Nationale de Solidarité pour l'Autonomie (CNSA) (Debrand and Or, 2005). The new fund was vested with about €2 million annually, financed by a tax on employers imposed in exchange for a day of unpaid work and a subsidy from the old-age insurance funds. The new resources have been used to increase the service infrastructure and to reduce the contribution of the *départements* to financing the APA. More recently, there has been talk about transforming the APA into a fifth branch of social security managed by the CNSA.

The introduction of the PSD and the subsequent amendments were strongly shaped by centre–local relations (Morel, 2006). Bearing a substantial part of the rising fiscal costs of frailty, the *départements* strongly supported the introduction of a new benefit. Keen on keeping the new responsibilities gained in the course of the decentralization of the 1980s, they opposed a social insurance solution and successfully argued in favour of a means-tested assistance benefit administered by themselves but partly financed by central government. Ever since the introduction of the PSD, they have lobbied for additional money from central government or the social insurance funds, but have opposed any uncompensated expansion of benefits. The resulting struggles over the financing of PSD and APA go a long way to explaining the frequent amendments of the French benefit schemes.

Alongside PSD and APA, there have been generous income tax deductions for different kinds of home service, including long-term care. Like PSD and APA, these deductions, which were originally introduced in the first half of the 1990s, have been seen as a means to foster formal employment in the service sector.

Long-term care reform in France has been associated with changes in the vertical and horizontal governance of services. Compared to the 1980s, central government, as well as old-age insurance funds, have increased their role both by increasing their share in financing and by reducing local discretion. At the same time, the introduction of the new benefit scheme has not put the *départements* out of business. By administering and partly financing APA, they are still involved in providing benefits to the frail. The increasing involvement of central government and social insurance funds has been accompanied by changes in the welfare mix (Da Roit et al., 2007, pp. 662–4). The introduction of PSD led to the large-scale employment of independent care workers rather than to flourishing established services offered by non-profit organizations (*services prestataires*). Because of lower rates, frail people preferred to employ unqualified care workers, often relatives, rather than to buy the more professional services provided by the non-profit sector. Meanwhile, this tendency has been reversed. From 2003 to 2005, the number of employees in *services prestataires* rose much more strongly than the number of employees working for individuals at home (ibid., pp. 662–3). However, the market share of the non-profit sector is still considerably lower than in the early 1990s.

Germany

Germany also saw the introduction of a new benefit scheme in the mid-1990s (Evers, 1998; Ostner, 1998). Unlike in France, the new Long-term Care Insurance Scheme (*Soziale Pflegeversicherung*) has survived its first decade without major changes.[7] The setting up of the new scheme was followed by a number of attempts at improving the quality of services. Compared to France, the overall effects of the new scheme on the welfare mix and the local government role in long-term care have been more dramatic. The German scheme differs from the French in a number of respects (Morel, 2006).

1. It is a social insurance scheme financed by social insurance contributions rather than taxes and administered by social insurance funds rather than by local governments.
2. Benefits are universal and not income-related. Moreover, they are not limited to frail people older than 60, even though the latter account for the large majority of recipients.
3. The German scheme puts more emphasis on strengthening informal care. In the case of domiciliary care, the frail have the choice between cash benefits (*Pflegegeld*), which can be freely spent, the reimbursement of professional care (*Pflegesachleistung*), and a combination of the two.[8] The cash benefit, which is substantially lower than the in-kind benefit, is seen as a pool of resources for 'acknowledging' informal care by relatives, friends or neighbours rather than as a personal budget for purchasing formal care services. In 2006, almost half of

all recipients of benefits provided by the Long-Term Care Insurance Scheme received the cash benefit (Bundesregierung, 2008, p. 24).
4. In Germany, the introduction of the new benefit scheme went hand in hand with an explicit attempt to change the welfare mix. Breaking with tradition, the legislation on the new scheme did not grant any privilege or priority to welfare associations, but was put on an equal footing with commercial providers, calling for the far-reaching commercialization of services.

The introduction and the stability of the Long-Term Care Insurance Scheme have been shaped by centre–local relations. As in France, local governments have been among the main advocates of a new scheme. Unlike in France, however, they have been less keen on retaining responsibilities in the field. Given their broad range of competencies and their strong overall position, they were much more willing to accept a declining role in long-term care. Once the new scheme had been established, the positions of French and German local governments continued to differ. Unlike their French counterparts, German local governments, which do not share the costs of the scheme but, on the contrary, have to step in when benefits are not sufficient, have fiercely opposed any cuts in benefits. Their commitment to the scheme has clearly contributed to its stability.

The introduction of the Long-Term Care Insurance Scheme has been associated with major changes in the governance of services and the role of local governments. As the law on the Long-Term Care Insurance Scheme has made the newly created long-term care insurance funds (*Pflegekassen*) responsible for licensing service providers and for concluding agreements on the price and quality of services, local governments have lost a substantial part of their traditional competencies and have been left with more general responsibilities such as ensuring an adequate local service infrastructure and organizing local round tables on long-term care (*Pflegekonferenzen*). According to critics, the loss of competencies has gone hand in hand with a 'process of de-municipalization and de-localization of care' that has eroded the 'embeddedness [of long-term care] in the local community' (Evers and Sachße, 2003, pp. 73–4). Moreover, many municipalities have reacted to the introduction of the new insurance scheme by reducing their voluntary activities in the field.

The decline in the role of local governments has gone hand in hand with the 'double marketization' (Bönker and Wollmann, 2000) of services. For one thing, welfare associations have lost substantial market shares to commercial providers. For another, the modes of service provision have changed and the welfare associations themselves have become more similar to their commercial competitors. Doing away with the traditional privileges of the welfare associations in service provision and policy formation, and accepting commercial providers as contract partners with 'equal rights', the new rules paved the way for the substantial expansion of commercial service providers, particularly in the field of domiciliary care. By 2005, the share of commercial providers in the total number of licensed providers of domiciliary care had increased to 58 per cent, while that of service providers associated with welfare associations had fallen to 41 per cent, much less than before the mid-1990s (Statistisches Bundesamt, 2007, Table 2.1).

The rise of commercial provision has been accompanied by changes in the relationship between local governments and welfare associations, as well as in the orientation of the welfare associations themselves. As welfare associations have lost their privileges, the close and exclusive cooperation between local governments and welfare associations has given way to a more market-like management of contracts inspired by the ideas of new public management. Finally, the welfare associations themselves have become more similar to commercial providers – partly forced by the new legal environment, partly attracted by the success of the apparently more successful and modern commercial providers.

Italy

In Italy, reforms in the field of long-term care have been less far-reaching, and more fragmented, than in the three other countries. Reform initiatives have been adopted at the national, regional and local levels, but have remained limited. Nevertheless, major changes have occurred, with the spread of 'grey' care markets transforming the provision of long-term care 'from below'.

As for the national level, three kinds of reform initiatives can be distinguished: the eventual adoption of a new national framework for personal social services; some changes in the regulation of non-profit organizations; and a number of attempts at fostering the integration of health and long-term care through the triennial national health plans. In 2000, the Italian parliament eventually adopted the much-awaited national framework law on social assistance and social services (Law 328/2000). The latter has given central government the right to determine an essential level of social services to be provided throughout the country. In order to implement this provision, the law called for the creation of a National Social Fund and a complex system of national and regional plans (Bifulco and Centemeri, 2008). In 2001, the national framework law was complemented by an act on the coordination of health and social care. However, the implementation of the new provisions has suffered from conflicts among the regions as well as among political camps. The essential level of services has not yet been determined. Nor has the envisaged National Social Fund replaced the old discretionary funding system.

Before the adoption of Law 328/2000, central government had already adopted some changes in the regulation of non-profit organizations with a view to making them more transparent and to reduce the scope for clientelism (Fargion, 2000, pp. 77–8). Law 328/2000 led to a new attempt by central government to induce a reorganization of the IPABs in 2001. It also contained a clear commitment to subsidiarity and strengthened the role of the non-profit sector in both service delivery and service planning (Ranci et al., 2005; Ciarini, 2008, p. 19).

Finally, central government has tried to use the triennial National Health Plans to promote the integration of health care and long-term care. Most notably, the 1992–94 National Health Plan included a special project 'Caring for the Frail Elderly', which called for the creation of integrated services for domiciliary health and long-term care (*Assistenza Domiciliare Integrata*, ADI) to be provided by the health authorities in cooperation with municipalities (Gori et al., 2003, pp. 65–7; Nesti et al., 2003; Ciarini, 2008, pp. 20–21). These services are provided free of charge and are supposed to be co-financed by the health authorities and local councils. At the beginning of the new millennium, 177 out of Italy's 197 Local Health Units provided ADI. The number of recipients, most of them elderly, increased from about 200 000 in 1997 to more than 300 000 in 2003 (Ciarini, 2008, pp. 20–21). In practice, however, cooperation between the health authorities and the regions/local governments has continued to be weak, so that in most cases ADI has amounted to home health care.

The failure to adopt and implement more far-reaching national reforms can partly be explained by centre–local relations. The great heterogeneity of regions and municipalities has made it difficult to arrive at national solutions. The richer regions have feared having to pay for the poorer ones. From 2002 to 2006, the fierce struggles between the regions and the Berlusconi government over the budget contributed to the failure to implement the provisions of Law 328/2000 (Fargion, 2006, pp. 284–8).

Alongside these national reform initiatives, regions and municipalities have themselves become active. Many regions have developed regional plans for services that are in line with the provisions of Law 328/2000. Moreover, a number of municipalities and regions, especially in northern and central Italy, have introduced subnational benefit schemes for frail people (Polverini et al., 2004, pp. 34–5, 60–61; Ciarini, 2008, p. 26). Most of the schemes are means-tested care allowances paid to frail people or their relatives in order to avoid their admittance to homes. So far, however, the coverage of the schemes and the size of benefits have been limited. The most prominent regional schemes in Emilia-Romagna and Veneto reach barely 1–1, 5 per cent of the population aged 65 or above and provide annual monetary support adding up to little more than between €1200 and €2200 on average (Da Roit et al., 2007, p. 661).

Arguably the most important engine of change in Italy has been the spread of 'grey' care by migrants. Since the beginning of the 1990s, the number of migrant care workers – most of them irregular, female and from the former Eastern Europe – has dramatically increased (Bettio et al., 2006). Migrant care work tends to concentrate in northern and central Italy and in large metropolitan areas. According to estimates, about 20–30 per cent of all households with frail elderly now employ migrants – a percentage that is much higher than in the three other countries.[9] The spread of informal migrant work has been a response to the lack of formal services and their high costs. Its effects on the provision of long-term care have been ambivalent. On the one hand, the cheap informal care by migrants has made long-term care available to broad strata of the population. On the other, it has raised concerns about the quality of care. Moreover, the availability of cheap informal care has reduced the pressure to improve formal care services. This is likely to become a problem in the medium run, when migrant inflows are likely to dry up.

COMPARATIVE ASSESSMENT: DIVERGENT REFORMS, SIMILAR OUTCOMES?

As we have seen, reforms in the four countries under analysis have taken rather different forms. In England, the various reforms adopted by the Thatcher and Blair governments have put benefits and services on a new footing without introducing a new benefit scheme; in France and Germany, different kinds of new benefits for frail people have been introduced; in Italy, reforms have been more limited and fragmented, with reforms at the national level focusing on ensuring the provision of a basic level of services throughout the country. The different trajectories reflect path dependencies resulting from different starting conditions, including, as we have seen, substantial differences in centre–local relations. Compared to other policy fields, long-term care has also been characterized by the lack of a clear, uncontested reform template (OECD, 2005) and weak pressure towards convergence by the EU.

While the reforms adopted have differed considerably from country to country, a number of broadly similar outcomes can be identified. A first striking similarity is the increasing role of central government and/or national social insurance funds in long-term care. In England, local governments have been subject to increasing control by central government; in France, central government and the old-age insurance funds have expanded their role in financing and regulating benefits for the frail; in Germany, the introduction of the Long-Term Care Insurance Scheme has resulted in the far-reaching 'de-localization' of care; in Italy, a national framework for personal social services has finally been adopted. The common move towards a greater role for central government in countries with quite different centre–local relations suggests that long-term care has become so salient and politicized an issue in the 1990s that politicians can no longer leave it to local governments. This finding echoes some of the observations made in Chapter 4 on child care.

As regards the horizontal dimension of governance, all four countries have seen a clear tendency towards the marketization of services. In England, independent – predominantly commercial – providers have replaced public providers; in France, individual care workers have become more important; in Germany, commercial providers have gained ground relative to non-profit organizations; in Italy, 'grey' care markets have spread. The common trend towards commercialization, which has been brought about by reforms 'from the top' as well as by changes in demand 'from below', points to a certain dissatisfaction with the traditional provider structures and a growing commitment to market solutions. Interestingly, the marketization of service provision has been much stronger in long-term care than in child care.

While marketization has been a common trend in long-term care in all four countries, its implications for the role of local governments have differed among countries. Only in England has the rise of commercial providers resulted in the far-reaching crowding out of local government. In France, Germany and Italy, by contrast, where the role of local governments in the actual delivery of services has always been more limited, the rise of commercial providers has primarily hit the non-profit sector and has thus had a less dramatic effect on the role of local governments. Unlike in England, and unlike in other fields of services, it thus makes little sense to speak of the local government role in long-term care being 'hollowed out' in these three countries.

NOTES

1. The chapter has strongly benefited from papers, presentations and comments by other members of the Vigoni group, most notably Enzo Balboni, Eugenio Caperchione, Martine Long, Francesco Longo, Yves Luchaire, Gilles Pollet, Hélène Thomas and Hellmut Wollmann.
2. The boundaries between long-term care, health care, social care and elderly care, as well

as between frail and handicapped people, can be drawn differently. In this chapter, long-term care stands for 'services for persons who are dependent on help with basic activities of daily living (ADL) over an extended period of time. Such activities include bathing, dressing, eating, getting in and out of bed or chair, moving around and using the bathroom' (OECD, 2005, p. 20). The large majority of the people requiring long-term care tend to be old people. Services can be provided in homes (residential care) or at home (domiciliary care).

3. Given the differences between England, North Ireland, Scotland and Wales with regard to personal social services, this chapter deals with England only rather than with the UK.
4. From 1946 to 1974, this even included the responsibility for home nursing (Lewis, 2001, p. 344).
5. For the sake of completeness it should be mentioned that the 1988 Act on Health Reform obliged the statutory health care funds (*Krankenkassen*) to pay highly frail members DM400 per month for home-based informal care and DM750 for professional care. At that time, the Kohl government still objected to the introduction of a comprehensive new benefit scheme for frail people and presented a combination of minor measures as an alternative. After the introduction of the Long-Term Care Insurance Scheme, the benefit was terminated.
6. These carers could be relatives, except for the spouse. Even for relatives, however, a formal employment contract was needed.
7. A reform of the scheme has been on the political agenda at least since the 2002–5 term. It took until March 2008 for the federal government to eventually agree on a reform package. The package leaves the basic features of the scheme untouched, but envisages a gradual increase in benefits from 2008 to 2012 and a rise in the contribution rate from 1.7 to 1.95 per cent starting in July 2008.
8. The level of benefits was left unchanged in nominal terms from 1996 to 2008. It depends on the type of benefit and the degree of frailty. From 2008 to 2012, cash benefits (in-kind benefits) for domiciliary care are scheduled to increase to €235 (450), €440 (1100) and €700 (1550). In case of residential care, benefits will increase to €1023, €1279 and €1550.
9. It further testifies to the size of the 'grey' care market in Italy that the estimated number of irregular migrant care workers exceeds the number of employees in the national health service, which stands at about 670 000.

REFERENCES

Alber, Jens (1995), 'A framework for the comparative study of social services', *Journal of European Social Policy*, **5** (2), 131–49.

Archambault, Edith (2001), 'Historical roots of the nonprofit sector in France', *Nonprofit and Voluntary Sector Quarterly*, **30** (2), 204–20.

Baldock, John and Peter Ely (1996), 'Social care for elderly people in Europe: the central problem of home care', in Brian Munday and Peter Ely (eds), *Social Care in Europe*, London: Prentice Hall, pp. 195–225.

Balloch, Susan (2007), 'Care, citizenship and community in the UK', in Susan Balloch and Michael Hill (eds), *Care, Community and Citizenship: Research and Practice in a Changing Policy Context*, Bristol: Policy Press, pp. 21–39.

Bettio, Francesca, Annamaria Simonazzi and Paola Villa (2006), 'Change in care regimes and female migration: the "care drain" in the Mediterranean', *Journal of European Social Policy*, **16** (3), 271–85.

Bifulco, Lavinia and Laura Centemeri (2008), 'Governance and participation in local welfare: the case of the Italian Piani di Zoni', *Social Policy & Administration*, **42** (3), 211–27.

Bode, Ingo (2007), 'Public–Private-Partnerships im Pflegesektor: Ein deutsch–englischer Vergleich wohlfahrtsmarktlicher "governance" und ihrer Folgen', *Sozialer Fortschritt*, **55** (3), 64–72.

Bönker, Frank and Hellmut Wollmann (2000), 'The rise and fall of a social service regime: marketisation of German social services in historical perspective', in Hellmut Wollmann and Eckhard Schröter (eds), *Comparing Public Sector Reform in Britain and Germany: Key Traditions and Trends of Modernisation*, Aldershot: Ashgate, pp. 327–50.

Bönker, Frank and Hellmut Wollmann (2006), 'Public sector reforms and local governments in Germany: the case of local social policy', in Vincent Hoffmann-Martinot and Hellmut Wollmann (eds), *State and Local Government Reforms in France and Germany: Divergence and Convergence*, Wiesbaden, Germany: VS Verlag, pp. 189–206.

Bundesregierung (Federal Government) (2008), *Vierter Bericht über die Entwicklung der Pflegeversicherung*, Berlin.

Campbell, Andrea L. and Kimberly J. Morgan (2005), 'Federalism and the politics of old-age care in Germany and the United States', *Comparative Political Studies*, **38** (8), 887–914.

Caperchione, Eugenio and Marcus Gudera (1995), 'Freie Wohlfahrtsorganisationen in Italien', *Zeitschrift für öffentliche und gemeinwirtschaftliche Unternehmen*, **18** (4), 398–415.

Ciarini, Andrea (2008), 'Family, market and voluntary action in the regulation of the "care system": a comparison between Italy and Sweden', *World Political Science Review*, **4** (1), accessed at www.bepress.com/wpsr/vol4/iss1/art4.

Da Roit, Barbara, Blanche Le Bihan and August Österle (2007), 'Long-term care policies in Italy, Austria and France: variations in cash-for-care schemes', *Social Policy & Administration*, **41** (6), 653–71.

Debrand, Thierry and Zeynep Or (2005), *Solidarity Fund for Financing Dependency*, October, Gütersloh, Germany: Bertelsmann Foundation Health Policy Monitor.

Department of Health (2005), *Independence, Well-being and Choice: Our Vision for the Future of Social Care for Adults in England*, London: Department of Health.

Evers, Adalbert (1998), 'The New Long-Term Care Insurance Program in Germany', *Journal of Aging & Social Policy*, **10** (1), 77–97.

Evers, Adalbert and Christoph Sachße (2003), 'Social care services for children and older people in Germany: distinct and separate histories', in Anneli Anttonen, John Baldock and Jorma Sipilä (eds), *The Young, the Old and the State: Social Care Systems in Five Industrial Nations*, Cheltenham, UK and Northampton, MA, USA: Edward Elgar, pp. 55–79.

Fargion, Valeria (1997), 'Social assistance and the North–South cleavage in Italy', in Martin Rhodes (ed.), *Southern European Welfare States: Between Crisis and Reform*, London: Cass, pp. 135–54.

Fargion, Valeria (2000), 'Timing and the development of social care services in Europe', *West European Politics*, **23** (2), 59–88.

Fargion, Valeria (2006), 'Changes in the responsibilities and financing of the health system in Italy', *Revue française des Affaires sociales* English edn, **60** (2/3), 271–96.

Glendinning, Caroline (2008), 'Increasing choice and control for older and disabled people: a critical review of new developments in England', *Social Policy & Administration*, **42** (5), 451–69.

Gori, Cristiano, Alessandra Di Maio and Alessandro Pozzi (2003), 'Long-term care for older people in Italy', in Adelina Comas-Herrera and Raphael Wittenberg (eds), 'European study of long-term care expenditure: investigating the sensitivity of projections of future long-term care expenditure in Germany, Spain, Italy and the United Kingdom to changes in assumptions about demography, dependency, informal care, formal care and united costs' Personal Social Services Research Unit discussion paper no 1840, University of Kent, Canterbury, pp. 59–76.

Häusler, Eveline (1996), 'Associations et fondations d'action sociale et sanitaire in Frankreich', in Peter Eichhorn (ed.), *Freie Wohlfahrtspflege in Europa aus betriebswirtschaftlicher Sicht I: Länderstudien Frankreich, Großbritannien und Italien*, Baden-Baden, Germany: Nomos, pp. 29–105.

Hill, Michael (2000), 'Trends in the marketisation of British social services', in Hellmut Wollmann and Eckhard Schröter (eds), *Comparing Public Sector Reform in Britain and Germany: Key Traditions and Trends of Modernisation*, Aldershot: Ashgate, pp. 304–26.

Köstler, Ursula (1999), *Pflegesicherung in Frankreich und Luxemburg: Ein institutioneller und empirischer Vergleich der Sicherung bei Pflegebedürftigkeit in Frankreich und im Großherzogtum Luxemburg*, Idstein, Germany: Schulz-Kirchner.

Land, Hilary and Jane Lewis (1998), 'Gender, care and the changing role of the state in the UK', in Jane Lewis (ed.), *Gender, Social Care and Welfare State Restructuring in Europe*, Aldershot: Ashgate, pp. 111–37.

Lewis, Jane (2001), 'Older people and the health–social care boundary in the UK: half a century of hidden policy conflict', *Social Policy & Administration*, **35** (4), 343–59.

Means, Robin and Randall Smith (1998), *From Poor Law to Community Care: The Development of Welfare Services for Elderly People 1939–1971*, Bristol: Policy Press.

Morel, Nathalie (2006), 'Providing coverage against new social risks in Bismarckian welfare states: the case of long-term care', in Klaus Armingeon and Guiliano Bonoli (eds), *The Politics of Postindustrial Welfare States*, London: Routledge, pp. 227–47.

Nesti, Giorgia, Stefano Campostrini, Stefano Garbin, Paolo Piva, Patrizia Di Santo and Filomena Tunzi (2003), *Providing Integrated Health and Social Care for Older Persons in Italy (PROCARE)*, Vienna.

OECD (Organization for Economic Co-operation and Development) (2005), *Long-term Care for Older People*, Paris: OECD.

Ostner, Ilona (1998), 'The politics of care policies in Germany', in Jane Lewis (ed.), *Gender, Social Care and Welfare State Restructuring in Europe*, Aldershot: Ashgate, pp. 111–37.

Polverini, Francesca, Andrea Principi, Cristian Balducci, Maria Gabriella Melchiorre, Sabrina Quattrini, Marie Victoria Gianelli and Giovanni Lamura (2004), *Services for Supporting Family Carers of Elderly People in Europe: Characteristics, Coverage and Usage (EUROFAMCARE). National Background Report for Italy*, Ancona, Italy: Istituto Nazionale di Riposo e Cura Anziani.

Ranci, Constanzo, Mauro Pellegrino and Emmanuele Pavolini (2005), 'The third sector and the policy process in Italy: between mutual accommodation and new forms of partnership', London School of Economics, Department of Social Policy TSEP working paper no 4, London.

Statistisches Bundesamt (2007), *Pflegestatistik 2005. Pflege im Rahmen der Pflegeversicherung – Deutschlandergebnisse*, Wiesbaden, Germany.
Stewart, John (2000), *The Nature of British Local Government*, Basingstoke and London: Macmillan.
Trifiletti, Rossana (1998), 'Restructuring social care in Italy', in Jane Lewis (ed.), *Gender, Social Care and Welfare State Restructuring in Europe*, Aldershot: Ashgate, pp. 175–206.
Wanless, Derek (2006), *Securing Good Care for Older People: Taking a Long-term View*, London: King's Fund.
Wollmann, Hellmut (2008), *Reformen in Kommunalpolitik und -verwaltung: England, Schweden, Frankreich und Deutschland im Vergleich*, Wiesbaden, Germany: VS Verlag.

6. Health services: issues and trends in Italy, France and Germany

Dieter Grunow, Francesco Longo and Martine Long

INTRODUCTION

Health as a Public Policy Reference Point and Goal

The health status of the population is one of the central issues for all societies: it is a question of general survival, life expectancy and quality of life. It is also a prerequisite for the functioning of society as a whole. Many health care problems cannot be solved by primary social networks. Specialized collective action is needed, incentives for preventive action, intervention against illness, or compensation of side effects (i.e. income for food, clothing and housing).

The three basic elements – causes, types of illness and forms of intervention – have been developing over time, and they now constitute a complex setting of health-related public issues. The definition, that is, the cognitive framework of health and illness plays the most important role in this setting. Health can be defined (negatively) as the absence of (known) diseases or (positively) – according to the World Health Organization (WHO) – as a status of complete physical, psychic and social well-being. It is evident that any type of definition has multiple effects on the search for causal factors – which more and more often are produced by society itself and not by nature. The development of infrastructure and treatment – curing, caring and compensating – is likewise influenced by the concept of health. There might also be some intervening factors stemming from societal belief systems and different systems of professionals or practitioners – that is, shamans, traditional Chinese medicine, and professional Western medicine.

Most of these observations refer to OECD countries. The following arguments concentrate, more specifically, on three countries in Europe: France, Italy and Germany.[1] These countries have functionally differentiated societies with a large public sector (up to 50 per cent of GDP is managed by the political–administrative system) and a well-developed health sector.

Features and Specifics of the Policy Field 'Health Services'

This book examines a wide range of policy fields. If they are to be compared, the similarities and differences must be identified. The field of health services can be truly described as a policy field – comprising a set of programmes, a set of actors participating in policy formulation, a set of actors engaged in financing and implementing policies, and an identifiable collective of policy addressees. To a large extent, health services have to be delivered close to the places where people live and/or work – because such services are normally produced and consumed at the same time (*uno actu* principle). But the different functions oblige the system to operate in a multi-level setting (Anderson and McDaniel, 2000). In comparison with other policy fields, therefore, the actor network is much more extended and resources cover about 10 per cent of GDP. The boundaries are especially open: health-related policies are often cross-cutting; that is, they affect many other policy fields and are influenced by many others, as well.[2] It is estimated that health-related services account for only about one-third of the envisioned outcome (health status of the population); the management of the system must therefore go far beyond organizing specific treatment practices. Nevertheless, a key element is the publicly guaranteed provision of services – which are in the nature of personal services – from person to person. Therefore the characteristics of the personal service (as opposed to public utility) have to be taken into account: it is an immaterial good, a confidence good;[3] it is not conservable, not easy to rationalize; a good that often needs the co-production by the users, and so on (McDaniel and Driebe, 2001). These features of personal services also have economic consequences – which have been termed 'cost disease' by Baumol (1967). Their productivity is lower than that of the material goods production. But service providers earn comparatively high wages. Many services cannot be provided profitably – owing partly to the small numbers of cases. Fiscal intervention by the state in combination with a broad definition of entitlements increases the number of cases – and probably the cost efficiency of each treatment – but this might lead to an escalating budget for health services. In sum, the financial and organizational arrangements of the health system have to be very complex; they are never optimal, and there are always many reasons or demands for further reform.

Five steps of analysis follow: (1) a brief introduction to the development of health policy in the three countries; (2) a comparative synopsis of local arrangements and services; (3) an analysis of the coordination of local/regional health issues; (4) a description of NPM reform and its effects on local health service arrangements; (5) a comparison of convergence and divergence in the latest reforms in the three countries.

BASIC CHALLENGES AND SOLUTIONS IN FRANCE, ITALY AND GERMANY

Many different 'histories' of health services development can be written, depending on the focus chosen. Complex landscapes have emerged in all modern OECD countries (Anderson and McDaniel, 2000). They involve many actors; many segments of knowledge and practices; many tools and instruments; and many subsystems of the societies are involved.

This chapter draws the attention to the involvement of the public sector ('the modern state') in this process. In very simplified terms, the process under observation is the development of health/illness related-activities into a 'public good'. The basic features of a 'pure' public good are non-exclusiveness and non-rivalry.[4] There are 'natural' pure public goods (like air), but they do not include health services: they have to be explicitly installed by societal actors. There are some basic and enduring issues that always have to be settled if a public-good 'health services' is to be installed:

- Financing of the system on the basis of politico-administrative regulation; this is the main reason for making health services a public good; otherwise many – if not all – services would not be accessible to large parts of the population: this raises the question of who makes the rules and who manages resource collection and spending.
- Coverage of problems and persons with regard to available services (entitlements): who decides about entitlements in principle and in specific treatment situations?
- Regulating and planning the health care system: who manages organization design and the distribution of services?
- The features of health care providers: who manages service organizations, who develops tools and who sets the standards of good practice?

Different answers and combinations of answers to these questions produce different health care systems. In all three countries, the development of public health policy started in the late nineteenth century in response to industrialization and urbanization. It was the self-organization of the rapidly growing industrial workforce that prompted development. In the event of illness, help from fellow workers was a question of survival.

Following these primarily local and self-organizational beginnings, central governments progressively extended social protection in the following decades, making social and/or health insurance obligatory for various groups of workers: in Germany in 1883 (starting with statutory health insurance), in Italy in 1878 with occupational accident insurance, and in France in 1910/1928/1930 with social insurance. It was a strategy of social integration and a move against the empowerment of labour organizations. In all three countries, the system was financed by worker and employer contributions. The first concern was to provide resources for the living expenses of the ill. The further development saw a continuous concern with treatment: more and more diseases were covered by entitlements defined by public policy. The number of occupational groups covered by insurance grew steadily. At the beginning of the twentieth century, important steps toward health insurance for the whole population were taken, including the dependants of workers and – later on – the unemployed and pensioners.

The expansion of social coverage and the scope of services covered by health insurance systems was similar in all three countries. After the two world wars, which imposed additional burdens on health services, the systems were rethought and restructured.

A review of historical developments (Thomson and Mossialos, 2004; Busse and Riesberg, 2004; Schwartz et al., 2005; Rico and Cetani, 2001) in the three health systems reveals that:

- they have a common starting phase prompted by urbanization and industrialization in central Europe in the nineteenth century;
- early provision for illness and its consequences for living conditions were tied to the local level (in villages, towns and cities), covering only a small section of the population and a limited range of problems as a kind of public good;
- the emerging nation-states accelerated development of the system through legislation in pursuit of welfare policies; overall development was driven by the expansion of compulsory membership, extension to greater sections of the population and more types of service;
- the three countries differed basically in four ways: (1) with regard to financing the system (tax-based in Italy; insurance-based in Germany and France); (2) with regard to the degree of public sector (Political Administrative System – PAS) involvement in organizing

the system (high in Italy and France, medium in Germany); (3) with regard to centralization of the decision-making system (high in France, medium in Italy, mixed in Germany); and (4) with regard to the role/power of professional groups (strong in Germany, medium in France, low in Italy);

- in all three systems reform is in constant demand, nowadays to cope with new demographic structures and emerging financial constraints. Common trends are: (1) the search for a balance between competition and collaboration (in Germany: competition or unification of sickness funds); (2) the search for a balance between centralization – to handle new challenges to the system – and decentralization – to make local agencies and providers responsible for results; and (3) the search for a balance between cost-cutting and efficacy improvement.

In the light of these similarities and differences, the overall cost and outcome of the three health systems (OECD, 2008) varies moderately in some distributional effects, and a great deal in terms of WHO ranking and subjective satisfaction (see Table 6.1).

It is not the aim of this chapter to interpret these data; it is clear,

Table 6.1 Health system indicators

	France	Germany	Italy
Expenditure (% of GDP, 2006)	11.1	10.6	8.7
* Expenditure (US $ per person) (almost 100% of the population covered)	3.937	3.718	2.837
* Percentage of public expenditure for health care (2006)	79.7	76.9	77.2
* Expenditure of ambulatory vs institutionalized care % (remainder being drugs/medication etc.)	26.8/42.3	29/36.6	34.3/41.2
* Beds/physicians (per 1000 inhabitants, 2006)	7.3/3.4	8.3/3.4	4.0/3.7
* Life expectancy (men/women, 2006)	77.3/84.4	77.2/82.4	77.9/83.8(2004)
* WHO ranking (1999)	1	25	2
* Consumer satisfaction 'very good' + 'rather good' (%)	78.2	49.9	26.3

Source: OECD (2008).

however, that the outcome of the systems is not a direct function of financial input.

THE DELIVERY OF SERVICES IN THE THREE COUNTRIES AND THE ROLE OF THE LOCAL/REGIONAL LEVEL

This section focuses on the local/regional[5] level. But, as the brief description of system development has indicated, various types of actors on different levels of administration are involved in planning and financing services. How much influence can, nevertheless, be exerted on the local (and regional) level with regard to the scope, quality and quantity of services?

A Comparative View of Context Factors in Service Production

Before we look in detail at local services, Table 6 2 provides an overview of the contextual factors guiding service production. It gives a first impression of the division of labour with regard to major functions in health services.

In Germany, different types of actor (public and semi-public) are responsible for various system functions (Schwartz et al., 2005). This has been described as a self-administrative institution mix. The local level has little influence on system design. Especially complicated is the variation in the jurisdictions of these actors: sickness funds can cover local, regional or national jurisdictions.

Italy has a clear hierarchical chain in a three-tier system: central government, regional government and local health authorities. Central government sets general rules and service standards, and guarantees every region the same per capita financial support (Tediosi et al., 2008). The pivotal SSN (Servicio Sanitaris Nazionale) administrative level is the *regione*, which controls the public provision network and the final purchaser of privately produced services. The power of the region depends on its financial strength (to purchase services), planning competence (allocation of functions to public providers and demarcation of contracted private services), and legal and political authority. The *regione* acts as a public service network holding. Municipalities are only consultants of LHA directors-general.

In France, the health system remains highly centralized, with the state playing a strong role. Since 1996, each region has had a regional hospitalization agency, which exercises control over public health institutions

Table 6.2   Contextual factors of local health services provision

Contextual factors	Germany	Italy	France
Sources of regulations	National law (few of European origin, state/Länder laws for public health office)	National general law and strong regional regulatory power. There are now 20 different regional health care regulations and systems	The state defines public health objectives and modalities of funding
Sources of institutionalization (planning function)	For the medical practitioners: Ärztekammer (regional jurisdiction); for the hospitals: state administration; for nursing care services: local administration; public health services: local health office, Länder administration	Rules derive only from public bodies (central government, regioni and LHA) Worker union and private providers networks act only as economic counterpart	Regulation of public health institutions and private providers by regional hospitalization agencies and by the departments of the state (DRASS, DDASS). For liberal practitioners there are professional rules and obligations
Sources of financing	Ambulatory and institutional treatment: sickness funds (multiple types; multiple jurisdictions); nursing care: care funds; multiple types and jurisdictions; public health services and crisis interventions: local budget (projects: often state budget)	National health care fund, divided on a per capita basis to the regional governments. Regional funds are divided on per capita basis to LHAs. The national health care fund is financed with general taxation (both national and regional)	Social security (70% of funds), itself financed by social contributions and respective taxes. Complementary insurances payments for the remaining 30%

Table 6.2 (continued)

Contextual factors	Germany	Italy	France
Sources of decision-making and participation by the population	Self-help group participation; choice of membership in sickness fund; choice of service (ambulatory and institutional)	Municipal control on LHAs and independent hospital performance. User committee as LHAs consultant. Choice of service and provider by the population	User associations are represented in public hospital forums. The decision to establish a private or public hospital is free. One physician per family for ambulatory services (freely chosen) was established
Modes of coordination	Regulation (national; state-level) (few elements of competition between private and public providers)	Strong central coordination of the regional level. Strong regional government coordination for LHA and independent hospitals (all owned by the region) and for nursing homes and private providers (entirely financed by the regional health care fund through LHAs)	Coordinated by the state and the ARH. A policy of concentration of institutions is carried out since 1996 in the public and private sectors and between the two
Focus of the allocation or addressing of services	Individual user (patient) (seldom: families, diagnosis-related groups; risk networks; local settings; general public via mass media)	Individual users. Target groups for screening, prevention programme and some disease management programmes (especially for elderly)	Individual users. Groups at risk for prevention

Table 6.2   (*continued*)

Contextual factors	Germany	Italy	France
Sources of information on allocation and effect of services	Special information primarily for the use of each actor and his function (little mandatory information given on infectious diseases; cancer statistics; statistics on cause of death); special surveys covering the general population	Population for public health programmes LHAs and regional databases and reports LHAs must report to municipalities. Regional government must report to the regional council and to the central government every three months	Essentially the family physician, who is the doctor allocated to an individual. The agency health monitoring and DDASS for contagious diseases or monitoring of certain diseases

Source: Summary by the authors.

and private institutions. The ultimate idea is to extend their scope to the entire health sector and medical and welfare systems to enhance coordination.

The Types of Local Service Delivered in Comparison

Table 6.3 attempts a direct comparison of local/regional responsibilities for service provision between France, Italy and Germany.

Not surprisingly, the table shows that most health-related services, especially primary care and community services, are offered locally. Depending on the degree of specialization and economies of scale, institutionalized services (hospitals etc.) may fall under other jurisdiction (regional, national). At the same time, Table 6.2 shows that the local public sector plays different roles in the three countries in the production and delivery of services.

In Germany, the local health administration covers very few of these services: health information, health protection, some elements of prevention, medical treatment substitution (if other providers fail), parts of institutionalized treatment and nursing care. In order to quantify these

Health services: issues and trends 129

Table 6.3   Local service-related activities

Activities (service-related)	Germany	Italy	France
Preparation and distribution of health-related information	Local health office (local practitioners – multiple types; sick funds – multiple types, non-local; pharmacies)	LHAs (departments for public health)	Family doctor
Individual-centred prevention	Local practitioners (sick funds – multiple types, non-local; local health office)	LHAs (GPs and department for public health). The department for public health has to have 5% of the LHA's budget	Family doctor. National campaigns for certain pathologies: cancer screening
Setting-centred prevention	Local health office (other local public institutions)	LHAs (departments for public health). The department for public health has to have 5% of the LHA's budget	National: prevention campaigns, sensitization. Compulsory vaccinations by municipality (*commune*)
Health protection, crisis management (SARS, bird flu)	Local health office (multi-level networks; special non-local institutions – RKI)	*Regione* and its LHAs in coordination with regional agency for environmental protection. The *regione* is the public holding for the public healthcare network and plays a steering role	National agencies; deconcentrated services by the state: *préfet*, DDASS DRASS; municipalities for risk through summer heat, (information and help for isolated persons)
Medical treatment (ambulatory)	Local practitioners – multiple types (local health office as substitute, especially for psychiatric treatment)	Local physician contracted or employed by LHAs and SSN independent hospitals	Family doctor, hospital emergencies, municipal free health centres

130   *The provision of public services in Europe*

Table 6.3 (continued)

Activities (service-related)	Germany	Italy	France
Complementary treatment (ambulatory)	Local professionals – multiple types	Local health care professional employed by LHAs and SSN independent hospitals	Specialists for certain pathologies. Care of the sick or hospital workers at home
Nursing care (ambulatory)	Local professionals – multiple organizational forms, some under public management	Local nurses employed by LHAs or nurses employed by private providers contracted by LHAs or nurses contracted by GPs under LHAs reimbursement	Freelance Agency nurses. Services of home care linked to municipality, municipal centre of social action or association
Nursing homes	Local professionals – multiple organizational forms, some under public management	Three types: LHAs in house nursing homes (10%); public non profit organizations under municipal control (45%); private contracted (45%)	Freelance Agency nurses. Services of home care linked to municipality, municipal centre of social action or association
Institutionalized medical treatment	Local clinics (with doctors and other professionals) – multiple organizations/ ownership (specialized clinics – e.g. psychiatric – non-local) – e.g. psychiatric	LHA or SSN independent hospitals facilities or private providers contracted by LHA	Public hospitals, private clinics (associative), private for-profit hospitals that participate in the mission of public hospital public utility
Rehabilitation	Mostly non-local clinics – multiple types, multiple organizational forms, some under public management	Private providers contracted by LHA under regional planning	Specialized services in hospitals and clinics: very often specific private structures

Source: Summary by the authors.

public components, budget data can be used: the public health system (in total, that is, at all levels) represents 8 per cent of the overall health budget.

In Italy, most health care services are run directly by local health authorities (LHAs), public agencies are controlled by the regional government and by independent SSN hospitals. LHAs are regional public agencies that manage health services for subsets of regional populations within a defined geographical area, delivering health prevention, primary and community care services, and hospital care in small and medium-sized hospitals. In a sense, LHAs also operate as purchasers in the system, since they buy and pay for health services for their population, delivered by independent SSN hospitals and private contracted providers. Independent SSN hospitals are public agencies running the biggest and most specialized hospitals, usually including care, teaching and research. In the country as a whole, there are 171 LHAs, each serving an average population of 341 800. There are 95 independent SSN hospitals with an average 672 beds in 2.2 facilities.

For France, Table 6.3 shows the important role of both central government and the private sector (liberal sector and private hospitals). The French system has always been dominated by an essentially curative approach; prevention is underdeveloped. The primary care doctor (GP or referring doctor) plays an essential role in orienting and informing clients.

PROBLEMS AND STRATEGIES IN LOCAL HEALTH SERVICE COORDINATION

Local coordination depends on the decision-making power of the local PAS. However complex the financing, production and delivery of services are, there is a demand to integrate all aspects into one local picture. This picture covers a specific territorial segment, the people living there and the service institutions available to them. The main pressure from users and stakeholders is on the local level, because that is where the PAS and the public come face to face. Independently of their formal responsibilities, local public actors are confronted with local health problems and – especially – scandals.

There are many options for coordination in Italian municipalities. In Germany, coordination is mainly a problem in cities and counties. Decentralization (more involvement of the regional and local levels) is proceeding in France and Italy. All this makes it particularly interesting to compare the issue of coordination in the three countries.

132   *The provision of public services in Europe*

Germany: Local Coordination Initiatives in the Health Sector

As Table 6.3 shows, few service areas in Germany are organized and financed by local actors. They are potential fields of strict local coordination (i.e. planning). However, structural variation is broad among the more than 13 000 local authorities in the country. But there are some topics of more general concern.

One of these fields is the provision of psychiatric services, which until the early 1970s was the domain of state institutions, with few local practitioners treating mainly neurotic diseases and the relevant department of the local health office responsible for treating drug problems and psychotic diseases. Under the reforms introduced in the 1970s, community psychiatric services (*Gemeindepsychiatrie*) were coordinated locally by the health office. Services were 'sectorized' and local networks (*psychosoziale Arbeitsgruppen*) established. This was counteracted by the increasing number of private professional service providers and the declining role of the health office. The last attempt to date to improve the quality of psychiatric service networks was the proposition of a team of experts commissioned by the federal government: they suggested setting up a community psychiatric services network (*Gemeindepsychiatrischen Verbund*) (1988).

The second example is the planning of ambulatory nursing care services. Earlier forms of service production and delivery by church organizations were reduced in the late 1960s while the demand for these services increased. The local PAS took the initiative, partly as financing agency and partly as service producer. The necessary and successful expansion of local services (social centres/*Sozialstationen*) led to an ever larger number of service providers operating with increasingly diverse and combined financial resources.[6] Thus local coordination efforts – that is, to sectorize services and merge service units – were not very successful. Nowadays service providers of all kinds (local authority, non-profit, private for-profit) are accepted. The local PAS uses the existing service backlog as an instrument to initiate competition between service providers. There is no longer any explicit coordination strategy.

This situation is different with regard to the provision of nursing homes. Because of the investment required, which is partly provided by local budgets, planning is more precise. On the basis of government forecasts, state legislation (e.g. *Pflegegesetz* – NRW) requires the local 'long-term care conference' (*Pflegekonferenz*), organized by local welfare (!) authorities to define future demand and investment requirements. Only if included in the local plan can investors draw on public funds to build nursing homes. The round table, which includes all kinds of local service providers, is responsible for preparation and preliminary decision. The final decision is taken by the local council.

As actors in local services have increasingly diversified, local coordination has become more and more necessary and demanding. Some states (such as NRW) have entrusted general coordination to local health conferences (organized by local health offices) with professional coordinators (originally financed by *Länder* projects). Such conferences include all local actors involved in local service financing, organization and provision. Although the conference is only advisory in capacity, its recommendations are important in the local policy arena. It meets two to four times a year. Typical topics include the situation of specific population groups; qualitative and quantitative problems in specific services; the relevance of long-term trends, reactions to new legislation, and agreement about specific local actions/projects. Providing for communication and mutual consultation, the conference fosters a territorially oriented and all-inclusive (and not only institutional or financial) view of health services. Studies have shown that this has already led to different sectors of local administration adopting common views (Grunow and Hüttner, 1998). This perspective is in keeping with the notion of the 'healthy city' propagated by the WHO in the 1980s.

Italy: the Role of Local Administration in Coordinating the Local Services Landscape

Because Italian municipalities are very fragmented (8000 for 60 million inhabitants) and the 110 provinces are politically and organizationally weak, there are general legal obstacles to municipalities establishing networks to run local services on a broader geographical scale. Sectoral legislation encourages the creation of local networks in water supply, public transport, public libraries, social housing, welfare and so on. Local networks can take many legal forms: consortium or agency regulated by public law, joint stock company, or private-law foundation. The mission of the network may differ: planning, purchasing, or operating in-house services.

There are various network models, ranging from huge, multi-scope networks covering different provinces (from 500000 inhabitants to a few million) to small, single-scope local networks focusing on a single sector.

A historical trend in the country was to seek to integrate social care with health care, and social care with education and labour policy, especially for the elderly, children, the disabled, immigrants, psychiatric patients, drug and alcohol addicts and for former criminal offenders. The integration of these public programmes is a major challenge, leaving little room for other considerations in implementation. However, in some places global experiments under the heading 'healthy cities' are also endeavouring to integrate all fields affecting public well-being, such as urban planning, transport, environmental policy and health care. Such exercises are rare, still very formal, and more or less abstract or academic in nature.

Integration is most advanced within the health care sector and between health and social care. The surprising success has been driven by three main factors:

1. LHAs integrate all health care services (from prevention to acute hospital care, from home care to nursing homes) within a single hierarchy since they generally serve a regional territory (on average 400 000 inhabitants). They decentralize services in health districts that seek to maintain the integrated organization of services at the micro level. Health care district boundaries coincide with those of intermunicipal social networks; there is accordingly a homogeneous organizational interface for integrating health care services with social care. The same board of majors acts in an advisory capacity in LHA strategic decision-making and governs the intermunicipal social network;
2. Municipalities have to implement the local social network to obtain additional financial support for their social programmes from central government. The network must establish a coordination office for social planning in order to be formally recognized by the government.
3. Health care districts and intermunicipal social networks must negotiate an integrated annual programme on the basis of a common, long-term strategy.

While the formal integration architecture is well diffused throughout the country, the results, not surprisingly, are less homogeneous. In some cases there is evidence only for formal institutional integration with poor operational consequences; in others a first attempt has been made at common planning and service design; in still others substantial integration to the benefit of users has been achieved. The latter includes disease management embracing the entire network, which, for example, allows an elderly patient to pass from hospital to rehabilitation centre, nursing home, and finally to domiciliary care through different organizations without really noticing, owing to the integration of social and health care support. However, it is clear that integration in welfare is a very difficult and complex undertaking, and data are lacking on final results and actual implementation rates.

Health-related Intervention and Coordination in France (Long, 2004)

From a historical point of view, the *communes* have made a far from negligible contribution to health issues. Mayors have policy-making competence in public safety, which includes public health and hygiene. Under the law of 1902, the role of public health is to promote collective protection against certain health hazards. All *communes* with more than 20 000 inhabitants must create offices of hygiene and health. Mayors must enact medical by-laws. However, *communes* can obviously play only a limited role in protecting health. The state, therefore, must reassume certain responsibilities. The Public Health Code provides for *département* medical regulation with the responsibility of the prefect to complement national regulation. Mayors can still introduce local arrangements – as long as they comply with those laid down at the central or *département* levels.

The law of 1983 abolished the obligatory character of the offices of hygiene. But all *communes* of a certain size have such a service today, providing necessary vaccinations and specific health protection services of (e.g. air quality monitoring). *Communes* also can organize specific campaigns or set up medical dispensaries for low-income or immigrant sectors of the population. Since decentralization in 1983, the *département* has provided maternal and infantile protection (PMI), which has responsibility for mother and child from birth to the age of six, when school medicine takes over. Until 2004, the *département* was responsible for 'the fight against social diseases'. This competence was recentralized, even though certain *départements* continue to take action in partnership with central government in this sector, in particular in combating cancer. Until 2000, the *département* performed a financially and socially important function in providing free medical assistance, a competence that has now been assumed by the social security system.

Although they maintain specific services, *communes* and *départements* now exercise only subsidiary responsibility in health matters, apart from PMI.

Health issues often lend themselves to communication and specific action. Elected officials accordingly tend to develop specific action in favour of a certain clientele or area. Certain networks, like the 'healthy city' programme, also exist in major cities.

Traditionally, the *régions* have no specific competence in medical matters. Indeed, control of structures and institutions was entrusted to state or quasi-state services (*agencies régionales de l'hospitalisation* – ARH).

However, the debate on reducing territorial differentials in life expectancy has now turned its attention to the regional level (Muller-Quoy, 2006). The field became an issue in the health sector with the law of 2004 on local freedoms and responsibilities. The *région* is responsible for schools of professional health training and can participate in financing medical infrastructures. But its role remains ambiguous, always on the periphery of decision-making.

NPM AND THE DEVELOPMENT OF LOCAL HEALTH SERVICES

This chapter has shown that the potential for designing local service provision is highest in Italy and rather limited in Germany and France. If the impact of NPM reforms is generally concentrated in local public administration, their effect on health services can be expected to be highest in Italy. But, here again, the picture is not so easy to draw. Cost efficiency problems are a permanent concern of health services units. Although the three systems under study are organized as mandatory public programmes, they all have private for-profit components or competitive options. Besides, economization or managerialism might find some limitations in the often very strong position of the medical professions. This raises the question of whether NPM concepts can offer local health services anything new and innovative.

Quasi-markets, Decentralization and Managerialism: How do They Affect the Steering Power of Local Authorities in Italy?

> In the 1990s, . . . a major reform [introduced] (1) quasi-markets, (2) regionalization and (3) managerialism. Quasi-market mechanisms require money to follow patients. Regionalization implies that each of Italy's 20 regional governments now have the opportunity to design its own funding arrangements. (Jommi et al., 2001, p. 347)

'Managerialist' scholars tried to introduce all the key NPM ideas into the Italian public sector (Hood, 1995). This reform package covered the following major aspects:

1. Quasi-market and public competition were introduced to foster responsibility for results. Since patients in the SSN are completely free to choose their health care provider throughout the country, competition has been introduced at three different levels: between similar public health care organizations; between public and private providers; and between different levels of care and approaches.

2. Italy undertook profound institutional decentralization, shifting political and legislative powers from central government to the intermediate level, the 20 *regioni*. The regional governments have, *de facto* since 1995, the power to design their own health care and social care systems. The main limitations are the general framework, which has to be a public health care system with free access for all citizens and financed by taxes, and the free choice of health provider across regions. All *regioni* have designed new institutional architectures, depending on the number and size of LHAs and independent hospitals, quasi-market rules, the market share of private providers, the allocation of resources in different health care clusters, and the degree of strategic autonomy enjoyed by providers. Twenty different regional health care systems are now in place, which makes the comparison of models and outcomes highly interesting.
3. Managerialism is a key concept covering many institutional and organizational innovations: less room for political involvement in policy-making, less room for bureaucratic procedures, more organizational power to control professional operations and outputs. Public health care organizations are headed by a general director, appointed by the *regione* for a 3–5-year term. The general director exercises legal and managerial power over the agency management. Local city mayors, as representatives of their local communities, have only an advisory role.

What are the consequences of these innovations for local political authorities?

1. The quasi-market has made the consumption of health care services more transparent, since every LHA is financed on an equal per capita basis. Consumption under or over the average is now more visible, involving the political agenda and, more precisely, equity issues. Big cities are usually overfinanced and rural areas underfinanced. Politicians are more aware of the resources and consumption of their constituents.

   The quasi-market has shifted priorities on the political agenda, placing greater emphasis on financial balance, competition and strategies. Local politics has lost the initiative in setting the agenda, which has increasingly depended on quasi-market dynamics. Even local political arenas have assumed a more competitive rather than solidary approach, analysing cross-community data, especially on resources.
2. There is evidence that regionalism has determined the development of different institutional models (Fattore and Longo, 2002). They diverge particularly in the following respects:

- the positioning and institutional governance of the purchaser function in the purchaser–provider split;
- the geography and mission of the different kinds of health care provider;
- the public–private mix on the provider side;
- the infrastructural development of the different levels of care.

'If decentralization continues, problems could arise owing to interregional differences in capacities to formulate and implement appropriate policies and tackle special interest groups' (France and Taroni, 2005, p. 169).

3. Managerialism has been a profound and broad process affecting many policy areas and, to some extent, even political language and rhetoric. Public policy is now expressed in managerial language. Institutional and organizational reforms, typical Weberian answers to emergent political problems, are now presented as managerial innovations (McLaughlin et al., 2002). In some cases, changes are ostensible, with new terminology not being coupled with new approaches. In other cases, managerialism has switched the focus from procedures to final results, outputs and outcomes.

The most important effect managerialism has had is to inaugurate a new era in management–politics relations. LHAs are headed by managers not answerable to a formal political board. The regional government is far away and the board of mayors has only advisory powers. Formally, the new framework is thought to clearly separate politics from management. How have matters developed? In some cases the new managerial framework is actually in place: regional politics sets goals and targets and managers manage. In others, a local politician has become general director. In still others, informal political pressure remains so strong that it substantially influences managerial decisions.

Local PAS Reform in Germany and its Impact on Health Service Provision (Grunow and Grunow-Lutter, 2000)

Local health services in Germany are produced by different kinds of provider. The key elements are autonomy and a welfare mix. Reforms are initiated and carried out in specific subparts of the system – often without regard for how they affect other subparts. Therefore reforms focus for the most part specifically on finance (cost-cutting: flat rates for types of case), therapeutical issues (standardized therapy), the organization and management of service institutions, alarm systems for infectious diseases and so on.

The most widespread modernization measures have concerned finance.

Many small local hospitals belonging to local government or church non-profit organizations have found themselves in financial difficulties, prompting their takeover by private for-profit organizations. How far-reaching this phenomena will prove is difficult to predict, but there is certainly room for change in the entrepreneurial landscape. Modern management methods have been introduced, especially in hospitals, obliging the medical profession to learn about accounting, cost-controlling and new ICT techniques. However, since the professionals can choose where to practise in an international market (EU), cost control is counteracted by rapidly increasing wage levels for doctors. This has prompted a wide range of changes: more and more hospitals are closing down; the length of stay per patient has been reduced; the number of semi-professional staff (i.e. nurses) has fallen; the (less costly) nursing or even untrained staff are being entrusted with (more) therapeutic tasks.[7]

On the local level, the effects of reform strategies are not easily discernible. If reforms are initiated at this level, they often have a 'gap-filling' or 'repair' function. Unexpected contradictions or problems in the health system are taken up by local actors – often in the context of health conferences. Some of the more enduring trends are demographic development, lack of doctors (because they increasingly find opportunities outside Germany) and diminishing population density in rural areas – especially in East Germany. The latest health service coverage scenarios do not exclude local health offices from employing doctors to provide basic medical services – not short of a revolution in the German health system.

Another impulse for change comes from local administrative reform. The many cutbacks and the introduction of NPM tools over the past ten years have influenced local health offices (Grunow and Grunow-Lutter, 2000). The overall effects have been slight. Reducing staff is complicated in an organization with up to 20 different professions and semi-professions. Cutbacks have often been renounced because scandals in the health service are politically highly sensitive. NPM tools have to some extent been tested; few are applied consistently. Those most often used, like the 'citizen office' or contracting out, do not affect health offices much, often only indirectly. As the local health office has little decision-making competence and few service-producing functions, the impact of NPM reforms on the health service landscape has been very slight.

Reforms in France Affecting the Local Level

While social welfare in France focused on decentralization (to the *département* level) after 1984, health policy has continued to devolve. The new organizational arrangements established in 1996 with legislation on social security financing, regional agencies and rationalization of the system with the *carte vitale* – health insurance card, have been proving insufficient. Subsequent reforms have tried to strengthen physician control and patient empowerment (de-reimbursement). However, there are limitations:

- ARH have reorganized the hospital sector (public and private) but not settled the question of the relationship between inpatient and outpatient care. The links between health and social care remain weak due to different levels of responsibility, while the ageing population requires better coordination.
- Since 2004, the *regions* have been involved in all major health issues. However, there is no clear affirmation of their role in the sector.
- Financing social security and access to care throughout the territory are recurring issues in the public debate. Various reports have recently been published, which should see some progress.

The following reforms are up for discussion:

- From a managerial point of view it seems important to re-establish links between the health and social sectors. The health agency that is to replace the ARH could play this role, but there is resistance within the sector.
- The position of the *région* in planning and programming must be consolidated. There are two goals:
  - To take account of local specificities, because certain pathologies are more prevalent in some *régions* than in others; and
  - To assure equal access to care for the whole population.

It is important for local and regional actors to organize an efficient dialogue with the liberal occupations and the conflicting interests of service providers and users.

Financing is also a crucial issue; the de-reimbursement of many treatments and medications implies private insurance or direct payments by the insured, with the disparities that such a system can generate. These problems can be reduced if service delivery becomes more cost-efficient.

SUMMARY

Although the three systems still differ considerably in their basic architecture, they face similar external demands for reform: how to make services demand-oriented and cost-efficient and how to find and combine different types of organizational solution. Table 6.4 summarizes the main features.

CONCLUSION

This chapter has shown that there are challenges common to all health systems in the OECD countries. Reaction to them goes back a long way. Path dependence is strongest in basic architectures. Their complexity includes many restrictions and veto positions, which reduce the likelihood of system change. Scenario details are similar in many comparable countries: demographic development and changes in the disease panorama; cost explosions and containment; new therapies and technologies – the daily subject of international exchange; new management methods for health services provision. Even though the problems are similar, the basic elements of the systems induce quite different reactions. Italy has a public health system financed by tax revenues; France has an insurance-based system with strong (central) government influence; the system in Germany is still predominantly self-organized subject to central government legislation. The basic difference between Italy and the other two countries is the mode of financing. However, owing to demographic developments and the risks in a globalized economy, it has become more and more difficult to tie health care contributions to employment contracts (Germany, France). There is a trend towards basic contributions on various forms of income – which might ultimately produce a system equivalent to tax-based financing. All three systems are thus slowly moving towards a national health care fund. Italy already has one, France has strengthened its central financial model, Germany has impressively reduced the number of sickness funds and has just (2009) established a common pool (*Gesundheitsfonds*) from which all resources are distributed to sickness funds. This development seeks to strengthen the role of central government as general planner of the system, with clear financial boundaries that cannot be exceeded. Every national policy has to be embedded in a financially balanced perspective.

This general institutional scenario for economic balance is accompanied by a trend towards decentralization at an intermediate level of government. Cost control goals are set at the central level, but strategies are decentralized step by step to the regional level because they have to be adapted to service organization and quality.

The regional level has gained more influence on the planning of local and regional infrastructure in Germany, France and Italy. The intermediate level of government has to steer the system, planning the number of facilities and personnel, monitoring providers' efficiency and efficacy, and

Table 6.4 NPM reforms

Contextual factors	Germany	Italy	France
External change drivers	Overspending Ageing Technological development	Overspending Ageing Technological development Federal reform of the state	Overspending Ageing Technological development State decentralization
Reform focus	Cost containment Quality improvement Managerial development Equal service accessibility	Cost containment Quality improvement Managerial development	Cost containment Quality improvement Equal service accessibility
Financial models Reforms	Competition between hospital and DRG system: succeeded Competition between sick funds: failed Competition between primary and ambulatory care physician: failed	Introduction of an organic quasi-market system LHAs are financed per capita and are purchasers of the system DRG for hospital, fee for service for other sectors	Competition between hospital DRG system
Meso planning models and tools	Empowerment of regional hospital planning Empowerment of local health conferences	Regional planning autonomy	Regional hospital plans In the future: ARS can facilitate plan
Providers Geography Development	Merger and acquisition of hospitals	Reduction of LHA Implementation of independent public hospitals Increase of the private providers' market share	Development of hospital networks Development of some rural primary and community care facilities

Table 6.4 (*continued*)

Contextual factors	Germany	Italy	France
Implemented managerial tools	Cost accounting Performance management ICT	Cost accounting Performance management Personnel MBO ICT	
Managerially strong providers	Hospitals Some municipalities	LHA and independent hospitals in the developed regions	Hospitals
Managerial weak providers	Primary care Ambulatory care	LHA and independent hospitals in the weak regions	Primary care Ambulatory care Integration between social and health care

Source: Summary by the authors.

consumption equity. Intermediate levels of government have come to regulate quasi-market mechanisms. The aim is to cut costs, improve quality and increase equity in a coordinated way. Monitoring and controlling health service providers to ensure adequate coverage and quality throughout the country strengthens regional (and local) agencies: they oversee the local situation[8] and, having more power than the provider's management itself, are more and more frequently able to intervene top-down in service organization, often contrary to the interests of professionals and other stakeholders.

Providers constitute the third level of the systems, and are increasingly mixed in nature: public, profit and not-for-profit organizations. Quasi-market models (public competition) put pressure on health care providers. Diagnosis-related groups (DRGs) or similar therapy-finance mechanisms have been implemented in all three cases, especially in hospitals, nursing homes and rehabilitation. The fee-for-service financial model, combined with regional hospital plans, has forced development of the hospital landscape: mergers and acquisitions, increase of for-profit market share, development of networks. Health care providers have introduced and developed new managerial tools to handle the new external pressure.

The biggest problems remain the delivery of primary care (issues of supply equity), ambulatory care and the integration of social and health care and of primary and hospital care. This is why new types of local health provider have been introduced, especially for primary and community care, employing doctors and other professionals to ensure a comparable distribution of services in all regions of the countries under study.

Altogether, the trend seems to be towards the Beveridge model – which might lead to meso-level (i.e. organization-level) tools of quality improvement and efficiency. The focus is on the health status of the population in local authorities and regions. The other components of the system architecture are more and more often evaluated in terms of their contribution to these standards. Traditional disease-related research has now been increasingly joined by health care evaluation research. This has the advantage of including factors beyond health system services, which account for two-thirds of local/regional health status.

NOTES

1. Whether these arguments hold for non OECD countries cannot be discussed here.
2. In a case study in Munich, a survey of all top administrators (*Dezernenten/Referenten*) revealed that all see their administrative domains as contributing to the health of the Munich population.
3. This means that you do not see and evaluate the good before you buy/use it; the good often cannot be returned or exchanged for another. Therefore a failure in a service often has more serious consequences than a deficiency in a technical product.
4. Non-exclusiveness means unrestricted access of everybody to the services. Non-rivalry means that the consumption of any person does not restrict the possibilities of any other consumer.
5. As the description of the three systems has shown, the definition of local and regional level is different from case to case. Therefore the legal terms of each case are used in the respective language. However, the primary focus of this part of the chapter is on the local level in the sense of local authorities or local authority networks (also in the sense of administrative districts) and municipalities (cities).
6. Since 1995 the financial basis has been covered by the national *Pflegeversicherung*, which defines three levels of individual entitlements (*Pflegestufen*).
7. According to a press release of 17 February 2009, the central government spent €3 billion of tax money to remedy these deficiencies. This indicates a new trend: the costs of the system are not sufficiently covered by the insurance system, so that tax revenues fill the gap.
8. For example, health reporting and increasing research about health provision in German local authorities (Kurth, 2008).

REFERENCES

Anderson, R.A. and R.R. McDaniel (2000), 'Managing health care organizations: where professionalism meets complexity science', *Health Care Management Review*, **25** (1), 83–93.

Baumol, W.J. (1967), 'Macroeconomy of unbalanced growth', *American Economic Review*, **LVII**, 415–26.

Busse, R. and A. Riesberg (2004), *Health Care Systems in Transition: Germany*,

Copenhagen: WHO Regional Office for Europe on behalf of the European Observatory on Health Systems and Policies.
Fattore, G. and F. Longo (2002), 'I modelli emergenti nei sistemi sanitari regionali' (titolo da controllare), in E. Anessi Pessina and E. Cantù (eds), *Rapporto OASI 2002, L'aziendalizzazione della sanità in Italia*, Milano: Egea.
France, G. and F. Taroni (2005), 'The evolution of health-policy making in Italy', *Journal of Health Politics, Policy and Law*, **30** (1–2), 169–87.
Grunow, D. and B. Hüttner (1998), *Gesundheitsbezogene Verwaltungslandschaft: die vernachlässigte Grundlage kommunaler Gesundheitspolitik und -förderung*, Bielefeld: Kleine Verlag.
Grunow, D. and V. Grunow-Lutter (2000), *Der öffentliche Gesundheitsdienst im Modernisierungsprozess*, Weinheim: Juventa.
Hood, C. (1995), 'Emerging issues in public administration', *Public Administration*, **73** (1), 165–83.
Jommi, C., E. Cantù and E. Anessi Pessina (2001), 'Funding arrangements in the Italian National Health Service', *International Journal of Health Planning and Management*, **16**, 347–68.
Kurth, B. (ed.) (2008), *Monitoring der gesundheitlichen Versorgung in Deutschland: Konzepte, Anforderungen, Datenquellen*, München: Deutscher Ärzteverlag.
Long, M. (2004), 'Les attributions des collectivités locales en matière sanitaire et sociale', in J.C. Douence and F.P. Bénoit (eds), *Encyclopédie des collectivités locales*, Paris: Dalloz.
McDaniel, R.R. and D.J. Driebe (2001), 'Complexity science and health care management', in J.D. Blair et al. (eds), *Advances in Health Care Management*, vol. 2, Amsterdam: Elsevier Science, pp. 11–36.
McLaughlin, K., S. Osborne and E. Ferlie (2002), *New Public Management: Current Trends and Future Prospects*, London: Routledge.
Muller-Quoy, I. (2006), 'Quelle régionalisation du système de santé?', *LPA 21*, **37**, 3.
OECD (2008), *Health Data 2008: Statistics and Indicators for 30 Countries*, OECD Publishing, Database 2008.
Rico, A. and T. Cetani (eds) (2001), *Health Care Systems in Transition: Italy*, Copenhagen: WHO Regional Office for Europe on behalf of the European Observatory on Health Systems and Policies.
Schwartz, F.W. et al. (eds) (2005), *Das Public Health Buch*, München: Urban & Fischer.
Tediosi, F., S. Gabriele and F. Longo (2008), 'Governing decentralization in health care under tough budget constraint: what can we learn from the Italian experience?', *Health Policy*, HEAP-2268 (DOI 10.1016/j.healthpol.2008.10.012).
Thomson, S. and E. Mossialos (eds) (2004), *Health Care Systems in Transition: France*, Copenhagen: WHO Regional Office for Europe on behalf of the European Observatory on Health Systems and Policies.
WHO, World Health Organization (2000), *The World Health Report 2000: Health Systems: Improving Performance*, Geneva: WHO Papers.

7. Comparative study of a local service: waste management in France, Germany, Italy and the UK

Magali Dreyfus, Annette Elisabeth Töller, Carlo Iannello and John McEldowney

INTRODUCTION

This chapter addresses waste management, an important public service, which provides a significant role for local government in France, Germany, Italy and the UK. There is a long history of local government responsibility for waste, going back to nineteenth-century industrialization and public health concerns. National governments passed legislation in the 1970s addressing waste management. The EU has been influential in linking waste management to protecting the environment. Waste management is also linked to tackling climate change through reductions in levels of carbon emissions from landfill sites. Any instability in oil prices can be avoided by meeting energy needs through heat recovery from waste disposal. The Landfill Directive in 1999 was a milestone in setting a new waste hierarchy and significantly reducing landfill use, with clear targets for reductions up to 2016. The waste hierarchy includes recycling and reuse targets and the use of waste for energy production. Municipal waste has grown throughout the EU. In 2005, municipal waste totalled 248 million metric tons (tonnes), with 78 per cent being collected in the four largest member states France, Germany, Italy and the UK (see Figure 7.1).

This chapter considers the institutional framework of waste management in France, Germany, Italy and the UK. The main questions addressed are: how have the four countries adopted municipal waste management strategies and are there any variations in practice? The overriding theme is EU convergence considered in terms of how each of the four countries has responded to waste management within its existing infrastructure and coped with the integration of a common set of EU rules and objectives in its national framework. Private sector involvement in

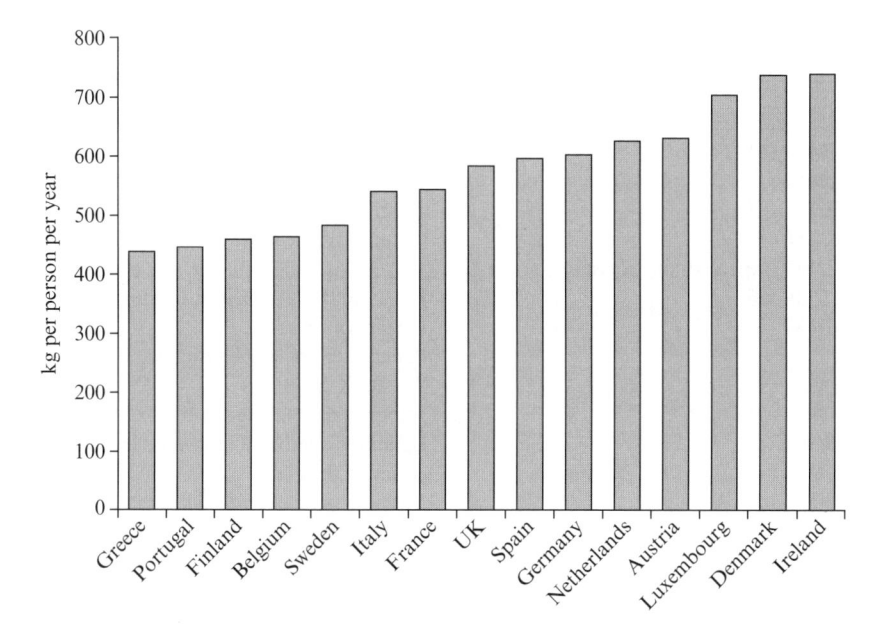

[Bar chart showing kg per person per year of waste by country: Greece ~440, Portugal ~450, Finland ~460, Belgium ~465, Sweden ~485, Italy ~540, France ~545, UK ~585, Spain ~595, Germany ~605, Netherlands ~625, Austria ~630, Luxembourg ~700, Denmark ~735, Ireland ~740.]

Note: The amount of waste falls within similar parameters for France, Germany, Italy and the UK.

Source: Eurostat.

Figure 7.1 The amount of waste in the main EU member states

waste management is common, as are strategies for adopting the polluter-pays principle through charges for waste disposal.

SITUATION AND TRENDS IN THE FOUR COUNTRIES

A Common Framework

The four countries have a common EU framework for local service provision in waste management. Article 1(a) of the Framework Directive on Waste (2006/12) defines waste in broad terms as 'any substance or object in the categories set out in Annex 1 (of the Directive) which the holder discards or intends or is required to discard'. Annex 1 to the Directive contains over 16 categories of waste covering a very wide range of products and substances. The shift from landfill to a new waste hierarchy

Table 7.1 Directives on waste

Directive	Specific field
75/439	Waste oils
75/442	General framework now amended
78/176	Titanium dioxide
91/156	General framework
91/157, repealed and revised by 2006/66	Disposal of batteries and accumulators
91/689	Hazardous waste
94/62	Packaging and packaging waste
96/59	Waste PCBs
96/61	Integrated pollution control
99/31	**Landfill directive: a milestone in waste policy in the EU**
2000/53	Management of end-of-life motor vehicles
2000/76	Incineration amended previous directives
2002/96	Waste electrical and electronic equipment
2006/12, repealed and revised by 2008/98	General Framework Codified Directive replacing 91/56

Source: Summary by the authors.

involving various options came after the Landfill Directive of 1999 as follows:

- Landfill is regarded as the bottom of the waste hierarchy and is the least desirable because it has the potential to generate up to 40 per cent of methane emissions.
- Recycling and composting are regarded as the most efficient because they are environmentally friendly and have the potential to reduce the costs of materials and conserve resources.
- Reuse is also regarded as good environmental practice and is generally encouraged as part of a sustainable development strategy.
- Energy from waste is possible in the production of electricity.

Table 7.1 sets out a number of relevant directives on waste. This illustrates the diversity of approaches – prevention through recycling; deterrence through landfill taxes; and precautionary principles through identifying dangerous waste.

The European Landfill Directive (99/31/EC) provides targets for the reduction of waste to be sent to landfill. Public authorities must guarantee to achieve the following:

- recovery or incineration in incineration plants with energetic recovery of a minimum of 60 per cent of package waste weight;
- recycling of a minimum of 55 per cent of package waste weight;
- recycling of 60 per cent of weight for glass, paper and paperboard;
- recycling of 50 per cent of weight for metals;
- recycling of 22.5 per cent of weight for plastics;
- recycling of 15 per cent of weight for wood.

We examine how waste management is undertaken in each of the four countries through the relevant legal framework and financial controls.

The Legal Framework for Local Service Provision

France

Waste management policy[1] in France is driven by strong decision-making at the local level and a major shift away from landfill in favour of recycling, reuse and incineration, providing energy. In the past, a public-health-led approach to waste management shifted to an environmental focus. The relevant law is in the Environmental Code of 2000 (Art. L110-1 to L110-2; L124-1; L511-1 to L517-2; L541-1 to L541-50 Code de l'environnement); the Local Government Code (Art. L2224-13 to L2224-17 Code général des collectivités territoriales) and the Public Health Code (Art. L1311-1 to L1311-3 Code de santé publique). There are four main guidelines applicable to waste (Art. L.541-1-I Code de l'environnement): preventing and reducing the quantity and harmfulness of waste, limiting the transport of waste, increasing recovery and enhancing information available to the public.

Two main laws regulate waste management. The first is dated 15 July 1975, inspired by a public health approach to waste. The law coincided with the first European Waste Directive (Directive of the Council 75/442/CEE of 15 July 1975). However, many local authorities favoured landfill and incineration, mainly because these activities were cheaper. Nevertheless, collection improved and by the 1980s more than 90 per cent of the population had access to the service.

The second law no. 92-377 of 13 July 1992 (amended law no. 75-633) adopted a more environmental approach in line with a new European directive (Directive 91/156/CEE of 18 March 1991) amending the Framework Directive of 1975. The main objective was to reduce the

Table 7.2   Waste management under the responsibility of communes *in France*

Household and assimilated waste		
Municipal waste		Economic activities waste
Maintenance waste	Household waste	Waste from economic activities
Forest maintenance, landscape refuse, garden and public spaces refuse, market waste etc.	Normal waste Occasional cumbersome waste	Industry, offices, shops, craft activities etc.
Local authority waste	Household waste	Assimilated waste (or DICB)

Source: Summary by the authors.

number of waste landfills by enhancing treatment and recovery. It also defined the concept of 'final waste', waste that cannot be recovered. By 1 July 2002, only this category could be received in landfills. Under EU influence a tax on landfill sites was also introduced alongside a law on packaging waste.

Finance and competencies   Waste disposal facilities are mainly publicly owned but privately operated. The 1975 law on waste management requires *communes* to ensure the removal of waste from households. The Environmental Code provides a broad definition of 'removal' (Art. L541-2), which covers collection, transport, storage, sorting, treatment and recovery. In discharging their responsibilities, *communes* collaborate with *régions* and *départements*. Waste management can also be handled by a group of *communes*[2] or syndicates. Pursuant to EU directives, waste management plans are adopted at the département level.

The compulsory competence of the *commune* concerns household waste (see Table 7.2). In many instances household and business wastes are mixed, except where hazardous and requiring special treatment,[3] when a special tax is levied to defray costs.

Communes may draw on one of the three sources of income to finance waste management. First, the TEOM (*Taxe d'enlèvement des ordures ménagères*) is an optional tax that *communes* are allowed to establish but which is levied by the state and is based on the rental value of housing. Second, the REOM (*Redevance sur les ordures ménagères*) is calculated on the full costs of the service and is recoverable by the local authority from the citizen. Third, since 1992, a fee is payable by waste producers of assimilated household waste, the *Redevance spéciale incitative,* based on the service provided (Art. L 2333-78, L-2224-14 CGCT).

Since 1999 there has been a further possibility: an incentive tax on classified facilities. The TGAP (*Taxe générale sur les activités polluantes*) is a substitute for a landfill tax. It is paid by the owners of storage facilities for household and dangerous waste. The tax is calculated as a function of the weight of waste received. The amount to be paid was doubled in 2002 for unauthorized landfill facilities and again in 2005 in an attempt to suppress such facilities completely.[4]

Waste management Most waste management installations are owned by municipalities or intermunicipal bodies. Waste collection is routinely carried out by private sector companies, which in some instances fully own waste management facilities. Waste management plans include the type, quantity and origin of the waste to be collected and treated; the policy priorities regarding the local circumstances; the authorities and companies acting in that field; the needs of the localities; and disposal facilities for 'final' waste.[5] Since 31 December 2008, the plans must be consistent with the national objectives fixed in the regulatory part of the Environmental Code and which directly transpose the 1994 Directive on Packaging. Local authorities must fulfil the objectives set by the European directives. For particular categories of waste, local governments act as coordinators. The *départements* establish plans for waste produced by public works and buildings. They have only incentive value, although planning is also organized at the regional level. Plans for harmful waste (*Plan Régional d'Elimination des Déchets Industriels Spéciaux* – PREDIS) and waste from the healthcare sector (*Plan Régional d'Elimination des Déchets d'Activités de Soins* – PREDAS) are adopted by regional councils after consultation with a commission composed of representatives from local authorities and central government. The responsibility for this waste falls to the producers and requires a competent company for disposal.

France has moved significantly away from landfill. In 2004, 37 per cent of household and assimilated waste was stored in landfill, 40 per cent was incinerated, 17 per cent recycled, and 17 per cent composted. This represents a decrease in landfill use in favour of recycling and incineration.[6] A survey conducted in 69 large cities and urban areas showed that in 2004 waste was collected directly by the authorities in 42 per cent of cases, in 15 per cent by an internal operator, in 2 per cent under concession and 41 per cent under public procurement contract. As for the waste treatment, 16 per cent was provided directly by the local authority or group of authorities, 3 per cent through an internal operator, 47 per cent under concession, and 34 per cent under public procurement contract. Landfill remains mainly in the hands of local government, 62 per cent of facilities being owned *en régie*, although collection and treatment are mostly delegated to external operators. In spite of the plurality of contracting authorities, the private sector waste market is a virtual duopoly of major contractors. Finally, the European Community has the oversight of directives and their implementation. France was censured for failing to transpose the 1992 directive in 1997. Delays in establishing the conformity of incineration plants with European standards also led to a conviction by the European Court of Justice (ECJ).[7]

The French experience is that, as a consequence of recent industrialization, *communes* will continue to delegate management responsibilities to specialized private companies. This reflects an increase in the market economic value of waste.[8] France has made some significant advances. The volume of household waste collected has decreased (from 34 500 000 tonnes in 2003 to 32 500 000 in 2004), recycling and incineration have grown as landfill has diminished (in 2006, 5.3 million tonnes of household waste was recycled compared with 3.8 million in 2000, an increase of 40 per cent, the recovery level of household waste in 2005 being 64 per cent compared with 53 per cent in 2000),[9] and waste-to-energy processes generated 6 per cent of total renewable energy production.

There has been slow progress in reducing the number of illicit landfill sites.[10] There are problems with financing and the distribution of responsibilities. The financial arrangements in place provide inadequate incentives and penalties. In terms of responsibilities, clarity is needed in policy-making and in interpreting directives. Definitions of waste and competencies need to be simplified to avoid wasteful and unnecessary legal tangles.

Germany
Waste management in Germany is a municipal task traditionally handled by landfill. In the 1960s and 1970s it was recognized that landfill contributed to air and land pollution. In the early 1970s the federal government, although it lacked clear legal competence in a field where state governments have the main say, was able to push through the first Federal Waste Management Act (1972). The *Abfallgesetz* required the municipalities to dispose of all kinds of waste, but insisted for the first time that all waste be disposed of at licensed sites (Lamping, 1997, p. 50). The 1980s saw a drastic increase in household waste. There was greater public awareness of the new waste disposal sites and incineration plants (Langmann and Schönwasser, 1998, p. 329; Beckmann, 2003, p. 374). The discussion in the late 1980s was dominated by the notion of a 'waste emergency' (*Müllnotstand*, SRU, 1998, p. 174) against a background of widely varying

regional waste management capacities (SRU, 1990, p. 194). The federal government addressed the regulation of disposal or recycling for particular groups of products outside the municipal waste system, placing responsibility on the producers. A 1993 law, the *TA Siedlungsabfall* (Technical Instructions on Waste from Human Settlements) laid down criteria for waste management treatment, making incineration the only legal method for disposing of municipal waste, even though the various *Länder* proved inventive, even creative, in dealing with these stipulations (Lamping, 1997). It was not until 2001 that the federal government, a coalition of Social Democrats and Greens, accepted (so-called 'cold') bio-mechanical treatment of waste as another legal option (SRU, 2008, p. 681).

The turning point in German waste management policy, however, was the 1994 Recycling Waste Management Act, which fundamentally reassigned responsibilities for waste management. The private producer or owner of waste was made responsible for recycling or disposal. Municipalities now have only clearly defined functions, reduced in fact to household waste. This was well in advance of the EU Landfill Directive in 1999. Over the past 40 years or so, waste management has been a major concern of policy at the national, state and local levels. According to a recent federal government study, waste management is a sector in which German companies cover more than one-quarter of the world market (BMU/UBA, 2009).

Finance and competencies Within the framework of the European and federal legislation, *Länder* and municipalities can pursue their own course in waste management. The *Länder* can legislate to assign responsibility for waste management to public authorities as they see fit. They prepare waste management plans to set capacities for waste management within their territory. Local authorities draw up local waste management concepts (Schulze Wehninck, 2008, p. 70). Within this legal framework, local service provision in waste management has been fundamentally transformed. The idea of separating groups of particularly problematic products from municipal waste goes back to the early 1980s. Starting with a voluntary agreement on the separate collection and disposal of used batteries, the federal government sought to make producers responsible for ecologically acceptable disposal of their products. The idea of producer responsibility was intended to motivate manufacturers to design products with stronger concern for recyclability and disposability. A particularly politically sensitive field is packaging waste, regulated by ordinance in 1991. Waste paper was regulated by a voluntary agreement in 1994, the separate disposal of scrap cars was regulated by voluntary agreement and regulation in 1996 and 1997, and by regulation later in 2002. The separate management of electrical waste and electrical equipment (WEE) was regulated only in 2005. Whereas some of these arrangements are genuinely German initiatives, others derive from complex combinations of German and European projects (Töller, 2007). Germany has led the way in the separate collection, recycling and disposal of different categories of waste.

The 1994 legislation on recycling waste management withdrew a second category of municipal waste management from the care of local authorities, namely commercial waste (not in terms of particular products, but ownership). Whereas local authorities were in charge of household waste, commercial waste was now considered an economic good that could be traded and treated in terms of profitability. There is more than anecdotal evidence that this incentive to dispose of waste under favourable market conditions often led to eco-dumping (e.g. in disposal sites with low ecological standards legally in operation until 2005).

The separation of certain categories of product and of commercial waste from municipal waste had four major effects. First, it led to the emergence of major markets for the recycling and disposal of certain products and waste, increasingly dominated by oligopolistic structures. Second, this private sector waste management has tended to be ecologically less exacting than municipal waste treatment (SRU, 1998, p. 183, Beckmann, 2003, p. 38). Third, the *TA Siedlungsabfall* put local authorities under pressure in the early 1990s to build new waste incineration plants. However, for local authorities, waste-sorting municipalities led not so much to overload but to a lack of waste. Since the operation of such plants is costly no matter how much waste they have to burn, unit costs rose sharply. They had to be met by the public through ever-increasing waste management charges. Conflict arose between municipalities and private waste management companies over waste (SRU, 2002, p. 448). Fourth, no matter how we judge this development in ecological terms, eliminating local authority responsibility for such major categories of waste considerably diminished local government control (Langmann and Schönwasser, 1998, p. 337).

Waste management In common with most local service provision, the nature of municipal waste management has been fundamentally changed by the various forms of privatization that swept the country – even though Germany privatized much later than other countries. Comparative studies of local service provision privatization conclude that privatization has been particularly strong in waste management (Bogumil and Holtkamp, 2006, p. 93), even though local authorities cannot completely relinquish their responsibilities in the field (Langmann and Schönwasser, 1998, p. 340).

Some municipalities delegated waste management entirely to private firms, but most privatized various combinations of collection, transport and treatment (e.g. incineration plants), also in conjunction with *Länder* governments (Schulze Wehninck, 2008). In the past, waste collection and transport had been in the hands of local authorities. During the 1990s many municipal enterprises were formally privatized by transforming them into companies under private law (e.g. Osthorst 2001, p. 124). Such merely formal privatization leaves control with the municipality, while more straightforward forms of privatization, such as selling the company to a private buyer or contracting, reduce local government control over waste management.

A recent study has found that about one-quarter of all local authorities have entrusted some aspect of waste management either partly or entirely to private companies, with about 9 per cent were still planning to do so (Ernst & Young, 2007, p. 16). In 20 per cent of small and middle-sized municipalities, the local authority collects and transports waste under various legal guises, in 9 per cent of cases through limited liability companies, and in 36.1 per cent through contracted private providers (a further 35.5 per cent of respondents gave no answer) (Bremeier et al., 2006, p. 40).

The 1993 *TA Siedlungsabfall* put pressure on municipalities to build incineration plants (see above), which in many cases they could not afford. This is where private companies entered the market. In this context, there are basically two forms of privatization. In the operator model the private partner agrees not only to build and finance the plant but also to run it for a contractually determined period (Schulze Wehninck, 2008, pp. 90f.). Cooperation models (public–private partnerships – PPPs) are basically variations of the operator model, differing mainly with respect to ownership. The building and/or operation of a plant is delegated to a mixed corporation, with the municipality usually owning 51 per cent. There are few reliable data. Some authors claim that of the 73 incineration plants in Germany roughly one-third are operated by a PPP (Schulze Wehninck, 2008, p. 93); other studies, for example Bremeier et al., 2006, estimate that 20 per cent of landfill sites and incineration plants are operated by local authorities. Almost 9 per cent are limited liability companies, while in only 29.8 per cent of cases is the operator a private firm (46.7 per cent of respondents gave no answer). An analysis by the news magazine *Der Spiegel* cites higher figures for private involvement: between 51 and 90 per cent (*Der Spiegel*, 2006, p. 108). All studies show major differences between *Länder*. The German experience offers three conclusions. The first is that the economization tendencies described have recently been criticized, even by those who had formerly advocated far-reaching privatization (such as the federal Scientific Advisors' Council on Environmental Matters; SRU, 2002).

The debate on the effects of privatizing local waste management services is no less critical. Privatization proceeded on the assumption that private companies can provide certain services better and less expensively, but much of the recent discussion has challenged this. One argument is that service provision efficiency depends less on the ownership of providers (public or private) than on their exposure to competition. In waste management, however, competition is problematic due partly to concentration trends and long contracts in the sector (Schulze Wehninck, 2008). Second, it is pointed out that efficiency is only one objective: social and ecological impacts are also important and cannot be adequately addressed by private, profit-oriented providers.

Partly due to the criticism of privatization and partly because waste management outsourcing contracts have expired, some local authorities have been considering complete 'remunicipalization' of privatized waste management services (collection and transport). Bergkamen in North Rhine–Westphalia, which had already led the way by buying the power grid from a private company in the mid-1990s, remunicipalized waste management logistics in 2006 (Schäfer, 2007). Many other municipalities have followed suit (Verbuecheln, 2009; Gruner et al., 2009).

The key motive for remunicipalization has been money. The expiry of contracts with private firms opens a window of opportunity, and a reconsideration of the costs and conditions of waste management services has indicated that public waste management firms (in various legal forms) are able to provide the service for up to one third less. This is partly because the public firms themselves have been through the NPM mill and partly because public enterprises do not have to make a profit or pay VAT. One point that had formerly been underestimated is that, due to oligopolistic structures in waste management, competition was insufficient to keep prices down. Saving money (and lowering tariffs) is the primary objective and legitimization of remunicipalization; but local authorities have other objectives, too. In most cases they want to tackle the problem of wage-dumping in waste management services and see an opportunity to create jobs in the region. For municipalities that operate waste management plants, the remunicipalization of waste collection and transport – when waste is in short supply – also appears to improve the chances of securing a share of the waste market. It is not yet clear whether remunicipalization will be the exception or become a major trend. Ernst & Young found that only 10 per cent of municipalities plan to remunicipalize (Ernst & Young, 2007, p. 16). A more recent study found 44 cases in which local authorities are considering such a step (Gruner et al., 2009).

However, some fundamentally challenge whether municipalities should be present as companies on waste management markets at all. This is, for example, challenged by European law. Some *Länder*, such as North Rhine–Westphalia, have recently restricted the economic activities of municipalities.

Italy

The law applicable to waste services is Law 152 (2006), which contains two major innovations. First, the current use of local public companies for waste services is to be gradually replaced by outsourcing contracts involving private companies. Second, the aim is to ensure the unitary management of waste through the waste hierarchy. This should provide more economical and effective management at each level (Optimal Territorial Area, *ambito territoriale ottimale*, ATO) (Montanaro, 2008). The significance of Law 152 (2006) is best understood in the historical context. The first legislation on waste management in Italy was Law 366 in 1941, which aimed to protect hygiene and urban health. Municipalities were given exclusive responsibility to ensure the management of services by granting collection, transportation and disposal rights. Town councils were free to choose between managing waste activities themselves and contracting waste services to the private sector. In the 1990s, a series of reforms allowed local authorities to modernize municipal companies and to change their legal form (from public to private company) while retaining legal control (Villata, 2008).

The Legislative Decree 152 (2006), amended by Law 4 (2008), resulted in local authorities losing exclusive legal control to private companies or mixed public and private institutions. Law 152 obliges the ATO authority to entrust waste service management to a single enterprise (Art. 202). A modicum of direct management (fully publicly owned companies to which service provision is directly entrusted) was reintroduced as an option in 2008 (Decree 112). This, however, is subject to many conditions that make it extremely difficult to put into practice. Under the new legislation, waste services have to be integrated. The collection, transportation, recovery and disposal of waste must be managed by a single enterprise replacing the multiplicity of operators currently managed by local authorities. Waste management companies will have to merge in order to be competitive and reorganize into the ATOs required by the legislation.

Finance and competencies ATOs are funded directly by local authorities. Each ATO is responsible for achieving targets and public tenderings. They have to conform to the Regional Waste Plan that sets out policy. There is increasing reliance on the private sector and ATOs have gained in popularity. The number of municipalities providing their own direct management has diminished except in the smallest towns. Northern regions favour

Table 7.3 Competency framework according to Act 152 (2006)

State	Legislative powers concerning environmental issues and the protection of free market competition to provide the administrative framework for waste services. Administrative powers to implement environmental targets and the administrative framework	Art. 195
Regions	Legislative powers to organize waste services in the region within the national legislative framework. Administrative powers to adopt waste plans for setting the technical axes of waste services (number and kind of waste facilities, general criteria to localize these) and to regulate all technical activities (e.g. granting authorization for waste facilities)	Art. 196, 199
ATO authority	Cross-municipal authorities to ensure self-sufficiency and reduce waste movement. Regulating powers, especially in the organization of service management (from public tendering to setting waste tariffs)	Art. 200, 201, 202
Provinces	Control and planning power to site waste facilities in accordance with regional guidelines. Under Law 244 (2007) provinces could assume the role of ATO	Art. 197
Municipalities	Municipalities have lost their main function (direct management and regulation). They participate in the ATO authority and still have autonomous powers to regulate service management in its territory (e.g. collection and transport modalities, health protection etc.)	Art. 198

Source: Summary by the authors.

ATOs while direct management by local authorities is more widespread in the south (Fise-Assoambiente, 2006).

Setting the boundaries for ATOs is often problematical. Act 152 (2006) favoured an industry-led boundary based on the size of operations rather than on regional boundaries. The Finance Act 2007 (244), however, reintroduced the provincial criterion for delimiting these areas. Act 152 (2006) had originally envisaged that each ATO would be governed by a specific authority with a legal personality, in which all municipalities in the area were to participate. In order to reduce public spending, the 2007 Act makes provision for the ATO Authority to be the province itself. The recent Finance Act for 2010 provides for the suppression of ATO Authority from 2011. Hence the region will remain completely free to deter municipalities which authorities will replace them (Act 291/2009, Art.186bis). The Emilia-Romagna Regional Law 25 (1999), amended in 2003, established the correspondence of ATO boundaries with those of the province. The municipalities belonging to these districts have to create, among themselves, a cooperative administrative body (freely chosen within the range fixed by the same law), where municipalities are represented in an assembly in accordance with the number of inhabitants. The peculiarity of this system is that the regulative functions are entrusted to an 'agency for public services' with an exclusive technical profile. In terms of funding, waste management privatization strategies and the use of private contractors have provided substantial cost benefits to municipalities. A tariff system has also been adopted. This system makes it possible to recover costs and measure the waste produced by a single user. Essentially, this has resulted in the adoption and implementation of the polluter-pays principle. It also provides greater awareness and transparency of the waste hierarchy (Iannello, 2007).

Waste management Despite the long history of waste management ownership by local authorities, the trend in Italy is now towards private management. The use of public procurement is common, although in many instances private and public companies have been amalgamated. Nearly 51 per cent of waste management companies are owned in some way by municipalities. Private waste management companies are still regulated by municipalities, and in carrying out their public functions are audited as public authorities (*osservatorio nazionale sui rifiuti*).

The main guiding principles in waste management stem from the EU waste hierarchy. There is a landfill tax and various initiatives to support environmental objectives. The aim is to reduce the amount of biodegradable waste that goes to landfill and, indeed, significantly reduce landfill use as a whole (APAT, 2007). There are marked differences between northern, central and southern regions of the country. For example, in 2006 Italy reached the target of 25.8 per cent for separated collection: a percentage well below the threshold (40 per cent) that Act 296 (2006) set as the objective to be reached by 31 December 2007. A closer scrutiny of the data shows that northern regions reached the 2007 objectives a year early (reaching 40 per cent of separated collection by 2006). Other areas of the country, in contrast, are very far from attaining this target. In central regions separate collection has reached only 20 per cent, and it has stagnated at 10.2 per cent in the south. A similar situation applies to reducing the use of landfill. Even though this method of disposal is in gradual decline across the country, falling from 59.5 per cent in 2002 to 47.9 per cent in 2006, there are regional variations. In 2006, Lombardy disposed of only 17 per cent of waste in landfills, but the story in the centre and south is very different. Lazio, Puglia and Sicily disposed of 85, 91 and 94 per cent of waste to landfill respectively. The marked regional variations in Italy reflect different cultural and social approaches to waste. The use of the market has great potential but is also dependent on local attitudes and aspirations. Consequently, market approaches have completely different effects in the north and south of the country. Northern regions make use of composting and incineration while the southern regions use mechanical and biological means of waste treatment. The north makes use of efficient waste utilities that provide a valuable source of revenue for municipal shareholders. In the south, public companies retain the anachronism of past inefficiencies but make some profit for the municipalities. It appears that future improvement in waste management will require further fundamental reform.

The UK

Waste management in the UK has shifted from the public health approach of the nineteenth century to an environmental focus in the twenty-first century. Local government continues to remain responsible for waste management but private companies are commonly used to deliver services. Municipal waste is defined as including household waste but also any waste collected by the various waste collection authorities. This includes waste from municipal parks and gardens, beach cleansing waste and commercial or industrial 'fly-tipping' waste (i.e. waste illegally disposed of or abandoned). Municipal waste is defined by the Waste Emissions Trading (WET) Act 2003. Domestic waste has been inadequately separated from commercial waste. The UK has a historical preference for landfill, which government has gradually attempted to reduce in favour of recycling, reuse and reduction. One innovation is the Local Authority Trading Scheme (LATS), a recycling trading system to encourage landfill reduction. It concerns 'all waste under the control of local authorities'.

Finance and competencies   Local government is involved in an integrated approach to waste and related services under the general supervision of the Environment Agency, established in 1995. This is an independent statutory agency receiving public funds and exercising a regulatory role independently of both local and central government. Under the Environment Act 1995, the Environment Agency licenses and supervises waste management activities. The responsibility for the actual collection and disposal of waste, however, is delegated to local authorities. They award contracts and monitor contractors, who are mainly private sector companies, many large enough

Table 7.4 UK institutions and responsibilities for waste

Organizational responsibility	Activities and jurisdiction	Sources of powers and role
Central government	Sets general waste policy and has monitoring and reporting roles	EU Directive and policy-maker
Environment agency	Licenses waste sites	General regulator: Environmental Protection Act 1990
District councils, England and Wales, and London boroughs	Waste collection authorities: responsibility for collecting waste and recycling	The Environmental Protection Act 1990 sections 45, 46–7 and 49
County councils in England	Waste disposal authorities: monitor and operate disposal sites	The Environmental Protection Act 1990, section 51 and the Waste and Emissions Trading Act 2003

Source: Summary by the authors.

to provide contractual services to different local authorities. Municipal enterprises are seldom involved. Local authorities oversee contractors, who have to meet environmental standards within the legal framework set and enforced by the Environment Agency. District councils in England and Wales constitute the waste collection authorities. Their role is to arrange for the collection and delivery of waste to sites approved by the waste disposal authorities. Collection authorities also draw up proactive recycling plans. Disposal authorities are mostly county councils in England and district councils in Wales (see Table 7.4). Both types of authority are integral to the work of local authorities but are organized separately within them. Their responsibilities include monitoring and operating disposal sites. UK waste management policy follows the direction set by the EU. In May 2007, the government announced a detailed national Waste Strategy for England (Defra, 2007). Local authorities are expected to meet targets and achieve a sizeable reduction in landfill to redress the excess use in the past.

The UK has a complicated system for financing waste management. Local authorities are financed by local taxes levied locally, and a proportion of local authority expenditure is devoted to waste management. The polluter-pays principle applies, industry and commerce paying market rates for waste disposal. Central government functions in the field are funded by national taxes. There are also a number of specialized taxes, including a landfill tax, levied on local authorities or organizations for the volume of waste sent to landfill. Since 1999 these taxes have increased annually; this is known as a landfill accelerator. A landfill tax credit scheme encourages eco-friendly disposal. Landfill owners are liable to taxation but can receive a credit of up to 6 per cent annually under the scheme.[11] In addition, licences for waste sites and disposal are payable as part of a self-financing waste management system.

Waste management Waste management falls under the Environmental Protection Act 1990 (sections 45–49) and the Household Waste Recycling Act 2003. The 1990 Act, together with the 1994 Waste Management Licensing Regulations, sets the main institutional and regulatory framework for licensing. In addition, the Control of Pollution Act 1989 provides a system of waste carrier registration. There have been some significant changes to the licensing regime:

- the Waste and Emissions Trading Act 2003 provides a quota system setting the amount that may be deposited in landfill sites;
- the Household Waste Recycling Act 2003 provides for the phased introduction of separate waste collection before 2010;
- the Clean Neighbourhoods and Environment Act 2005 provides a regulatory structure that includes fixed penalties for certain waste offences.

There are various strategies for implementing the Waste Framework Directive (75/442) as amended in 1991 by Directive 91/156 and Directive 91/689 on hazardous waste. The Household Waste Recycling Act 2003 places a legal duty on local authorities to provide kerbside collection for recycling, composting and energy recovery by 2010. This has created an incentive for all local authorities to meet their targets based on performance indicators (Defra, 2007). In order to meet the demanding requirements of the European Landfill Directive (99/31/EC), the UK has embarked on a strategy to reduce landfill (to 3 per cent of that produced in 1995 by 2020).

To achieve this, the government introduced a Landfill Allowance Trading Scheme (LATS) in April 2005. This provides the 121 waste disposal authorities with tradable allowances that ensure an overall reduction in landfill disposal but allows authorities who expect to discharge more to landfill to trade with those disposing less. This system encourages local authorities to reduce landfill use. A waste strategy board and a focus group to work with stakeholders have also been established under the Waste Strategy 2007. It remains to be seen whether the current reduction in landfill use will meet the targets.

In the UK, economic instruments are commonly used to provide effective pollution control. Taxes on particular types of waste disposed to landfill can encourage best practices and a reduction in landfill. The taxation scheme also allows waste disposal authorities to trade in landfill allowances in conjunction with recycling strategies. The link between land use and landfill sites as part of the planning system remains in place, despite the complex system of waste management regulation and licensing. Thus the deposit of waste on land is part of a deemed development and requires planning permission. Land used for waste management purposes is treated similarly. The storage of waste and the incidental collection of waste may constitute a material change of use that also requires planning permission.

There is, therefore, a significant input from local planning authorities into waste planning, which may involve the use of compulsory purchase schemes or regional spatial strategies. The Planning and Compulsory Purchase Act 2004 and regional spatial strategies are used to replace current planning guidance.

The details of development control and its application to waste are found in section 55(3) (b) of the Town and Country Planning Act 1990. There are important overlaps between the implementation of the Framework Directive on Waste and the Integrated Pollution Prevention and Control (IPPC) Directive 96/61. Waste management facilities may be covered by both directives. There are also related issues associated with the control of groundwater contaminated by waste, and civil liabilities that may emerge through the unlawful disposal of waste. In the latter case this may be because of common-law action or through the statutory arrangements under section 73(6) of the Environmental Protection Act 1990.

COMPARATIVE ANALYSIS

The study of the four countries provides evidence of converging and diverging trends in response to EU law and waste policy. The main impact of the EU is to transform waste management from a public health issue to one of environmental policy. The main finding is that waste management strategies in the four countries, operating within a common set of EU rules, have revitalized the role of local authorities as pivotal actors in the development of policy, the enforcement of good practice and in the management of resources. All four countries have adopted strategies

Table 7.5   Municipal waste recycled (kg) per capita

Country	Paper and cardboard	Bio-waste	Glass and metals	Bulky	Other
France	6.5	56.5	28.8	39.8	26.3
Germany	94.5	92.6	99.8	12.1	73.4
Italy	18.5	41.5	28.8	10.0	32.6
UK	31.1	45.1	33.7	10.6	50.9

Source: EIONET (2009).

to reduce landfill; engaged with the waste hierarchy; and adopted policies for the recycling, reuse and incineration for energy production. The 1999 Landfill Directive has been of fundamental significance in limiting landfill. Germany was the first country of the four to tackle landfill reduction, and is consequently far in advance of the others, notably the UK, in recycling and thereby reducing waste. Germany has also taken a major lead in generating electricity from waste. The *Länder* deal with waste in different ways. Italy, also, has regional variations between the north and south in waste treatment and reduction, and in the introduction of private contractors. France and the UK take a more uniform approach to waste management, although there are some variations in waste treatment from local authority to local authority. The UK is struggling to meet its landfill reduction targets, as is Italy. At the same time, the UK has attempted to encourage recycling and reuse but has only recently addressed the use of waste for energy generation.

Experience diverges widely in waste disposal and good practice in waste management. The reuse of resources and recycling are important elements in a strategy to save costs and protect the environment, but some of the four countries are better at adopting good practice than others. Table 7.5 shows their varying success.

Historical and cultural reasons probably underlie this divergence. Member states with strong municipal waste planning and well-developed infrastructure have made the most significant advances. In this respect the UK has begun to make changes that bring it into line with the other countries.

There are a number of innovative and divergent practices in some countries but not in others. In France, the tradition of public service remains strong despite the move towards privatization. As activities become more and more specific and technical, private companies, often multi-utilities, are contracted to provide the service. Public and private actors are therefore collaborating in various waste management tasks, but policy choices remain in the hands of public authorities. In Germany, the distinction drawn between municipal and commercial waste is important, one not so easily replicated in other member states, and which makes recycling, reuse and implementation of the waste hierarchy easier. In Italy, the range and variety of waste disposal operators is remarkable. Special territories for the management of the activity, the so-called ATOs, provide the optimum area for service provision. This has led to separate regions developing their own waste management programmes with regional differences, notably between the north and the south. Northern regions have adopted composting and incineration, while the south uses more biodegradable processes. In the UK the need to bring landfill use under control has led to incentives in the form of the Landfill Allowance Trading Scheme (LATS). This allows high-performing waste authorities to trade with poor performers and provides incentives for better performance. This is slowly improving waste recycling and reuse. The distinctions between countries are important reminders that common rules may encourage a juridical form of harmonization while maintaining divergence in the range and vitality of national and cultural differences. France has always maintained a close link between waste and energy policy due partly to the lack of fossil-fuel resources. Germany has increased its use of waste for generating electricity and Italy is moving slowly in that direction. All countries have poor experience with landfill management. France and Germany define waste as all waste produced in the municipality, including industrial, construction and commercial waste. Both countries have a collective social responsibility at the municipal and regional levels. Italy stands out as accepting mixed waste irrespective of sources. In composting and recycling, France, Germany and the UK have increased their recycling capacity. In Italy, composting plants operate at 50 per cent or less of capacity. Only France and Germany have stepped up composting. Extracting energy from waste in landfill has reached a considerable level in France and Germany. High standards in the use of composting have helped Germany and Italy to make more effective agricultural use of waste than the other countries. Landfill has declined, especially in Germany and Italy, but remains high in the UK. It is remarkable that a common set of rules should enable such diversity of options.

NOTES

1. Blessig (2003) gives a description of this policy until the year 2000.
2. Art. L2224-13 CGCT.
3. They are also called *déchets industriels commerciaux banals* (DICB), normal commercial industrial wastes.
4. €36 per tonne, instead of €9.15 for authorized landfill plants (Buclet et al., 2000).

5. The notion of *déchet ultime* lies in French law (L.13 July 1992). It refers to waste that cannot be treated any more and has reached the last stage of its value. It corresponds to some extent to European Directive 99/31/EC, which provides that only waste that has been treated, as well as inert waste, can be placed in landfill (Art. 6-a). In principle the law had foreseen that, by 2002, only 'final' waste should be placed in landfill. This objective, quite unrealistic, has not been reached and has led to a great deal of litigation in the French courts (see, e.g., CA Paris 23 May 2003, *S.A. Clinique Ker Yonnec c/ Société Travaux et Services*, RDImmo, 2003, p. 551, F.G. Trébulle).
6. Data on France are based mainly on the reports of ADEME (2001 and 2002) and on Association des Maires de Grandes Villes (2004).
7. Respectively, ECJ C-60/01, *Commission contre République française*, Rec. 2002, p. I-5679 and C-292/99 *Commission contre République française*, Rec. 2002, p. I-04097. For implementation of European norms by local governments, see Conseil d'Etat (2004).
8. Between 1993 and 2000 the turnover of the waste sector increased by 48 per cent from €3.34 billion to €4.95 billion.
9. Data source: Institut français de l'environnement, www.ifen.fr.
10. There are currently 45.
11. Standard rate of tax: £21/tonne. Net receipts £0.73 billion.

REFERENCES

APAT (2007), *Rapporto sui rifiuti*, Rome, accessed at www.apat.gov.it/site.

ADEME (2001), *La gestion des déchets en France: les évolutions essentielles depuis 1992*, December.

ADEME (Direction des déchets municipaux – Département des observatoires des déchets et planification) (2002), *Intercommunalité et gestion des déchets: approche statistique, situation fin 2001*, December 2002.

Association des Maires de Grandes Villes (2004), *Les services publics locaux*, Direction des Etudes de Dexia – Crédit Local.

Beckmann, M. (2003), 'Abfallrecht zwischen staatlicher Lenkung, kommunaler Daseinsvorsorge und privatem Wettbewerb', *Verwaltungsarchiv*, **94** (3), 371–88.

Blessig, E. (2003), *Rapport d'information de l'Assemblée Nationale sur la gestion des déchets ménagers sur le territoire*, Paris: Assemblée Nationale.

BMU (Bundesministerium für Umwelt, Naturschutz und Reaktorsicherheit)/ UBA (Umweltbundesamt) (2009), *Umweltwirtschaftsbericht*, Berlin.

Bogumil, J. and L. Holtkamp (2006), *Kommunalpolitik und Kommunalverwaltung – Eine policyorientierte Einführung*, Wiesbaden, Germany: VS Verlag.

Bremeier, W., H. Brinckmann and W. Killian (2006), 'Kommunale Unternehme in kleinen und mittelgroßen Kommunen sowie Landkreisen', in W. Killian, P. Richter and J.H. Trapp (eds), *Ausgliederung und Privatisierung in Kommunen*, Berlin: Sigma, pp. 25–53.

Buclet, N., C. Defeuilley and S. Lupton (2000), 'Municipal waste management in France', in N. Buclet and O. Godard (eds), *Municipal Waste Management in Europe. A Comparative Study in Building Regime*, Amsterdam: Kluwer.

Conseil d'Etat (2004), *Collectivités locales et obligations communautaires: étude adoptée le 23 octobre 2003 par l'assemblée générale du Conseil d'Etat*, Paris: La Documentation française.

Defra (Department for Environment, Food and Rural Affairs) (2007), 'Waste strategy for England', London, accessed at www.defra.gov.uk.
Der Spiegel (2006), 'Kampf um den Müll', **9**, 108.
Ernst & Young (2007), *Privatisierungen und ÖPP als Ausweg? Kommunalfinanzen unter Druck – Handlungsoptionen für Kommunen*, Stuttgart: Ernst & Young.
Fise-Assoambiente (2006), *Report: Le forme di gestione dei rifiuti urbani*, Italy.
Gruner, R., B. Klippel and F. Wisskirchen (2009), 'Das Pendel schwingt zurück', *Recycling Magazin*, **7**, 34–5.
Iannello, C. (2007), *L'emergenza rifiuti in Campania: I paradossi delle gestioni commissariali*, in *Assegna di Diritto pubblico Europeo*, **2**, 137 ff.
Lamping, W. (1997), 'Mit Phantasie die Ketten der Hierarchie abstreifen – am Beispiel kommunaler Umsetzung der Zechnischen Anleitung Siedlungsabfall', in H. Heinelt and M. Mayer (eds), *Modernisierung der Kommunalpolitik. Neue Wege der Ressourcenmobilisierung*, Opladen, Germany: Leske + Budrich, pp. 48–67.
Langmann, A. and S. Schönwasser (1998), 'Umweltpolitik in den Kommunen – das Beispiel Abfallpolitik', in U. Andersen (ed.), *Kommunalpolitik in Nordrhein-Westfalen im Umbruch*, Cologne: Kohlhammer, pp. 327–44.
Osthorst, W. (2001), *Die De-Kommunalisierung der Abfallwirtschaft in den Städten. Sieben Fallstudien*, Bremeu, Germany: Universität Bremen.
Schäfer, R. (2007), 'Daseinsvorsorge kommunal oder privat? Erfolgreiche Kommunalisierung der Abfallentsorgung in Bergkamen', paper presented at the 16th Kölner Abfalltagung.
Schulze Wehninck, R. (2008), *Public Private Partnerships und Wettbewerb. Eine theoretische Analyse am Beispiel der kommunalen Abfallentsorgung*, Wiesbaden, Germany: VS Verlag.
SRU (Sachverständigenrat für Umweltfragen) (1990), *Sondergutachten des Rates von Sachverständigen für Umweltfragen: Abfallwirtschaft*, BT-Drs. 11/8493.
SRU (1998), *Umweltgutachten des Rates von Sachverständigen für Umweltfragen. Umweltschutz: Erreichtes sichern – Neue Wege gehen*, BT-Drs. 13/10195.
SRU (2002), *Umweltgutachten des Rates von Sachverständigen für Umweltfragen: Für eine neue Vorreiterrolle*, BT-Drs. 14/8792.
SRU (2008), *Umweltgutachten des Rates von Sachverständigen für Umweltfragen: Umweltschutz im Zeichen des Klimawandels*, SRU: Stuttgart.
Töller, A.E. (2007), 'Die Rückkehr des befehlenden Staates? Muster und Ursachen der Veränderung staatlicher Handlungsformen in der deutschen Abfallpolitik', *Politische Vierteljahresschrift*, **48** (1), 64–94.
Verbuecheln, M. (2009), *Rückübertragung operativer Dienstleistung durch Kommunen – am Beispiel der Abfallwirtschaft*, Deutches Institut für Urbanistik papers, Berlin.
Villata, R. (2008), *Servizi pubblici. Discussioni e problemi*, Milan, Italy: Giuffrè.

8. From public service to commodity: the demunicipalization (or remunicipalization?) of energy provision in Germany, Italy, France, the UK and Norway[1]

Hellmut Wollmann, Harald Baldersheim, Giulio Citroni, Gérard Marcou and John McEldowney

INTRODUCTION

In the five European countries under discussion, the provision of energy started out as a core function of municipalities but has gradually been demunicipalized. This chapter outlines how the transformation was achieved and discusses the implications for the scientific study of public administration.

There were three components of demunicipalization: (1) the creation of a national electricity system made possible by the establishment of national grids; (2) the functional and organizational separation ('unbundling') of generation, transmission and distribution; and (3) the transformation of electricity from a local service into a commodity. Another common development is the return of municipalities in the regulation of energy consumption. From being active producers and purveyors of energy, municipalities are becoming overseers of its use and conservation.

The converging paths of these countries are highly surprising given the different starting conditions and historical backgrounds to municipal involvement in the supply of energy, especially electricity, with which this chapter is mainly concerned. From the point of view of historical institutionalism, a dominant theoretical position in the study of public administration, such an outcome would appear highly unlikely. Instead, path-dependency could be expected to keep these countries on different, perhaps even diverging, tracks. In order to account for change, historical institutionalism has often resorted to metaphors such as 'shock' or 'windows of opportunity'. In the concluding section of the chapter the adequacy of such explanations will be discussed.

HISTORICAL BACKGROUND ('STARTING CONDITIONS')

In all the countries under consideration, the provision of energy – of gas and of electricity – for the local population and local industry was an early concern and responsibility of the municipalities. While gas and electricity provision also involved private investors and entrepreneurs, municipalities needed to establish corporations of their own, often in an effort to 'bail out' failed private enterprises.

In Great Britain, a European front-runner in industrialization and urbanization, local authority engagement in energy provision dates back to the beginning of modern local government, at least to 1835, when energy was seen as falling to local authorities as part of a wider functional profile. At that time gas and later electricity production was often linked to local coalmines (McEldowney, 2007).

In Germany, the provision of gas and electricity was also seen as an early responsibility of the municipalities and as essentially pertaining to what in German is called *Daseinsvorsorge*, the 'provision (of public services) for (well-) being' (Wollmann, 2002, 2007). As Germany was a latecomer to industrialization and urbanization, the need for 'provision' emerged and rapidly expanded from the mid-nineteenth century. To begin with, services such as water, sewage and electricity were provided by private commercial entrepreneurs, but in the wake of bankruptcies or to meet public needs, municipalities took over *Daseinsvorsorge*, including the provision of electricity, establishing what conservatives and liberals came to decry as 'municipal socialism'. (It should be noted, however, that some services, particularly water supply, were already provided at least in a basic form – through publicly accessible fountains – by medieval towns.) Designed to serve the 'best interests' of the local business world and the local population, service provision was typically organized in the form of 'city-works' (*Stadtwerke*), multi-utilities vertically integrating a broad range of public utilities, including energy as a core responsibility of local government.

In the Italy of the late nineteenth century, the energy business was controlled mainly by a small number of private enterprises, which held regional or interregional monopolies. In 1903, the shortcomings of this system provoked national legislation to set a legal frame for public utilities, including electricity, to be provided by (public-law) municipal corporations (*municipalizzate*) – a system already operating in some places but which gained impetus from the legislation, offering an alternative (especially in northern Italy) to market domination by a small number of large operators that had gradually come to constitute an oligopoly, or rather a set of regional monopolies. Due to the limited geographical scope of the phenomenon, and the fact that they served only urban (and not industrial) needs, *municipalizzate* has only a 6 per cent share of power generation at the national level, but their political role and their incidence in urban power transmission and sales were more significant than this figure implies (Prontera and Citroni, 2008).

The Fascist regime imposed some restrictions on the diffusion of *municipalizzate* in the mid-1920s, dissolving and liquidating a number of them, on the grounds that they constituted 'municipal socialism' and were an element of decentralized power, but no consistent policy of centralization or privatization was actually implemented, so that the expansion of municipal enterprises continued in the later 1920s and the 1930s (Bolchini, 1994a).

In France, by contrast, concessions awarded to private enterprises became the dominant instrument for the development of energy supply – gas and later electricity. However, municipalities had the power to establish their own public enterprises (*en régie*), as public corporations or as enterprises under direct municipal management, and a number of them did so, either as a political choice ('municipal socialism') or to bail out concessions following concessionaire failures. With growing urban concentration and the increasing needs of industry, central government took over organization of an electricity transmission network on the basis of concession contracts with private companies (Marcou, 2007).

In Norway, the early engagement of the municipalities was conspicuously shaped by the geographical features of the country, with an abundance of waterfalls that put the country on a hydropower track; many (small) municipalities, located in and isolated by fjords, had their own power station and transmission grid for local supply. Early legislation (1906, 1917) discouraged foreign investors from purchasing the financially attractive waterfalls and has given public institutions (municipalities, counties and the state) almost complete control over the Norwegian energy sector to this day (Baldersheim and Claes, 2007).

In short, developments in the five countries up to the First World War showed broad similarities in that municipalities, operating either directly (*en régie*) or through municipal corporations, were engaged in local energy provision. While in Norway this responsibility fell almost entirely to the public sector, particularly municipalities, the other countries entrusted it to a mix of private corporations and municipal corporations. France provided the chief contrast in this respect: until the late 1940s, energy supply was based on the private sector, with extensive use of concession contracts for generation and network provision and operation.

DEVELOPMENTS AFTER 1945

After 1945, energy provision diverged strongly in the five countries under discussion, as France, the UK and later Italy began to nationalize the energy sector, while Norway and Germany continued on the traditional trajectory of giving the local level a dominant role (Norway) or a significant position (Germany) in energy provision.

In the UK, the Labour government that took office after 1945 made nationalization of the energy sector a crucial element in an all-out attempt to restructure the country's public sector and national economy (McEldowney, 2007). The 1947 Electricity Act transferred local power plants as well as private energy enterprises to a single, nationalized industry. Later, under the Electricity Act of 1957, the Central Electricity Generating Board (CEGB) was established, which was intended to create a unified system for generating and transmitting electricity across the UK. Thus the historical direct involvement of local authorities in the energy sector came to an end.

In France, the law of 8 April 1946 (expropriation with compensation) nationalized the generation, transmission and supply, but not the distribution, of electricity. Local distribution networks have since remained in municipal ownership (through specialized joint authorities usually established for each *département* but operated by the newly created state monopolies for electricity (Electricité de France – EdF) and gas (Gaz de France – GdF) on the basis of concession contracts. The new national monopolies were the only possible concessionaires; indeed, they have replaced the former private concessionaires. Furthermore, the municipal enterprises (500 in 1945) were exempted from nationalization and have survived to this day, sometimes under new legal forms (mixed-economy companies) but always in the same distribution areas; there are now 157, serving 2500 municipalities and 3 million inhabitants, and representing about 5 per cent of electricity consumption (Allemand, 2007). At the local level, EdF and GdF have established joint operations for serving retail customers. The legal monopoly has been narrower than the scope of nationalization. For electricity, the legal monopoly extended to transmission, distribution network operation and supply except in areas covered by municipal enterprises; for gas, the legal monopoly extended to importation, the distribution network operation and supply.

In energy provision in Italy after the war, private and public corporations, as well as municipal corporations (*municipalizzate*) initially coexisted. A small number of private enterprises and state-owned or mixed public–private corporations (formerly private, then integrated into IRI – the national holding company for industrial development – under Fascist rule after the 1929 crisis) operated under national concessions over wide regional and interregional territories; only about 250 municipalities were engaged in energy production and provision, either through a *municipalizzata* (about 50 municipalities), or through direct management or concessions to private enterprises (Lanza and Silva, 2006).

In a dramatic policy move in 1962, the Italian government embarked upon nationalization of the energy sector, establishing ENEL as a public corporation that absorbed all private and public energy companies. *Municipalizzate* could survive nationalization of electricity production and distribution on two accounts: by continuing their expansion in other service sectors, most notably water (see Chapter 9 in this volume) and gas (which was a growing business especially in the 1970s, see Bolchini, 1994b, p. 201); and by virtue of concessions that ENEL could issue to existing *municipalizzate* at its own discretion for continued electricity-related activities. Along with industrial 'self-producers' (i.e. industrial plants that produce energy for their own needs, and – following nationalization – are not allowed to sell surplus energy), existing *municipalizzate* were thus able to continue operating, but several factors made the impact of nationalisation no less fatal to their role: no new *municipalizzate* could be created in the field of electricity, so that expansion was stopped; changes in the market (with an increased role of international energy trading) and in the regulatory framework (built as a top-down planning structure) made most strategic policy-making converge to the centre; the legal definition of the relationship between ENEL and *municipalizzate* – including the concessions system – was ambiguous, and allowed for many issues to be settled through 'power struggles' that invariably favoured the state-owned and politically stronger ENEL. Indeed, ENEL developed a strategy whereby it would delay the issuing of concessions to *municipalizzate* for so long that the uncertainty under which they had to operate forced them to suspend investment, making it progressively impossible for them to prove their efficiency and self-sufficiency in local production and distribution network operation (Bolchini, 1994b, p. 191). So, from 1962 on, Italy's energy sector was largely dominated by ENEL (Prontera, 2008). As Figure 8.1 shows, the 'mere' survival of *municipalizzate* is characterized by the stable amount of energy they produced over three decades when production by ENEL increased dramatically; their share of the national net production thus decreased from 6 per cent to about 4 per cent.

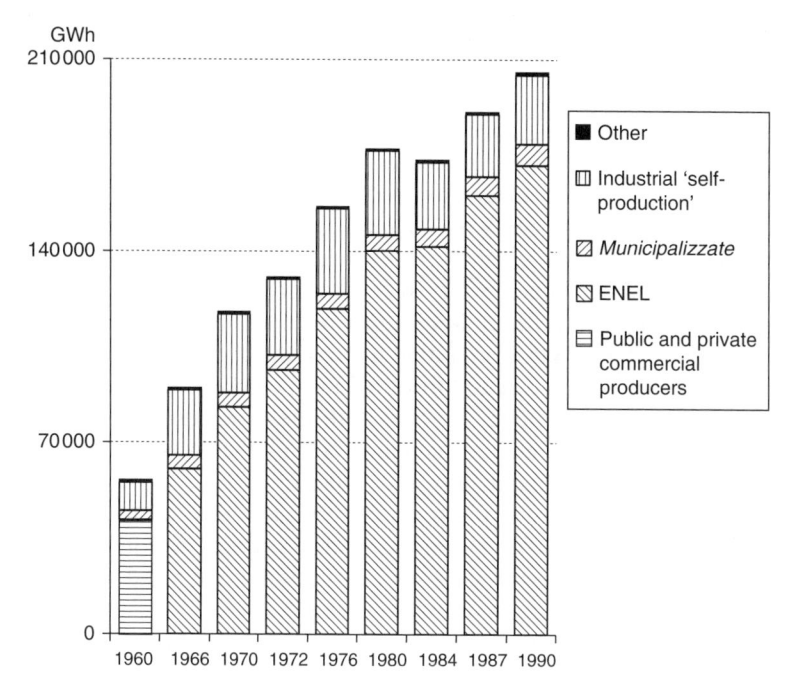

Figure 8.1 Net production of energy by type of producer (GWh)

Source: Adapted from Bolchini (1994b).

Legend: Other; Industrial 'self-production'; Municipalizzate; ENEL; Public and private commercial producers

By contrast, hydro-based local power corporations and local transmission grids continued to predominate in Norway. In 1973, energy was supplied locally by 337 distribution companies, 76 per cent of which had fewer than 5000 consumers (Baldersheim and Claes, 2007). However, a national power grid was slowly developed under state control to ensure transmission between electricity-rich and electricity-deficient regions. The state also took on a role in electricity production and was the single largest owner of production facilities by the 1980s. By this time the national energy agency was also operating an energy exchange system that allowed local energy companies to feed excess capacity into the national grid.

Until well into the late 1980s, the electricity market in Germany was characterized by a mix of private sector and municipal providers. The former comprised nine large electricity and transmission ('grid') companies and some 60 regional distributors (see Praetorius and Bolay, 2009). They were organized as private-law stock companies in which municipalities also had an interest, as in the case of the largest of them, RWE. These private sector companies generated about 80 per cent of the electricity, owned most of the long-distance high-voltage transmission grids, and distributed/supplied about 70 per cent to the end-consumer. The large providers managed largely to divide the market between them under 'regional agreements', constituting oligopolies.

On the other hand, municipalities continued to hold a significant segment of electricity transmission and distribution/supply. Particularly through the traditional 'city-works' (*Stadtwerke*) (some 900), they retained ownership of 'last mile' of the grid, the short-distance distribution networks to the end-consumer. Some 30 per cent of electricity and 70 per cent of gas were supplied to the end-consumer by municipal corporations (see Reidenbach, 1995, p. 84). Committed to serve the 'local community', they tended to carve out and defend 'protected local markets', seeking to cross-subsidize other, deficit-ridden services with the proceeds from profitable energy provision. In defending such local 'turfs', they often amounted to local 'monopolities' (see, critically, Ude, 2006).

A German peculiarity is the right of municipalities to charge energy companies, whether *Stadtwerke* or external enterprises, a 'concession fee' (*Konzessionsabgabe*) for allowing the use of public space and local roads in setting up and operating transmission grids. Such fees for electricity, gas and water have become a handsome source of revenue for local authorities (totalling €1.6 billion for electricity, gas and water in 2008, of which 63 per cent was for the electricity sector; see VKU, 2009).

DEREGULATION AND MARKET LIBERALIZATION SINCE THE 1980s/90s

From the 1980s, the prevailing forms and structures of energy provision in their various legal and organizational guises faced increasing criticism that a lack of competition caused production and price inefficiency. While reform was triggered in the UK and Norway by national factors, in the other three countries – most noticeably in Germany – it was induced by EU promotion of market liberalization.

The UK

In the UK, the privatization and deregulation drive of the 1990s was launched by the Conservative government under Margaret Thatcher. After taking office in 1979, the Tories embarked on neoliberal policies in which deregulation and competition were guiding precepts. The Energy Act of 1983 made a first attempt to liberalize the energy market (i.e. to dismantle the state-run energy sector) – with meagre results (McEldowney,

2007). Privatization began with the British Gas Act of 1986, followed by the Electricity Act of 1989, which established private energy corporations. The 1989 legislation also aimed at separating ('unbundling') production, transmission and distribution in electricity provision in the new private energy sector. At the same time, however, the Electricity Act of 1989 offered local authorities the opportunity to supplement local supply with more environment-friendly sources of energy (McEldowney, 2007).

Since then, the UK has discovered renewable and CHP (combined heat and power) technologies, encouraging local authority initiatives. The relevant legislation includes the Utilities Act 2000 the Enterprise Act 2002 and the Energy Act 2004. The recent Energy Act 2008 strengthens the local use of renewable energy and small-generation capacities up to 5MW. Through the new central Department of Energy and Climate Change, this has provided new opportunities for local authorities to promote energy schemes.

Norway

In 1990, Norway was set for a fundamental change in traditional energy provision. On the one hand, the basic structure of hydropowered plants and local transmission grids owned and operated predominantly by local authorities and municipal corporations remained in place and unimpaired. On the other hand, the previous distribution system, which hinged on local markets, was profoundly revamped in two main ways. First, the law required all energy companies that had so far bundled production and transmission functions to split into separate enterprises for production and transmission. The most dramatic change occurred in the electricity trade system. While customers had previously been bound to a single supplier, the law of 1990 overnight created a fully open market for trade in electricity for all customers, regardless of size. The Norwegian electricity system now operates as a marketplace where all producers deliver power into the grid and all customers use power without knowing where the power actual originates from. The price of the electricity supplied fluctuates according to supply and demand. Sweden and Norway have set up a joint power exchange – Nord Pool – for trade and clearing in both the physical and financial electricity market. The individual producer does not have to balance the amount of electricity sold with the amount of electricity produced. The producer can simply buy or sell electricity in the market in order to balance his obligations. The producer can also adjust the level in reservoirs according to anticipated price changes. A number of financial instruments are also available for risk reduction, in addition to the possibility of entering into long-term contracts. The system-level price is set by the Nordic electricity exchange – Nord Pool – each hour. It also sets spot prices for electricity the next day, hour by hour. After this spot price has been set, the actor responsible for the system – Statnett – engages in trade with producers and customers for upwards or downward regulation of supply and demand in order to balance the entire system. This trade compensates the imbalances that open trade on the exchange might create. As owner of the high-pressure transmission network, Statnett is responsible for providing sufficient voltage throughout the system.

The customer's bill is divided into three parts: electricity consumed; use of the net, and taxes. As far as the electricity actually supplied is concerned, most customers (60 per cent) have a contract under which the supplier can change the price at short notice. About 23 per cent of customers have spot-related contracts, while the rest have some kind of fixed-price contract. The number of foreign actors in the Norwegian electricity system is very limited. A few foreign companies have been licensed to trade, but they operate mostly on the gross and spot markets. Some foreigners hold shares in Norwegian electricity trading companies and have also invested in production and distribution companies (Baldersheim and Claes, 2007). In adopting this course, Norway became a front-runner that preceded the EU deregulation policy of 1996, thus serving as a model for a liberalized electricity sector.

EU PUSHING FOR MORE COMPETITION IN THE 'SINGLE EUROPEAN MARKET'

In pursuit of the 'single European market', EU efforts to introduce competition into member states' energy markets have come in two main rounds.

First, in 1996 the European Commission issued Directive 96/92/EC, which obliged EU member countries to ensure price competition in national electricity markets. It largely failed because, as developments in Germany showed, it paradoxically entailed a wave of mergers between energy companies, thus jeopardizing competition instead of fostering it. The transposition of the Directive into national law lacked effective regulation of discrimination-free access to transmission grids as the crucial component of the generation, transmission and distribution/supply cycle.

In reaction to the shortcomings of the 1996 Directive, the European Commission then introduced the Acceleration Directive 2003/54/EC, which sought to ensure discrimination-free access to transmission grids for all energy producers and consumers by legally and organizationally separating ('unbundling') transmission energy provision from production and distribution.

By 1 July 2004, all non-household (industry and business) consumers, and by 1 July 2007, all household consumers were also required to be given freedom of choice in selecting an energy supplier. Moreover, by 1 July 2004, each member country was to create a regulatory transmission ('grid') agency to ensure indiscriminate access to transmission grids and oversee tariffs and fees.

Germany

Transposing EU Directive 96/92/EC into German law with a two-year delay, the (federal) Energy Management Act (*Energiewirtschaftsgesetz*) was designed to introduce competition to the energy market. However, it had quite the opposite effect, triggering an unprecedented wave of mergers producing ever fewer and larger enterprises – with E.on, RWE, EnBW (private stock corporations) and Vattenfall (the Swedish state-owned energy company) emerging as the 'Big Four' dominating the German energy market.[2] Expectations that the energy giants would practise some form of self-regulation (so-called 'negotiated grid access') were disappointed (see Praetorius and Bolay, 2009).

Since market liberalization began in the mid-1990s, municipal energy companies have faced considerable challenges, which at times have threatened *Stadtwerke* with demise. Over the past 15 years or so the number of *Stadtwerke* has been dwindling, from about 900 to some 600, as a growing number of municipalities, including big cities such as Berlin, Hamburg and Düsseldorf, have seen reasons (not least for budgetary) to sell their assets to the private sector. Furthermore, the 'Big Four' have been eager to extend their influence over *Stadtwerke*, especially local transmission grids or grid companies (see Vorholz, 2006) by acquiring an interest in them. Thus RWE and E.on have established subsidiaries (Rhenag and Thüga), each with a minority interest in about 100 'city works'. In the meantime, only 30 per cent of the energy companies of the major cities are still fully owned by the municipalities (as in Munich and Leipzig), whereas more than 70 per cent have external (minority) shareholders (see Trapp, 2006).

Furthermore, in view of this market and price pressure, municipalities have felt threatened in their traditional role and responsibility for pursuing environment-friendly local energy policy (particularly through CHP or 'co-generation') as a crucial local government task. In order to alleviate these local government concerns (and step up federal environmental policy strategy), the federal government introduced legislation in the early 2000s, the 2000 Renewal Energy Act and the 2002 Combined Heat and Power Generation Act (see Deutscher Städtetag, 2001, p. 111).

When the European Commission prepared its Acceleration Directive to debundle energy provision, German municipalities and their umbrella organizations were in the forefront of opposition to the 'debundling' concept being applied to *Stadtwerke* since it would lower proceeds to the point of finally pushing them out of local energy provision (see Deutscher Städtetag, 2005, p. 131). With the federal government strongly supporting the local authority position in EU negotiations, a compromise was finally reached under which all energy providers with fewer than 100 000 clients were to be exempt from debundling (which, in practice, exempted most *Stadtwerke*).

However, the establishment of the Federal Network Agency (FNA – *Bundesnetzagentur*), another major requirement of the Acceleration Directive, has had an immediate impact on *Stadtwerke* since it affects all transmission companies, whether unbundled or not. Thus *Stadtwerke* with a transmission component (which is usually the case) fall under the regime of FNA with respect to grid management. Most importantly, as operators of transmission networks they can only charge the user fees (*Netznutzungsgebühren*) (which make up about 30 per cent of the consumer energy price) as approved by the FNA.

On 1 January 2009 the federal government introduced a procedure for incentive regulation (*Anreizregulierung*) that allows the FNA to check and eventually reduce grid user fees by way of a benchmarking procedure oriented on the most effective (and least expensive) provider in the market segment. In an immediate response, *Stadtwerke* have raised concerns that this new instrument may squeeze them out of the local energy market as it would not allow them to take specific local conditions and needs into account, for instance the 'cross-subsidizing' strategies pursued hitherto.

Thus municipal corporations have a significant position in the country's energy market, particularly in distribution/supply.

By and large, however, *Stadtwerke* have coped remarkably well with the new competitive context by adopting various strategies. First, they have formed transmission grid operation companies (*Netzbetriebsgesellschaften*) to economize, pool capacities and join forces. Second, they have set up joint offices to purchase energy collectively from the European Energy Exchange (EEX). Third, they have established 'shared services' (for billing, book-keeping, call centres etc.) to cut operational costs. Fourth, they have set up and invested in new power plants of their own to strengthen their role in energy production and to get a direct grip on production prices.[3]

Finally, two important shifts in national and European actor and policy constellations suggest that local energy provision has recently seen a remarkable 'comeback' and 'remunicipalization' (Rekommunalisierung). First, national environmental and energy policy has been placing growing weight on local government for promoting and implementing environment-friendly and energy-efficient 'alternative' electricity generation (see Müschen, 1999), particularly co-generation (CHP), which constitutes 80 per cent (sic!) of the electricity produced by municipal corporations (according to VKU, 2009).

This policy approach is evident in the 2008 amendments to the Renewal Energy Act and the CHP Act, designed to enable local energy companies to feed alternative energy into the wider grid. It is also evidenced by the federal government's 2008 Integrated Energy and Climate Programme, which aims to increase the share of CHP electricity from 12 per cent to 25 per cent by 2020 (see Praetorius and Bolay, 2009, p. 7).

Second, a powerful coalition has taken shape between the European Commission, the federal government and the local authorities to strengthen local energy companies as a key strategy for promoting competition vis-à-vis the 'Big Four' that dominate, and other big international providers entering, the national market.

Thus, quite recently RWE and E.on have been singled out by the EU Commission's antitrust strategy, which attracted a great deal of media attention when company offices were searched on suspicion of price-fixing. In the meantime both companies have at least partly given in to the pressure, E.on having agreed to sell its entire transmission grid in a conspicuous step of 'ownership unbundling',[4] while RWE is said to be willing to unbundle its gas sector legally and organizationally from the electricity sector. Similarly, in 2001 the Federal Cartel Office (Bundeskartellamt) stipulated that minority interests of external shareholders in *Stadtwerke* must not exceed 10 per cent. In reaction to changes in the EU and national policy climate, E.on has recently decided to sell its subsidiary Thüga, that is, its *Stadtwerke* holdings. In a spectacular move, in August 2009, a consortium of *Stadtwerke* purchased Thüga from E.on for €3 billion with the declared intention to challenge and compete with the 'Big Four' on Germany's energy market and possibly beyond.[5] Vattenfall may see itself under pressure to also give up its *Stadtwerke* holdings.[6]

In sum, the stage appears to be set for local government and its energy companies to reposition themselves on the energy market and embark upon the 'remunicipalization' (*Rekommunalisierung*) of energy provision. A crucial lever in exercising this new local authority self-confidence in the energy sector is the renewal of the concession contracts (*Konzessionsverträge*), many of which will expire and need to be renewed by and in 2013. An increasing number of municipalities is considering buying back the minority holdings they sold to outside providers during the 1990s, particularly to the 'Big Four', or the municipal energy companies they privatized completely. In the meantime, a considerable number of municipalities has founded new *Stadtwerke* and repurchased transmission grids[7] or are seriously considering strengthening their position in energy provision. In sum, a distinct trend towards re-municipalization is in evidence.[8] This trend is being fostered by a new 'coalition' between the European Commission, federal and *Länder* governments, and local authorities to reinforce the engagement of local authorities and their *Stadtwerke* in energy provision with the aim of competition *vis-à-vis* the market dominance of the 'Big Four' and to safeguard the *Stadtwerke* generation of alternative energy, especially CHP, where they have proved to be champions.

To summarize:

- As of 31 December 2008,[9] 604 municipal corporations (most of them in the form of *Stadtwerke*) are engaged in electricity provision. This is 56.9 per cent of all municipal electricity, gas, water and sewage enterprises.
- Municipal corporations generate 10.4 per cent of total electricity production themselves.
- Their share in total electricity provided to the end-consumer is 56.8 per cent.

France

In France, the liberalization of the energy sector began only with the Electricity Act of 2000, and the Gas Act of 2003. These reforms were induced by EC directives alone, because there has been little criticism in France of the national public service provision by EdF and GdF, from either industry or the general public. The reason was quite simple: the public monopoly and vertical integration produced retail prices among the lowest in Europe for domestic customers and for industry. Furthermore, the development of capacities was ahead of demand and also yielded an export capacity, plus energy independence with nuclear energy generation.

French governments and both national enterprises therefore sought to resist or circumvent deregulation adoption of the first Electricity Directive (1996) and also tried to conserve some features of the existing system. But EdF and GdF soon changed their strategies when it became clear that liberalization was unavoidable. They decided to take advantage of their economic power to expand abroad in order to compensate the market shares they had to give up on the domestic market. In 2004, EdF and GdF were transformed from public corporations into commercial holdings with majority public control, making it possible to unbundle generation and supply from network operation while maintaining integration through a holding structure. On the basis of the 2006 Energy Act, the door was opened to privatizing GdF by absorbing Suez instead of GdF being bought by the Italian ENEL. The law requires the state to hold more than one-third of the capital. EdF's main competitor is GdF, since the latter can now offer electricity jointly with gas, and it has generation capacity after absorbing Suez, which owns Electrabel, the main provider in Belgium.

This was the apparent situation in France. Backstage, however, something else was happening from the 1980s onwards: municipalities were making a comeback. New ecological conceptions deploying new micro-generation technologies stimulated local policies devoted to satisfying local needs (small hydropower, co-generation, later wind energy). A new role for local governments in energy conservation has been outlined. Several years have passed between the first reports and the first legislative amendments. Nevertheless, the opportunities for local governments to play a part in the energy sector have increased step by step. At present, municipalities can play a role in the energy sector on three fronts: (1) developing energy-saving policies – informing and advising domestic customers, taking account of the energy balance in planning and development; (2) developing their own generation systems when this can save network expenses and (from 1999), in local authorities without a gas distribution network, contracting with any company, not only GdF, to establish networks (in practice the coverage of the GdF network usually makes it cheaper to contract with GdF for an extension of its network); (3) the municipal ownership of distribution networks is becoming a new source of revenue for local policy. In the context of liberalization, tendering out network operation could become an attractive issue for municipalities, since EdF is now inclined to save in network maintenance in less populated areas. This would require legislative changes, but is not ruled out, and this changes the balance between municipalities and operators (EdF and GdF). According to the law, concessionary authorities are entitled to negotiate concession contracts and supervise the fulfilment of public service distribution obligations. Last but not least, the 2006 Energy Act states that municipalities as owners of distribution networks are 'organizing authorities' of the public gas and electricity supply services to customers connected to the network. These provisions still have to be developed, and further legislative changes are needed. But they could be taken to mean that municipalities (or their joint authorities) will deal with suppliers willing to make offers on the local market.

For the time being, the debate in France has focused on tariffs. The decision of the Constitutional Council has invalidated the provisions of the Energy Act 2006 on regulated tariffs because they were in conflict with the constitutional obligation to transpose into French law the objectives of Directives 2003/54 and 2003/55 to develop a competitive energy market, since they were not based on clear public service objectives, and were discriminatory since only to EdF and GdF were granted the possibility to offer regulated tariffs. But the directives do not rule out such tariffs, although the Commission sometimes claims the contrary: member states may impose public service obligations on energy supply prices (Art. 3.3). The Law of 5 March 2007 confirms the guarantee of regulated tariffs for domestic customers, and gives professional customers the opportunity to return to regulated tariffs under certain conditions. The Law of 21 January 2008 allows consumers in new consumption sites to opt for regulated tariffs until 1 July 2010, and for those having opted for market tariffs to return to regulated tariffs. In parliament this is a non-partisan issue.

Italy

In the wake of nationalization in 1962 in Italy, the electricity sector came under the sway of ENEL as the dominant state corporation. At the beginning of the 1990s, ENEL had no fewer than 112 000 employees (Prontera, 2008, p. 292). Since the early 1990s, however, steps have been taken to reduce this dominance.

First moves to limit ENEL's monopoly were taken by the national government to increase production and not to liberalize the market as an end in itself. In 1991, Law 9 effectively ended the monopoly in energy production, and in 1992 a decision by the Committee on Price Regulation (CIP) established incentives for private producers.

However, from 1992 onwards a proper liberalization policy was pursued. In 1992, ENEL was transformed into a stock company (albeit still fully in state ownership!). In 1997, an independent regulatory agency (Autorità per l'energia elettrica ed il gas) was set up while ENEL continued to be the main player on the energy market. In 1999, legislation was finally adopted (*Decreto Bersani*) to implement the 1996 EU Directive, actually going beyond its requirements as to the pace, scope and intensity of liberalization. While *municipalizzate* could once again engage in transmission and sales, some also took the opportunity to buy significant interests in the power plants ENEL was forced to sell off. The larger and richer *municipalizzate* (and hence the larger and richer municipalities) thus regained and increased their role, while also recurring to stock markets and PPPs to find strategic international partners. At the same time, multinational corporations such as Endesa, Suez, Electrabel and EdF have entered the Italian market by two different means: by acquiring shares in former ENEL power plants, and acquiring minority shares in *municipalizzate*. The sale of ENEL power plants to multinationals and *municipalizzate*, or alliances of the two, and the minority privatization of *municipalizzate*

Table 8.1 Number, size and ownership of public and public–private energy companies in Italy, 2003–5

	2003		2005	
	Electricity	All sectors	Electricity	All sectors
Number of companies	103	3512	120	3769
Employees	10139	238393	12274	255529
% owned by local governments	58.9	64.3	57.6	62.3
Regions	5.1	4.7	0.1	4.5
Provinces	1.0	3.6	4.1	4.1
Municipal consortia	0.0	0.1	0.0	0.1
Municipalities	52.7	55.9	53.5	53.6
Number of owner authorities	1281	6729	1086	7313
(average number of owner authorities)	12	2	9	2
Regions	6	20	3	20
Provinces	11	101	11	100
Municipal consortia	6	224	4	221
Municipalities	1258	6384	1068	6972

Source: Unioncamere (2008).

to these same multinationals and on the stock market have broadened the scope of activities and profitability for larger municipal corporations while weakening the smaller ones (Prontera and Citroni, 2007). A handful of large *municipalizzate* (in big cities such as Turin, Venice, Brescia) are in full or majority ownership of their parent city; in most other cases they have national or international energy corporations as co-shareholders. On average, municipal corporations operating in the electricity sector have a slightly higher percentage of private (non-public) ownership than municipal corporations in general (see Table 8.1).

Municipalities as such have thus had an opportunity to regain their role in the energy sector through their *municipalizzate*, now converted into joint stock companies. However, they have no role as regulators other than that as owners: according to the *Decreto Bersani*, concessions for operating local services (i.e. distribution of energy, since production and sale are liberalized) are issued by the Ministry of Industry (now Ministero delle Attività Produttive) for a term of 30 years – thus confirming the strongly centralized nature of energy policy in Italy. Moreover, concessions to local enterprises cover only a marginal part of the distribution market, since ENEL still holds a share of over 86 per cent, followed by Electrabel/ACEA (a partnership between the ex-*municipalizzata* of Rome and the Belgian multinational) with under 4 per cent and another 136 operators sharing the remaining 10 per cent of the market (AEEG, 2008).

The sale of energy to private end-users having been liberalized only as of July 2008, data are still lacking on customer trends to take advantage of the free market and to move from ENEL to other providers (AEEG, 2008).

The national grid and high-voltage installations that had belonged to ENEL have been transferred to new state-owned companies, while the gradual privatization of ENEL has started. Planning and policy-making in the energy sector have recently been redefined as 'concurrent competence' giving the regions' (*regioni*) wide legislative powers. However, most regions are not legislating and planning in due time, so that in the more general field of energy planning (incentives for alternative sources, location of plants etc.) municipalities still find their (modest) regulatory powers hampered when they cannot operate through their own company.

On the whole, no consistent trend or strategy is apparent in the Italian energy sector other than a strong liberalization drive throughout the 1990s – which has not effectively dismantled the role of ENEL other than obliging it to sell plants – generating new strategies and alliances in the market and involving *municipalizzate* and multinationals on a more or less level playing field. The distribution of energy – the sector that has not been liberalized – is still strongly centralized as regards both the national grid (operated by a state-owned company) and local networks (where local companies have only a small share of the market and only on the basis of a concession issued by the ministry). Sales have been liberalized too recently to be assessed. But local regulation and planning have certainly been marginalized by the overall framework of energy policy and business – with the exception of the few dozen municipalities that own a company, either fully or with a majority share.

After heavy dependence on coal in the past, there is now greater diversity in fuel in the UK. Gas, oil, renewable sources, coal and nuclear power are in common use. National Grid Transco (NGT) is responsible for overall security of supply, with increases in transmission costs of 3 per cent per annum owing to price fluctuations. There are concerns that an increasing reliance on imported fuels has given rise to fluctuations in prices, and a rate of 38 per cent gas-fired generation produces some vulnerability. The regulatory regime is 20 years old and a two-year review is being undertaken of its operation and effectiveness. The energy market is inexorably linked with environmental issues, and the government plans new nuclear generation plants and renewable technologies in line with the Kyoto Agreement to be considered in Copenhagen in December 2009.

One important breakthrough is the 2007 consultation on barriers for local electricity generation. There is ongoing consultation on the following issues:

- making it easier for local schemes, including local authorities, to sell small amounts of electricity;
- encouraging and licensing small operators;
- promoting subcontracting with large generators to encourage small generation.

The UK is slowly accepting the idea of micro-generation of electricity, and this will encourage communities and local government to become involved. This will have an impact on future electricity needs and planning. There are some concerns that low-carbon electricity generation projects may be delayed because of network access. Ofgem, the main regulator, is considering ways of avoiding delays. Future gaps in electricity generation owing to increasing demand are likely to give small generators, including local authorities, considerable scope for innovation provided they adopt 'green technologies'. The financial markets in electricity are likely to remain buoyant for some time to come.

COMPARATIVE DISCUSSION AND CONCLUSIONS

As a result of the nationalization of the energy sector in 1948 and of its privatization in 1987, local authorities in the UK have lost all direct involvement with the production, transmission, and distribution of electricity. This is also the case in post-communist Hungary. In Italy, the 1962 nationalization of the energy sector embodied in ENEL has recently been mitigated by the advance of European champions such as Endesa and EdF, private corporations and large municipal energy companies (*municipalizzate*). In France, municipalities were not fully deprived of their competence in the energy sector through nationalization, and this may allow them a comeback in a new phase of decentralization and liberalization.

Among the other countries, Norway stands out as a country where hydropowered electricity generation is almost entirely in public (state and municipal) ownership and control (while the private sector's share is only 13 per cent). However, municipal in-house electricity supply is mostly a thing of the past in Norway, too. Municipalities may be owners but they are not operators in the generation and distribution of energy. However, they play a growing role in energy conservation. Thus a mixed overall picture emerges. In Sweden, municipal corporations still play a major part in energy distribution. In Germany, too, municipal corporations, primarily in the form of *Stadtwerke* ('city-works') continue to be involved in electricity production (20 per cent) and distribution (30 per cent share).

Since the 1990s, and regardless of the ownership and operation issues, energy markets have been largely liberalized in terms of separating the transmission function from the other functions. Furthermore, regulatory agencies have been established to regulate and control players on the energy market. Yet the difficulties such as those encountered in Germany by the new network agency (particularly *vis-à-vis* the 'Big Four' energy giants) in regulating, controlling and enforcing access fees and prices indicate that much still needs to be done to establish stable regulatory regimes.

Why has the supply of energy changed in the ways outlined above? There are two aspects to this question: why did all five countries undertake a shift from local or national monopolies to competitive regimes, a course entailing the de-municipalization of energy supply? And why was it decided to unbundle functions, a strategy that has now been accepted if not fully adopted by all five countries?

The first of these questions can probably be answered by reference to a combination of technical developments, economic inefficiencies and political opportunities and constraints. At the beginning of the twentieth century, electricity had to be consumed close to the point of generation; long-distance transmission resulted in too heavy losses. Technical developments enable the construction of long-distance transmission lines, gradually forming a national grid. The very existence of a national grid (or something close to it) made local and regional inefficiencies and variations in supply capacity conspicuous. In many countries the initial solution was to nationalize all supply functions. The switch to competitive regimes between the mid-1980s (UK) and the mid-2000s (France) owes much to a combination of political ideology, windows of opportunity, and leadership. The UK is an example of both the role of ideology and windows of opportunity. The Thatcher government came to power committed to the pursuit of market-oriented liberalism and could do so against the backdrop of the preceding Callaghan years, when striking coalminers could bring electricity supply to a standstill. Before the new regime of 1991, local and regional authorities in Norway had successfully resisted the vertical integration of electricity supply into large regional conglomerates. The introduction of a competitive regime was a way of circumventing or working with rather than against a large number of local and regional producers and distributors. The key actors agreed that something had to be done to address the inefficiencies of the existing system, so the field was ripe for new initiatives; but few perceived the radicalism of the proposal until it was enacted and under implementation. The cases of France, Germany and Italy are probably best understood as adaptations to external constraints imposed by the EU. As core members of the EU, France and Germany are committed to eliminating trade-distorting practices. The supposedly hidden subsidies and opaque price policies inherent in the old energy regimes were natural targets for EU (re-)regulatory policy. In the long run, non-compliance is not an option for core members and central European players, although the actual regimes put in place also demonstrate how much room for negotiation there is in European multi-level governance.

The choice of an 'unbundling' regime for electricity supply may perhaps be explained in terms of network regulation theory, which has emerged in economics in recent years (for an introduction to this particular subfield, see, e.g., Newberry, 1999; Cowan, 2006 or www.regulationbodyofknowledge.org). Spulber and Yoo (2005) suggest that deregulation regimes may focus on opening up five different types of access: (1) retail access; (2) wholesale access; (3) interconnection access; (4) platform access; and (5) unbundled access. The choice of regulation regimes may be accounted for by the specificities of the network in question. What unbundling implies with regard to electricity supply has been outlined above. Retail access means that a supplier has to sell to any customer who makes a demand. This is fundamental to consumer choice. Wholesale access means that a supplier may buy in bulk from another supplier and sell to 'its' customers. Interconnection access implies connection between networks. Platform access refers to technical standardization that allows the development of secondary services related to the network. Unbundled access means that other suppliers may route their traffic through your network. In the case of electricity supply under competitive regimes, all five types of access are in place. But in the case of electricity it is unbundling that makes the other types of access possible. Without unbundling there can be no retail or wholesale access, which are the driving forces of competition.

NOTES

1. This chapter is based on the country reports that originally appeared (in French translation) in the *Annuaire 2007 des collectivités territoriales*; see Baldersheim and Claes (2007), McEldowney (2007), Prontera and Citroni (2007), Wollmann (2007a, 2007b). The papers were also submitted (in English) to the reserarch conferences held at Villa Vigoni in 2007.

2. E.on, RWE, EnBW and Vattenfall E.on (with some 100 000 employees in Europe and branches in France, Germany, the UK, Italy, Austria, Hungary) and RWE (with 78 000 employees and branch companies in Germany, the UK, Sweden, the Netherlands, Slovak Republic, Czech Republic, Hungary) are the second and third largest European energy companies behind EdF (with 155 000 employees in Europe and branches in France, Germany, the UK, Italy, Austria, Hungary) (figures for 2004); see Bergelin (2004), p. 6.
3. See Ernst & Young (2003) for the results of a survey of the directors of 105 city-works and regional energy providers according to which 28 per cent plan to become shareholders in power plants, while 10 per cent even intend to invest in a power plan of their own.
4. See *Süddeutsche Zeitung*, 28 November 2008.
5. See *Süddeutsche Zeitung*, 13 August 2009: 'Energy rebels on buying trip. A consortium of Stadtwerke acquires the E.on subsidiary Thüga for 3 billion E and is poised to compete with the established energy companies in Germany'.
6. See *Frankfurter Allgemeine Zeitung*, 11 April 2009.
7. On the example of Bergkamen (52 000 inhabitants), see (Bergkamen's mayor) Schäfer 2008. As the time of writing, in at least six cases new (energy-related) *Stadtwerke* have been created and in at least four cases local transmission grids have been re-municipalized (information courtesy of Hans Bolay). At least five new *Stadtwerke* have been founded: '"Private better than public" is a thing of the past: Re-municipalization – fashion or new political phenomenon?' See, for example, *Hamburger Abendblatt*, 20 May 2009: 'Hamburg follows the general trend and founds *Stadtwerke* of its own'.
8. See, for instance, with further examples, www.lbd.de/ob/trend-zur-rekommunalisierung-lv1499.htm. See also *Hamburger Abendblatt*, 20 May 2009: '[The City State of] Hamburg follows the general trends and founds Stadtwerke of its own', *Frankfurter Allgemeine Zeitung*, 11 April 2009.
9. These and the following data are from VKU (2009).

REFERENCES

AEEG (Autorità per l'Energia Elettrica e il Gas) (2008), *Relazione annuale sullo stato dei servizi e sull'attività svolta – Anno 2007*, AEEG: Rome.
Allemand, Roselyne (2007), 'Les distributeurs non nationalisés d'électricité face à l'ouverture à la concurrence', in Hellmut Wollmann and Gérard Marcou (eds), *Annuaire 2007 des Collectivités Locales*, Paris: CNRS, pp. 31–47.
Baldersheim, Harald and Dag Harald Claes (2007), 'Comment un marché de l'énergie a été créé sans que (presque) personne le remarque. La révolution de 1990 de l'approvisionnement en électricité en Norvège et l'évolution du rôle des collectivités locales', in Hellmut Wollmann and Gérard Marcou (eds), *Annuaire 2007 des Collectivités Locales*, Paris: CNRS, pp. 131–43.
Bergelin, Sven (2004), *EU Binnenmarktrichtlinien Elektrizität und Gas*, ver.di Bundesvorstand Fachbereich Ver- und Entsorgung.
Bolay, Sebastian (2009), 'Einführung von Energiemanagement und erneuerbaren Energien. Untersuchung von Erfolgsfaktoren in deutschen Kommunen', dissertation, University of Potsdam.
Bolchini, Piero (1994a), 'Le aziende elettriche municipali', in Valerio Castronovo (ed.), *Storia dell'Industria Elettrica in Italia. Vol. 4: Dal Dopoguerra alla Nazionalizzazione, 1945–1962*, Rom–Bari, Italy: Laterza, pp. 631–63.
Bolchini, Piero (1994b), 'Le ragioni del decentramento: enti locali, aziende municipalizzate ed ENEL', in Giovanni Zanetti (ed.), *Storia dell'Industria Elettrica in*

Italia. Vol. 5: Gli Sviluppi dell'ENEL, 1963–1990, Roma–Bari, Italy: Laterza, pp. 175–220.
Cowan, Simon (2006), 'Network regulation', *Oxford Review of Economic Policy*, **22** (2), 248–59.
Deutscher Städtetag (2001), *Geschäftsbericht 2001*, Cologne, Germany: Deutscher Städtetag.
Deutscher Städtetag (2005), *Geschäftsbericht 2005*, Cologne and Berlin: Deutscher Städtetag.
Ernst & Young (2003), *Stadtwerke 2003*, Eschwege, Germany: Ernst & Young.
Held, Friedrich Wilhelm (2002), 'Neue Entwicklungen im Gemeindewirtschaftsrecht', *Deutsche Zeitschrift für Kommunalwissenschaften*, **41** (1), 91–109.
Lanza, Salvatore and Francesco Silva (2006), *I servizi pubblici in Italia: Il settore elettrico*, Bologna, Italy: Il Mulino.
Marcou, Gérard (2007), 'Le cadre juridique communautaire et national et l'ouverture à la concurrence: contraintes et opportunités pour les collectivités territoriales', in Hellmut Wollmann and Gérard Marcou (eds), *Annuaire 2007 des Collectivités Locales*, Paris: CNRS, pp. 9–29.
McEldowney, John (2007), 'La fourniture d'énergie et l'administration locale: une étude de cas du Royaume-Uni', in Hellmut Wollmann and Gérard Marcou (eds), *Annuaire 2007 des Collectivités Locales*, Paris: CNRS, pp. 121–31.
Müschen, Klaus (1999), 'Kommunale Energiepolitik', in Hellmut Wollmann and Roland Roth (eds), *Kommunalpolitik*, 2 edn, Opladen, Germany: Leske + Budrich, pp. 662–75.
Newberry, David M. (1999), *Privatization, Restructuring, and Regulation of Network Industries*, Cambridge, MA: MIT Press.
Praetorius, Barbara and Sebastian Bolay (2009), 'Implementing energy efficiency innovations: the strategic role of local utilities', unpublished manuscript.
Prontera, Andrea (2008), *L'europeizzazione della politica energetica in Italia e Francia: il cambiamento della politica elettrica fra pressioni europee ed evoluzioni nazionali*, Macerata, Italy: EUM Edizioni Università di Macerata.
Prontera, Andrea and Giulio Citroni (2007), 'Energie et administrations locales en Italie: dénationalisation, libéralisation et concurrence', in Hellmut Wollmann and Gérard Marcou (eds), *Annuaire 2007 des Collectivités Locales*, Paris: CNRS, pp. 191–208.
Püttner, Günter (1999), 'Kommunale Betriebe und Mixed Economy', in Hellmut Wollmann and Roland Roth (eds), *Kommunalpolitik*, 2 edn, Opladen, Germany: Leske + Budrich, pp. 541–51.
Reidenbach, Michael (1995), 'L'Allemagne: l'adaptation graduelle', in Dominique Lorrain and Gerry Stoker (eds), *La privatisation des services urbains en Europe*, Paris: La Découverte, pp. 81–104.
Schäfer, Roland (2008), 'Privat vor Staat hat ausgedient. Rekommunalisierung: Modetrend oder neues Politikphänomen?', *Frankfurter Allgemeine Zeitung*, 19 June, p. 3.
Spulber, Daniel F. and Christopher S. Yoo (2005), 'Network regulation: the many faces of access', *Journal of Competition Law and Economics*, **1** (4), 635–78.
Trapp, Jan-Hendrik (2006), Ausgliederung und Privatisierung in den dreißig größten deutschen Städten', in Werner Kilian, Peter Richter and Jan-Hendrik Trapp (eds), *Ausglliederung und Privatisierung in Kommunen*, Berlin: Sigma, pp. 85–110.
Ude, Christian (2006), 'Stadtwerke – Eckpfeiler kommunaler Selbstverwaltung', *Der Städtetag*, **3**, 21–5.

Unioncamere (2008), *Le società partecipate dagli enti locali. Rapporto 2007*, Rome: Retecamere.
Verband Kommunaler Unternehmen (VKU) (2009), *VKU Kompakt*, Berlin.
Vorholz, Fritz (2006), 'Vom Stromschlag getroffen', *Die Zeit*, **30**, 20 July.
Wollmann, Hellmut (2002), 'The traditional model of local self-government in Germany becoming defunct?', *German Journal of Urban Studies*, **1**, http://www.difu.de/index.shtml?/publikationen/dfk/en.
Wollmann, Hellmut (2007a), 'L'engagement des collectivités locales (les communes) dans la fourniture d'énergie (l'électricité), une perspective internationale', in Gérard Marcou and Hellmut Wollmann (eds), *Annvaire 2007 des Collectivités Locales*, Paris: CNRS, pp. 111–19.
Wollmann, Hellmut (2007b), 'La fourniture d'énergie, l'administration locale et le marché – le cas d'Allemagne', in Gérard Marcou and Hellmut Wollmann (eds), *Annuaire 2007 des Collectivités Locales*, Paris: CNRS, pp. 161–71.

9. Neither state nor market: municipalities, corporations and municipal corporatization in water services – Germany, France and Italy compared

Giulio Citroni

MUNICIPAL WATER SERVICES: DEFINITION

The provision and regulation of water and sanitation services constitute a complex sector that includes such disparate activities as the collection, potabilization, transport, distribution and sale of drinking water, and the collection and purification of domestic wastewater.

This industrial chain, the subject of this chapter, is just one relatively small part of what international agreements[1] define as 'Integrated Water Resource Management' (IWRM), which includes policies relating to other uses of water – for instance in industry and agriculture – as well as the environmental protection of water basins in general. EU countries are presently implementing Directive 2000/60, setting a framework for water policy by introducing water basin planning, systematizing and streamlining standards and objectives, and providing for stakeholder engagement in water pollution policy.

This wider concept of water management will be dealt with only marginally, not because non-domestic uses of water are quantitatively less relevant than urban water consumption (Table 9.1), but because they tend to lie outside municipal competence.

The relevance of domestic water services is not limited to the environmental aspects that link it to IWRM and make it part and parcel of sustainability policy; it arises from the importance of a constant and accessible supply of water to the population for their nourishment and hygiene, and to the 'water business' involved in constructing, maintaining, and operating plants and networks, and in collecting charges from the population.

Table 9.1 Uses of water

	Agricultural use (%)	Industrial and energy use (%)	Urban/domestic use (%)
World	70	22	8
Low- and middle-income countries	82	10	8
High-income countries	30	59	11
European Economic and Monetary Union	21	63	16
Italy*	46	37	18
Germany*	3	84	13
France*	13	71	16

Note: * European Commission's Environment Water Task Force, 1997.

Source: UNESCO–WWAP (2003).

While these characteristics of water services generally apply for most local public utilities, the water sector has certain distinctive characteristics. First, a single network can be put in place, implying a monopoly in the distribution of water. Second, mixing water from different sources and plants must be avoided to obviate hygienic and bacteriological consequences, implying a local monopoly in collection and treatment, too. Third, the transport of water across long distances is not recommended due to its environmental consequences;[2] this favours direct involvement of local authorities in the planning and operation of water networks and plants. These factors exclude any form of unbundling similar to that experienced in the energy sector.

A LEGACY OF MUNICIPALISM

A general trend in Europe has indeed been the involvement of local authorities in water services since the very dawn of modern urban water supply in the eighteenth century,[3] when the pressures of urbanization, industrialization and growing scientific awareness led to increased attention being paid to the provision of safe water to households. Interestingly, most cities facing the construction of modern aqueducts initially resorted to (mainly French and British) private enterprises, which built and operated the plants and networks. Only when the life cycle of a first wave of investment had ebbed and private investors lost interest in expanding services to poorer areas or maintaining networks for long-term development did local authorities in many European countries proceed to 'municipalize' services: in Great Britain, so-called 'municipal socialism' (also ironically referred to as 'water-and-gas socialism') lead to the widespread, direct involvement of local authorities; on the eve of the twentieth century the Netherlands, Germany, Switzerland and Italy were experimenting with municipal enterprises as an innovative model for water service delivery. Thus local governments throughout the twentieth century were able to exercise a supply-side 'water policy' consisting essentially of increasing coverage of the population and below-cost pricing. Growing difficulties in public finance and more stringent environmental legislation have challenged this model, and several reactions to the 'crisis of the municipal model' have emerged (Barraqué, 1995) including increased recourse to concession contracts ('French-style privatization'), multi-utility integration, adoption of private-law status by public enterprises, and centralization or intermunicipal cooperation/integration. Uneasiness with fragmented and subsidized municipal provision has been rather widespread across Europe, sometimes, as in England and Wales, leading to dramatic centralization, or as in Italy and Germany, to the progressive introduction of private-law status implying formal separation of the (public) 'purchaser' from the (private-law) 'provider'.

The evolution of municipal water services in Europe can thus be described as a 'pendulum' swinging from original private sector involvement through concessions to direct municipal provision in a phase of service expansion, and (half-way) back to private-law, private-capital or quasi-private organizations.

What has not changed is the ultimate responsibility to provide services, which still lies with municipal governments who own networks and plants and define the form of management to be implemented. Rather, economic and environmental considerations have led to the realization that the boundaries of individual municipalities seldom represent an optimal level for water management. Environmentally, what EC Directive 2000/60 describes as 'river basin districts'[4] represents the areas within which water management can be regulated – or exercised – with due consideration for environmental and political issues. From the economic perspective, economies of scale can be gained by aggregating the smallest municipalities, especially in areas (as in much of France and Italy) where local authorities are extremely small.

National and European legislation tends to respect municipal competencies in the provision of water services. National and state/regional legislation concentrates on regulating water quality, environmental standards, conflicting uses of water, and the general framework for municipal activities in the field of public utilities. Similarly, European decision-making has focused on the regulation of 'output' standards for drinking water, water purification, and public-interest orientation, while the 'input' side of provision has been only marginally influenced by EU policy and case law.

Competition and single-market regulation imply that, once a local government decides to deliver water services through private, potentially competing firms, such enterprises must comply with all relevant norms on state aid and competition. On the other hand, the Stability and Growth Pact and the Maastricht process have imposed 'confining conditions' that limit the freedom of local governments to choose among different forms of service provision.[5]

WATER SERVICE PROVISION IN GERMANY, FRANCE AND ITALY

This section describes the major characteristics and trends in water service management in the three countries under scrutiny; it should be noted that, while each case study presents the basic information on legal frameworks, forms of provision and means of municipal oversight/steering, the focus shifts in each case due to the varying relevance of different aspects in the specific comparative context, in the national debate, and in the academic and managerial literature. The account of the German situation thus pays greater attention to the forms of provision while the Italian account concentrates more on the evolution of the legal framework, and the French report focuses on the regulation of concession contracts.

Management and governance issues are the focus of the discussion. An economic analysis of the consequences of management choices about prices and environmental protection standards is beyond the scope of this chapter. However, in order to show the major trends and the state of the art of water pricing in the different countries under discussion, Table 9.2 offers an overview of some such indicators. Comparisons are hard to draw, since standards of measurement differ from country to country, prices vary considerably within each country, and the levels of public investment and public subsidization differ substantially (not to mention the complexity of accounting).

Germany

According to Art. 28 of the constitutional Basic Law (*Grundgesetz*), German municipalities have full autonomy in regulating local issues, including water service provision. Hence many legal and organizational

Table 9.2 *Water prices for households in selected European countries: prices, investments and trends in the 1990s*

Country	Price 2003 (€/m³)*	Annual investment for water and sanitation services**	Years	Nominal aggregate % increase	Average real annual % increase
Italy	0.68	...	*1992–98*	*39.0*	*2.0*
Sweden	2.32	...	1991–98	35.0	1.9
Belgium	2.50	...	1988–98	65.0	2.7
Finland	2.56	...	1982–98	234.0	3.8
France	*2.58*	*68*	*1991–96*	*55.0*	*7.0*
UK	2.69	95	1994–98	22.0	2.0
Netherlands	3.35	70	1990–98	73.0	4.6
Germany	*4.45*	*115*	*1992–97*	*36.0*	*3.8*
Denmark	4.53	...	1984–95	175.0	6.3

Notes:

*   Price paid for 120 m³/yr per household (weighted average of the price of water supply, sanitation and taxes in the five main cities of each country in 2003).

** Investment in drinking water supply and sanitation; in €/cap.: Spain (2000), France (2003), UK (2001), Netherlands (2002), Germany (2001).

Source: NUS Consulting and BIPE/SFDE, 2005 (quoted in OECD, 1999, 2000).

forms exist across the country. Among other things, autonomy has implied extreme fragmentation in water service provision, which is entrusted to no fewer than 6500 operators in water supply and 6700 in sewage disposal and treatment (BMWA, 2005, p. 5). Fragmentation is particularly strong in West Germany, where the history of municipal autonomy has not suffered the interruption experienced in the East. Under the GDR regime, water services were provided by 15 state enterprises (VEB–WAB, Volkseigene Betriebe der Wasserversorgung und Abwasserbehandlung), and when these were dismantled after reunification, the same level of fragmentation as in the West was not attained – although there is in fact a trend towards progressive fragmentation (ibid.).

A potential factor in further diversification – *Länder* legislation – is not very relevant in this sector, since state regulation of water services (mainly pertaining to local utilities in general) is rather uniform (Cronauge and Westermann, 2006, pp. 158 f.): thus, in all *Länder*, direct municipal involvement in economic activities must be limited to objectives of general

Table 9.3   Forms of water services management

Forms of privatization	Models of service delivery
Public-law	*Regiebetrieb* (direct management)
	Eigenbetrieb (public-law municipal enterprise)
	Anstalt des öffentliches Rechts (institution under public law)
	Zweckverband (intermunicipal consortium)
	Wasserverband and *Bodenverband* (intermunicipal consortium)
'Organizational' privatization	*Eigengesellschaft* (private-law enterprise fully owned by municipality)
'Functional' privatization	*Pachtvertrag* and *Betriebsführungsvertrag* (lease contract)
	Betreibermodell (outsourcing of management)
'Asset' privatization	*Kooperationsmodell* (PPP mixed company)
'Service' privatization	*Dienstleistungskonzession* (service concession)

Source: Adapted from Kluge et al. (2003), pp. 11ff.

interest, must be confined to the municipal territory, and must balance revenue and expenditure. These criteria, however, apply only to 'sovereign duties' (*hoheitliche Aufgaben*), which include sewage disposal but not water supply, and are being progressively eroded by the use of private-law models of service provision and the integration of different (sovereign, and commercial) activities in multi-utility enterprises (Scheele, 2006, p. 31). Regional legislation is thus not decisive in explaining or determining municipal choices not only because it is uniform across the country, but also because the more municipalities tend to adopt integrated, public–private or corporatized forms of service delivery, the less such legislation can influence local authority choices.

What does contribute to diversification in water services management is the wide range of institutional forms that may be adopted by municipalities; scholarly analysis has provided classifications of these forms of service management (see Table 9.3), but some are so leniently regulated that freedom of 'institutional design' is almost complete: in the case of the *Anstalt*, for example, a public-law institution can be set up that is not regulated by any specific law and can thus be designed totally à la carte (Ochmann, 2005) as regards institutions, powers, and public or private partners.

The models that pertain to the domain of public law are most influenced by state (*Land*) legislation as part of the more general competence of

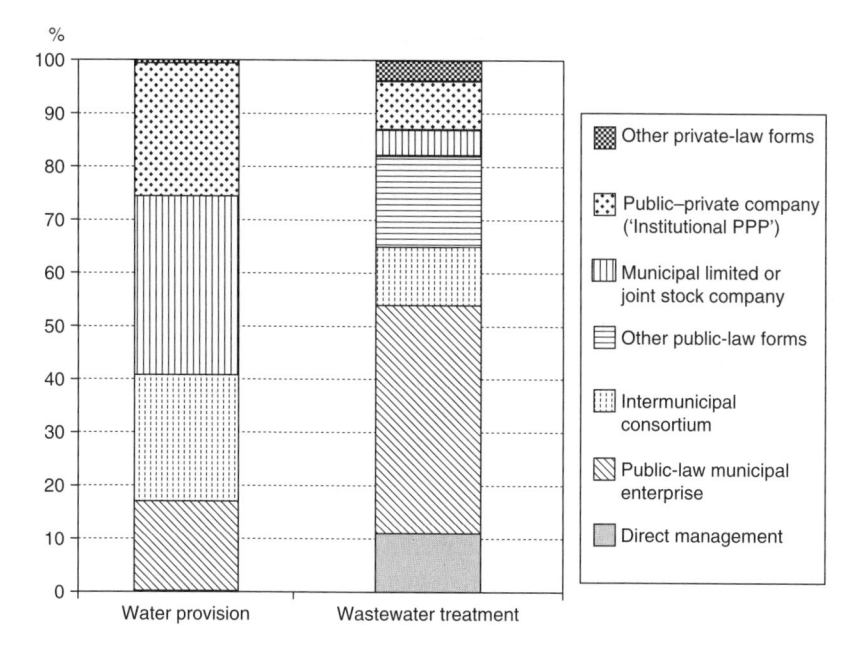

The corporatization of water services compared 197

Source: BMWA (2005).

Figure 9.1 Water service providers by model of management (% of the population)

Länder concerning the functioning of municipal administration, whereas the models that pertain to corporate and joint stock models are regulated by the several federal laws on companies.

The share of the population served by enterprises of various forms is summarized in Figure 9.1 (the classification is slightly simplified). As the graphs show, the situation differs widely in the two sectors of water supply and wastewater treatment. In water supply, public-law models cover just over 40 per cent of the population, while the other 60 per cent are served by private-law corporations; of these, only a marginal proportion are fully private corporations (0.6 per cent), while a vast majority are mixed companies (24.9 per cent) and fully public companies (33.7 per cent). The situation in wastewater treatment is quite different, in that public-law models cover 82 per cent of the population, with a significant share of direct municipal provision (11 per cent). The remaining 18 per cent is made up mainly of mixed companies, as well as fully private and fully public enterprises.

The explanation for these differences lies mostly in the different legal regimes governing each sector; sewage and wastewater treatment is treated

Table 9.4 *Provision models of different public utilities in a sample of cities over 50 000 inhabitants*

	Water and sanitation services	Electricity	Public transport	Housing
Direct municipal management (%)	12	0	3	6
Municipal enterprise (%)	24	2	5	0
Other public-law model (%)	13	1	8	10
Private-law model (%)	51	97	84	84
no.	270	124	140	100

Source: Richter et al. (2006).

in German legislation as a 'sovereign duty', while water supply is an 'economic activity': sovereign activities, such as wastewater treatment, are not subject to VAT and other taxes as long as they are managed by public-law bodies. Thus the incidence of 'formal' (or 'organizational') privatization (i.e. the transformation of public bodies into private-law enterprises without private partners) is much lower since it is quite inconvenient from an economic point of view – which points to the 'pragmatic' perspective (Feigenbaum et al., 1999) that German local authorities seem to take towards corporatization. The reform of wastewater services through the adoption of 'privatized' models appears more a consequence of integrating water and wastewater management than an autonomous policy of the (sub)sector itself.

All in all, the water sector in Germany is much more 'backward' in privatization and corporatization reform than other public utilities (see Table 9.4).

Privatization in its various forms seems to take place most often in larger cities. This is shown in Table 9.5, where the data on population served by different types of companies can be compared with data on the number of companies serving the population: the percentages in the last column are higher than those in the middle column in all public-law types, except for *Wasserverbände* (water associations), which typically serve many municipalities.

Finally, private-law models are more common in what used to be 'East' Germany than they are in 'the West' (Richter et al., 2006a, p. 68): in the eastern *Länder* private-law companies make up 60 per cent of water service providers, while the figure for western *Länder* is just under 50 per

Table 9.5 Models of water service provision

	Water supply: % of population served*	Water supply: % of number of enterprises**
Direct management	0.2	1.3
Public-law municipal enterprise	16.8	36.7
Intermunicipal consortium	23.8	20.4
Municipal limited or joint stock company	33.7	28.0
Public–private company ('institutional PPP')	24.9	11.9
Other private-law forms	0.6	1.7

Sources:
* BMWA (2005), p. 7.
** Kluge et al. (2003), p. 15.

cent. Two alternative – but not incompatible – explanations can be given for this phenomenon: one is that the very bad state of infrastructure and service in the East (Kluge et al., 2003) required the most innovative and potentially effective models for new investment to be carried out at a sufficient pace; the other, suggestive but unconfirmed, hypothesis (Richter et al., 2006b, p. 119) is that the weaker and sparser network of post-reunification eastern *Länder* may have been a favourable 'laboratory' for the innovative provision models that scholars and consultants had devised in the West (of Germany, and of Europe) – paradoxically, a *more* favourable laboratory than the western municipalities where they had been invented.

Whatever the service provision model, the ultimate responsibility for service conditions and performance lies with local authorities, which accordingly tend to maintain some form of control over the operations of the service provider depending on the structure chosen. Several supervisory or steering tools may be combined:[6]

- the appointment of directors and/or president of the service provider company: this is generally the case in municipal enterprises and in 100 per cent public joint stock or limited companies, but may also be the case in mixed companies according to specific shareholders' agreements;
- the creation of a supervisory board (*Aufsichtsrat*) in joint stock companies, where the municipality nominates at least a majority of members;

- the safeguarding of specific local authority powers (executive and/ or legislative bodies or committees) as regards decisions on tariffs, investments, or changes in the corporate identity and structure.

Most supervision is in the hands of elected politicians, who form the core of supervisory boards in joint stock companies, while the directors and presidents appointed to public enterprises are non-political professionals, control being exercised directly by the municipal administration. In private-law companies the chain of control is thus slightly longer and heavily influenced by what has been called the 'double double position' of political members on supervisory boards (Schäfer and Roreger, 1998, pp. 27f.), characterized by potential conflicts of interest both between (1) the competing goals of profit maximization and of fulfilment of public ends, and between (2) the political activity and expertise of supervisory board members in their capacity of mayors, councillors, city managers, and their involvement in the technical and economic control of service providers. The potentially ineffective position of supervisory board members as political guarantors is further weakened by the strict confidentiality of a great deal of the information they receive from the firm – making it impossible for them to report on much of the debate and the issues at stake to colleagues in party and office and to the population at large.

The data available do not permit any clear-cut statement on a decrease in political and administrative steering and controlling powers. However, some remarks can be made:

- The exercise of control 'at arm's length' requires specific innovations in the structure and functioning of the controlling administrations, which do not always seem to have taken place on a scale that can guarantee, for example, the demarcation of competencies between units responsible for asset management and for public service goals.
- Elected councils are progressively excluded from control and steering, while mayors and executive councillors maintain – or even gain – a more prominent role (Bogumil and Holtkamp, 2002) due to their direct participation in steering bodies, their power to nominate municipal representatives, their ease of access to restricted policy networks, and the fact that they usually direct and control the processes of privatization in a more concrete and 'hands-on' way than do the elected councils.
- In the case of 'asset privatization', that is, when private partners are included among the shareholders of water companies (25 per cent of water companies, Figure 9.1), possible partners for municipalities

are either huge energy corporations (E.on and RWE) or a combination of these with German and international banks and French water multinationals. The economic and political power of these actors can create an imbalance in local relationships, especially in small and medium-sized municipalities.

These aspects combine to create the sort of uncertainty that is common where administrative power is 'unbundled'. Peculiar to the water sector, however, is that political and democratic control appears to play a stronger role than in other sectors owing to the specific characteristics of the public good at stake. Political and administrative actors (Citroni, 2007; Fitch, 2007) seem to view the water sector as slightly different from other local utilities because of certain technical, environmental and 'emotional' characteristics: the impossibility of establishing the conditions for market competition, but also the need to integrate water service management within the framework of water resource management, are the main elements of this different regime. This attitude is not as strong as in Italy (see next section), nor is it as strong as in some of the social services: full cost recovery through tariffs, for example, is a widely accepted norm; and yet this 'peculiarity' of water is clearly visible in the much lower recourse made to various forms of privatization than in other local utilities.

Italy

The water sector in Italy has long been as fragmented as in Germany, with 8000 enterprises or administrative units responsible for one or more aspects of water service provision – on average, almost one firm per municipality.

Water services have always been a responsibility of municipalities. Until the reform of 1994, legislation on service provision models had been very fragmented but overall quite stable since the very early 1900s when the act on *municipalizzate* was adopted. Besides direct municipal provision and concessions to private firms, municipal enterprises could be set up for the purpose. These enterprises – enjoying autonomous legal status and some freedom in operation – had already developed in the late eighteenth century, and have been a persistent component of the local utilities sector for a century. Other forms of provision, such as direct municipal management and – to a much lesser extent – concessions to private firms, have survived the 'municipalization wave', especially in smaller towns and rural municipalities. In addition, 'public bodies' have been in charge of water adduction and delivery in wide areas of southern Italy where the scarcity of water has made it impossible for individual municipalities to cater for

Table 9.6 Water service providers in Italy, by subsector

	Operation of aqueducts	Water supply	Wastewater treatment	Sewerage	Overall
Municipality	3714 (80.1%)	4534 (84.6%)	3644 (85.8%)	6340 (95%)	6463 (82.6%)
Municipal enterprise (*municipalizzate*)	83 (1.8%)	88 (1.6%)	60 (1.4%)	59 (0.9%)	107 (1.4%)
Consortium	400 (8.6%)	329 (6.1%)	170 (4%)	100 (1.5%)	528 (6.7%)
Public body	28 (0.6%)	19 (0.4%)	33 (0.8%)	8 (0.1%)	53 (0.7%)
Joint stock company	130 (2.8%)	144 (2.7%)	148 (3.5%)	100 (1.5%)	215 (2.7%)
Other	280 (6%)	246 (4.6%)	190 (4.5%)	70 (1%)	460 (5.9%)
Total	4635	5360	4245	6677	7826

Source: Istat (1999).

their own needs. Finally, consortia could be created among a number of neighbouring municipalities, subject to norms similar to those regulating *municipalizzate*.

Table 9.6 shows that an overwhelming majority of service providers before the 1994 reform (which had not yet been implemented in 1999) were administrative units of municipalities, nearly 83 per cent of all water services and 95 per cent of sewage services. Municipal enterprises in fact represent a very limited proportion of service providers, less than 2 per cent in each subsector. However (Table 9.7), they carry over 40 per cent of the water: this indicates that *municipalizzate* have been a feature of the larger, northern and central Italian cities, while direct municipal management is a characteristic feature of smaller municipalities (which often boast populations of between 50 and 500!). Table 9.7 also shows that the 'public body' providers are for the most part huge enterprises that deliver water across entire regions in the South, where the scarcity of natural resources has required massive intervention by the state to provide water to all communities. One such aqueduct is the Acquedotto Pugliese in Apulia, the largest in Europe.

What is apparent from these data is the extreme fragmentation of water services in Italy: nearly 8000 providers were serving an average of just over 7000 citizens each, and operating completely independently of one

Table 9.7   Models of aqueduct operation (number of providers and amount of water carried)

	% number of providers	% water carried
Municipality	80.1	34.42
Municipal enterprise (*municipalizzate*)	1.8	42.54
Public body	0.6	18.75
Private firm	2.8	3.78
Other	14.6	0.52
Total	100	100

Sources: Istat (1999) on number of providers; Caselli (1993) on water carried.

another. Direct municipal management, but also 'public body' management in the South, generally implied heavy subsidization of services with pricing which failed by far to meet costs (Caselli, 1993; Malaman and Cima, 1998). A sound investment policy was hard to attain.

Several converging factors came to a head in the early 1990s, prompting reform by central government. They included:

- a worsening fiscal and monetary crisis, fostering the conviction that service provision, let alone investment, could not be sustained without new sources of revenue and capital;
- corruption scandals that upset the political system involving mismanagement of local utility and administration contracts, resulting, for example, in the majority of the board of governors of ACEA, the Roman water and energy utility, being charged and or jailed in connection with crimes pertaining to works, supply and service contracts between 1992 and 1993 (Citroni, 2007);
- enhanced environmental awareness, including a 1989 act on water basin regulation and the EU Urban Waste Water Directive issued in 1991;
- administrative reform at the local level, with Law 142 of 1990 providing for a clearer separation of competencies between political and managerial personnel in accordance with NPM principles.

Thus a wide parliamentary coalition agreed on legislation that appeared to respond to these different stimuli; after years of parliamentary discussion, the 'Galli' reform – named after the MP who proposed it – was passed in 1994 under a so-called 'technical' (non-partisan) cabinet.

Four main points define the Galli reform:

- vertical integration of the water industry: contrary to the 'unbundling' to which other sectors were subject, water services were to be regulated and managed as a whole, covering adduction of water from sources, distribution and sale of water to households, collection and treatment of wastewater, and all aspects of service provision, construction, maintenance and operation of facilities;
- horizontal integration: territories, so-called 'optimal territorial areas' (ATO, *ambiti territoriali ottimali*) within which a single service provider can operate were to be clearly defined by regional authorities according to water basin criteria;
- regulation was to be clearly separated from service provision: an 'authority' was to be established in each ATO responsible for selecting and controlling a service provider operating throughout the territory and across 'integrated' water services; these authorities are in fact a consortium of municipalities situated within the ATO;
- full-cost recovery through user tariffs: the definition of tariffs by ATO authorities was to enable the service provider to deliver services and to construct, maintain and operate facilities without public subsidization.

The implementation of this complex, somewhat revolutionary, reform design has been slow, piecemeal and uncertain.[7] Some regions have taken as long as five years to define the geographical boundaries of ATOs; municipalities have taken years to establish ATO authorities and make them operational; as of 2006 the award of ATO-wide, 'integrated' concessions had been accomplished in 43 of the 91 existing ATOs.

The model of provision envisaged – and imposed on all municipalities – by the Galli Law is that of a concession awarded by a consortium of municipalities to a formally autonomous firm. What the reform does not define, however, is the nature of such firms: this is regulated by another strand of legislation concerning the functioning of local administration in general. Municipalities or consortia may choose to confer the task of service provision in one of three forms:

- competitive tendering for the award of a concession to a private firm;
- direct (non-competitive) award of a concession to a mixed public–private company, as long as the private partner is selected by competitive procedures;
- direct (non-competitive) award of a concession to a fully public, 'in-house' firm.

Over the years, the legal rules have repeatedly changed, as has their interpretation by tribunals and successive national governments. The persistent fear of compulsory competitive tendering being imposed has now subsided, but has long influenced local choices.

Of the three options for the award of concessions, competitive tendering has been by far the least frequently employed by ATO authorities – that is, by municipalities. In only four of 43 cases has competitive tendering been successfully carried out – one in central Italy, three in the South; in a few more cases it was attempted but failed owing to a lack of competitors or other procedural problems.

A number of factors explain why concessions were not awarded at all or at least not by means of competitive tendering in almost all ATOs. First, in ATOs where no concession was awarded, agreement on procedure and on outcomes was difficult to reach among the numerous municipalities composing the authority (on average almost 90), especially in the absence of strong leadership from a central, influential city or a political party assembling a majority of mayors. Second, and more generally, the political influence – or patronage – of previous municipal management may have induced mayors to avoid dismantling old firms by either boycotting the whole process or by ensuring that the outcome could be settled consensually rather than competitively.

Leaving aside the four cases of successful competitive tendering, where an ATO-wide concession was awarded (43 cases), the process was usually a careful and slow one that permitted all existing municipal units and enterprises, consortia and public bodies to be merged into a single company to which the concession could then be awarded. Intense negotiations took place on the financial, organizational and occupational aspects of merging dozens of existing service providers. In 14 cases, this process culminated in the partial privatization of a minority of shares (40–49 per cent) to form 'temporary associations of enterprises' composed of varying combinations of French multinationals, some Italian *ex-municipalizzate* (now public–private stock companies),[8] local banks, builders, and other industrial and financial partners.

Much public attention has been drawn to the corporatization and partial privatization of water companies by the media and by protests led by organizations such as Attac and supported in particular by the left-wing party 'Rifondazione Comunista'; keywords for these campaigns are 'renationalization', 'common good' and 'basic human rights'. The idea that formal and 'material' privatization distorts the aims and functioning of water companies is at the root of these protests. Doubts about the democratic quality of Italian water companies, however, arise from several 'details' of the implementation of the Galli reform as much as from the adoption of private law as such:[9]

- the conflict of interest between owner-municipalities and regulator-municipalities is at the very heart of the system devised by the Galli reform, since it was implemented in a situation where over 80 per cent of companies were (and still are) owned by municipalities;
- the progressive exclusion of elected councils, and the concentration of powers in the hands of mayors as both ultimate 'owners' of the companies and representatives of public and consumer interests in ATO authorities, reduce transparency and pluralism;
- the inclusion of private partners is not accompanied by sufficient guarantees of transparency, either in the selection of private partners (competitions are organized and run by mayors and their staff, and the number of competitors is always extremely limited) or in the functioning of privatized companies (competencies are not clearly defined, and all-powerful boards of governors of up to 18 or 20 public and private members constitute new – opaque and ademocratic – bodies for the governance of water services;
- the tendency to appoint political personnel or politically oriented professionals to represent municipalities on corporate and regulatory bodies; they seldom have the necessary expertise in commercial law and corporate governance, which may weaken control and regulation.

All in all, municipal administrators appear to distrust their ability to control service provision 'from outside', seeking rather to maintain an active role within the corporatized or partly privatized companies. This only partly satisfies the demands of anti-privatization activists, but does point to the malaise felt by some mayors in abandoning all direct control. Minority privatization, when it does occur, is thus often organized politically rather than competitively, which explains the low credibility of the few competitions for privatization, and the consequent poor participation.[10]

France

The provision of water services in France has been the sole responsibility of municipalities since the Revolution, and is handled by about 15 000 municipal and intermunicipal units (Assemblée Nationale, 2001, p. 15) across the over 36 000 French *communes*. Municipal competence in this sector was confirmed in an act of 1928, and survived the nationalization waves of the twentieth century.

While the regulation of competing uses of water and the environmental protection of land and water resources (Assemblée Nationale, 2003) are regulated centrally and implementation is entrusted to mandatory public corporations (*établissements publics*) composed of local administrations and representatives of central government (*agences de l'eau*), the actual delivery of water services is strictly in the hands of municipalities, who are free to choose from among a wide set of management regimes:

- *régie directe*, or direct municipal management, under which administrative units of the municipality carry out all activities pertaining to water and wastewater services;
- *régie autonome* (municipal enterprise), under which the administrative unit delivering water services enjoys relative organizational and financial autonomy;
- *régie personalisée* (self-standing public agency), under which the administrative unit is formally constituted as a juridical person under public law;
- *régie intéressée* and *gérance* (management contracts), under which a private contractor takes on management duties and is remunerated by the municipality at a fixed rate or depending on levels of service;
- *affermage* (lease contract), under which a private contractor takes on management duties and collects tariffs from users; the contractor thus assumes the commercial risk, while the municipality is in charge of investment, which is financed through a specific quota of the tariffs collected by the contractor;
- *concession* (concession), under which a private contractor is in charge of management and investment to be covered by the tariff levied on users;
- *société d'économie mixte* (public–private joint stock company), a kind of local enterprise subject to public procurement regulations, where the concessionaire is a joint stock company in which the municipality has a majority holding (between 50 per cent and 85 per cent), the rest being owned by one or more private partners.

The first three models are fully public forms of service management and delivery, while the latter four imply varying degrees of involvement by private sector partners. Interestingly, French legislation does not allow municipalities to create joint stock companies unless they are at least partly privatized: thus no 100 per cent public-owned joint stock companies exist, which somewhat simplifies the distinction between public and private models of service management.

However, a complex and much-debated mixture of public and private law comes to bear in water services[11] under the legal heading of '*services publics industriels et commerciaux*' (SPIC – industrial and commercial public services), which, under whatever model of management, are subject to ordinary jurisdiction in so far as the relationship between user and provider is concerned, while regulatory and authoritative aspects are to be found, for example, in the strongly asymmetrical relationship between municipalities and concessionaires in delegation models. Generally speaking, all water services serving over 3000 users must comply with the principles of organizational and accounting separateness, and must cover all running and maintenance expenses from their own revenues, so that no cross-subsidization is allowed (Assemblée Nationale, 2001, p. 16).

The situation is made even more complex by the fact that each of the models described may in fact be exercised by a single municipality or by an intermunicipal body: there are many intermunicipal organizations (especially in the form of *syndicat intercommunal à vocation unique*, SIVU) involving about 55 per cent of all French municipalities (Cour des Comptes, 2003, pp. 67ff.).

Moreover, each municipality or intermunicipal district may and often does opt for a different form of delivery and different public or private actors for each segment of the water service cycle. Furthermore, the territories of intermunicipal bodies responsible for water delivery and for wastewater and sanitation may differ and intersect.

Notwithstanding this great variety and complexity of viable options, water service management in France is widely known for the widespread use of concessions and lease contracts, generally under the heading of *gestion déléguée*, and sometimes referred to in other European countries as 'French-style privatization' (Finger and Allouche, 2002).

This management model has been used in French municipalities ever since the first aqueducts and water plants were established, and has survived all the nationalization and municipalization waves experienced in France and Europe during the twentieth century.

As Table 9.8 shows, the various forms of delegated management cover almost 80 per cent of water delivery and over 50 per cent of wastewater management; it must be noted, however, that the incidence of delegated management over the number of municipalities served is much lower, which points to the tendency of private providers to become involved in medium-sized and large cities rather than in the smaller municipalities most in need of ways to exploit economies of scale. Unfortunately, no reliable data are available on specific modes of service delivery other than the general *régie* versus *gestion déléguée* dichotomy; however, about 90 per cent of *régies* are run in the form of *régie directe* (Duval, 2006), while over 85 per cent of *gestions déléguées* consist of lease contracts (*affermage*). In most concessions a high proportion of investment is always financed by public agencies and central government (Assemblée Nationale, 2001).

Table 9.8   Incidence of water service models in France, 2000

		Water		Wastewater and sewage	
		% municipalities	% population	% municipalities	% population
Régie	Régie directe (Direct management) Régie autonome (Municipal enterprise) Régie personalisée (Public agency)	48	21	62	48
Gestion déléguée	Régie intéressé (Management contract) Affermage (Lease contract) Concession (Concession) Société d'économie mixte (Mixed company)	52	79	38	53

Source: Hansen and Herbke (2004) in Kuhlmann (2008).

It must also be stressed that, although generally considered characteristic of French water services, the delegation model has not been consistently as strong as it is now (see Table 9.9), so that France has also experienced the more general trend described in an earlier section as 'pendulum' from original private management to municipal provision and back to *gestion déléguée*.

Besides legal complexity and the increasing diffusion of delegated management, a third characteristic element of French water services should be mentioned, the well-known phenomenon of oligopoly that distinguishes the water services market in France, dominated by three major corporations covering about 98 per cent of the market. Such concentration of the market is not new in France; the two main corporations have been

Table 9.9 Incidence of gestion déléguée *in water delivery*

Year	1936	1954	1962	1968	1975	1978	1982	1990	1999
Population served (million people)	7.1	13.5	16.9	22.2	26.0	30.5	33.5	42.4	46.2
Population served (%)	16.9	31.6	36.3	44.7	50.0	57.5	61.7	75.0	79.0

Source: Guérin-Schneider and Lorrain (2003) in Kuhlmann (2008).

Table 9.10 Market share of water companies in France (%)

	Own market share	Through participation in joint ventures	Total
Vivendi – Générale des Eaux	51	5	56
Suez – Lyonnaise des Eaux	24	5	29
Bouygues – SAUR	13	–	13
12 other companies	2	–	2

Source: Conseil de la Concurrence (2000).

operating for over a century. But the 1990s witnessed further acquisitions by Suez and Générale des Eaux (Conseil de la Concurrence, 2000), producing the situation shown in Table 9.10. A number of joint ventures between the two 'oligopolists' further block the water services market.

Closely associated with this market structure, as both cause and consequence, is the insufficient regulation and opaque practice of concessions that was revised only in the early 1990s.

Until the *Loi Sapin* was issued in 1993, followed by *Loi Barnier* and *Loi Mazeaud* in 1995, concessions were awarded and renewed with no transparent and competitive procedure, according to public-law principles that differed radically from those regulating public procurement (West, 2005): *intuitu personae* (whereby trust prevails on formal competition), *fait du prince*, *théorie de l'imprévision* and *force majeure* (whereby an asymmetrical relationship is recognized and regulated between local authority and contractor). The first principle has come under particularly strong attack after a series of corruption and bribery scandals showed that the oligopoly was not a 'natural' outcome of economies of scale and efficiency: direct, personal contacts, informality, repeated extensions of contracts, formal or informal 'entry fees' imposed on new operators, and a lack of information and control contributed to weaken the capacity of municipalities to guarantee effective service at reasonable prices. Prices grew by 170 per cent between 1975 and 1985, by 5 per cent each year between 1985 and 1990, then again 11 per cent each year between 1991 and 1994, slowing down to about 2–3 per cent a year more recently (Assemblée Nationale 2001, p. 8).

To counter these tendencies, the above-mentioned regulations have introduced stricter norms on the competitive tendering of concessions and limits to their renewal; on accounting and reporting to increase transparency; on uniformity and transparency of tariff formation; on fair conditions for the entry of new contractors. Such regulation has only partly solved the problems of opacity and inefficiency (Conseil de la Concurrence, 2000): renewals are rare (concessions usually run 25 to 30 years) and are still almost always granted to incumbent providers (95 per cent of renewals), also due to implicit agreements among the three major corporations; tariff transparency is not accompanied by sufficient cost transparency, so that efficiency is difficult to assess; the cost of remunicipalization appears too high to pose a serious threat to private firms. Regulation is not transparent enough to allow competition from foreign corporations.

These *gestion déléguée* issues have contributed to making water prices under public provision (Assemblée Nationale, 2001) 13 per cent lower than under private provision; the difference in 1992 was 22 per cent, so that some improvement in delegation procedures seems to have taken place.

The problem of transparency also plagues direct municipal service delivery, where accounting procedures are not always up to the standards required by law (Assemblée National, 2001, p. 25) and management and internal control are lacking (Cour des Comptes, 2003, p. 9). The know-how needed for investments necessitated by increasingly demanding environmental and safety regulations is also not always available in small *régies*, nor are the funds needed to renovate or even maintain infrastructure (ibid.). Legislation in the 1990s has concentrated on strengthening the rules on *gestion déléguée* rather than improving conditions for *régie*, and the steering and control instruments in the hands of mayors (let alone municipal councils, who detain essentially formal powers; see Kuhlmann, 2008) appear outdated and insufficient to govern the complexity of present water and sanitation regulation and practice.

It is therefore all the more surprising that there should be widespread debate in France on a supposed return to direct municipal delivery. This is indeed taking place in some notable cases, which assume rather strong symbolic value, as in the city of Grenoble, but no overall trend is yet apparent. Indeed, if the difficulties in controlling water service are nearly as great under *régie* as in *gestion déléguée*, one reason for opting for public delivery – democratic control – is weakened. Another strategy seems to prevail: that of letting the private sector take at least part of the blame for tariff increases needed to pay for increased investment imposed by stricter environmental regulation (Assemblée Nationale, 2003; Conseil de la Concurrence, 2000). This strategic political explanation for the diffusion of *gestion déléguée* is rendered plausible by the observable lack of any correlation between left-wing and right-wing administrations and model of service delivery, or any 'rational' tendency for smaller municipalities (most in need of economies of scale) to privatize more than larger cities (Kuhlmann, 2008).

Unlike their Italian and German counterparts, French local politicians thus appear to be willing to 'escape' responsibility in the water service sector, or at least to have wanted to do so in the past; recent trends suggest that wider and better use is progressively being made of the steering and control instruments provided by the legislation of the early 1990s (Cour des Comptes, 2003). Thus, what started as a 'blame-shifting' strategy up until the 1980s, and produced a shock in the early 1990s with the realization that tariff increases and corruption were as politically dangerous under privatization as under *régie*, might now very slowly and tentatively be developing into a learning process towards greater efficiency and accountability. And from this example many other countries must learn, *volens nolens*, given the ever-increasing role of the French model and French corporations across Europe and the world.

CONCLUSIONS

Analysis of the data confirms that there is a shift in water management towards innovative forms characterized by the increasing involvement of private partners and private corporate forms of organization. This is true of Italy and Germany, where municipalization had been radical and widespread, and the present trend towards corporatization and partial privatization is now all the more evident; and it is also true of France, where the involvement of private actors has always been common but has increased dramatically over time. At the same time, all countries appear to have neglected the 'modernization' and 'maintenance' (Pollitt and Bouckaert, 2004) of public administration, including the guarantees of effective steering and control capacities made all the more necessary by partial privatization, public forms of management in legislative reforms and administrative processes.

Increasing recourse to corporate models and privatization can be explained by varying configurations of several elements:

- the search for effectiveness and efficiency combined with a 'new public management' rhetoric according to which these are found in private models of management;
- increasingly demanding environmental regulations requiring investment which public authorities alone cannot sustain;
- an attempt – also provoked by the need for more investment – to shift the blame for tariff increases to 'somebody else' than elected politicians.

In the two countries where municipalization has been most radical, enabling autonomous actors (*Stadtwerke* and *municipalizzate*) to gain power, corporatization appears to be the most viable outcome, and privatization tends to be limited to minority holdings; in France, on the other hand, there is much less resistance to 'tougher' privatization in the form of lease contracts, and very limited recourse to mixed companies.

The outcomes of corporatization and mixed ownership (Italy and Germany), on the one hand, and of concessions on the other (France), seem to differ in one major regard: the roles of public and private actors and rationales are more clearly defined in concessions. However, French municipalities find this difficult to achieve under market competition conditions and under the pressure exerted by oligopolist corporations on local politicians and administrations. Transparency, accountability and economic efficiency do not automatically spring from contractual arrangements, and are problematic in direct municipal provision, as well as in public, mixed and private corporations. Relationships of trust, and the continuous renegotiation of roles and collective aims are to be found formally and informally in all institutional settings observed, where neither hierarchy nor market competition appear to be the main sources of regulation or coordination. This is a common issue in processes of administrative and institutional 'unbundling' (Pollitt and Talbot, 2004), but not necessarily an unexpected or miscalculated outcome. The interests at stake in the water business and the political relevance of water as a common good might not only induce politicians to opt for provision models allowing for accountable political control, but also for some area of legal and institutional uncertainty (Crozier, 1963) that leaves them an additional share of power in local governance. What appears rather to have been an unwanted consequence of reform is the progressive centralization of water governance networks, prompted by intermunicipal integration (Italy) and especially the various forms of privatization (in all three countries), opening the way for national and multinational players to operate in a strictly oligopolistic market.[12]

NOTES

1. For example the Dublin Statement on Water and Sustainable Development of 1992.
2. The German Federal Water Act (*Wasserhaushaltsgesetz*, Article 1) states that 'the need for public water supply is to be covered giving priority to local water resources'.
3. The historical reconstruction is based on Barraqué (1995), Bigatti et al. (1997), Marquand (2004).
4. Directive 2000/60/EC of 23 October 2000, establishing a framework for Community action in the field of water policy; see Articles 2(15) and 3(1).
5. Compare Héritier (2001); the specific exclusion of water services from norms concerned with services of general interest and from the issuing of a sector-specific directive has been demanded by the European Parliament, 'in view of the distinctive regional characteristics of the sector and local responsibility for provision of drinking water', European Parliament Resolution of 13 January 2004 on the Green Paper on services of general interest [A5-0484/2003].
6. The discussion on the forms and effectiveness of control draws largely on a set of expert interviews carried out in 2006; these are listed and more amply analysed in Citroni (2007).
7. For a detailed description of the implementation process and outcomes, see Citroni et al. (2008).
8. The larger and stronger water companies – the *municipalizzate* – of Rome (Acea), Genova (Amga), Turin (Smat), compete for concessions all over Italy and even across the Mediterranean and in Latin America – while being awarded concessions without competition on their home ground.
9. Again (compare note 8), the discussion that follows is partly based on case studies more amply discussed in Citroni (2007) as well as Citroni et al. (2008).
10. See the *Antitrust authority* decision of December 2007, which condemned ACEA and Suez for forming a cartel in the competitions for water privatization in Tuscany; see also Gilardoni and Marangoni (2004).
11. See, for example, the decision of *Tribunal des Conflits* no. 3450, 21 March 2005, Mme Alberti-Sott/commune de Tournefort.
12. In France, the law of 28 May 2010 allows local governments, for exercising their competencies, to establish local public companies in which they may hold 100 per cent of the capital. Thus they will be devised to be in house companies with regard to EU law. They can be involved in development projects or in public service provision. The legislation on local mixed economy companies remains unchanged.

REFERENCES

Assemblée Nationale (2001), *Rapport d'information présenté par M. Yves Tavernier, Député, sur le financement et la gestion de l'eau*, Paris, 22 May.
Assemblée Nationale (2003), *Rapport d'information présenté par M. Jean Launay, Député, sur la gestion de l'eau sur le territoire*, Paris, 3 November.
Barraqué, Bernard (1995), *Les politiques de l'eau en Europe*, Paris: La Découverte.
Bigatti, Giorgio, Andrea Giuntini, Amilcare Mantegazza and Claudia Rotondi

(1997), *L'acqua e il gas in Italia: La storia dei servizi a rete, delle aziende pubbliche e della Federgasacqua*, Milan, Italy: Franco Angeli.

BMWA (Bundesministerium für Wirtschaft und Arbeit) (2005), *Wasserleitfaden*, Berlin.

Bogumil, Jörg and Lars Holtkamp (2002), 'Liberalisierung und Privatisierung kommunaler Aufgaben – Auswirkungen auf das kommunale Entscheidungssystem', in Jens Libbe, Stefan Tomerius and Jan Hendirk Trapp (eds), *Liberalisierung und Privatisierung kommunaler Aufgabenerfüllung*, Berlin: DIFU, pp. 71–87.

Caselli, Renata (1993), *Pubblico e privato nella gestione dei servizi pubblici locali. Uno studio per la Toscana*, Milan, Italy: Franco Angeli.

Citroni, Giulio (2007), *Tra stato e mercato: L'acqua in Italia e Germania*, Acireale, Italy and Rome: Bonanno Editore.

Citroni, Giulio, Nicola Giannelli and Andrea Lippi (2008), *'Chi governa l'acqua?' Studio sulla governance locale*, Soveria Mannelli, Italy: Rubbettino.

Conseil de la Concurrence (2000), *Avis n° 00A12 du 31 mai 2000, relatif à une demande d'avis de la Commission des finances, de l'économie et du plan de l'Assemblée nationale sur le prix de l'eau en France*, Paris.

Cour des Comptes (2003), *La gestion des services publics d'eau et d'assainissement: Rapport au Président de la République suivi des réponses des administrations et organismes intéressés*, Paris, December.

Cronauge, Ulrich and Georg Westermann (2006), *Kommunale Unternehmen. Eigenbetriebe – Kapitalgesellschaften – Zweckverbände*, 5th edn, Berlin: Erich Schmidt.

Crozier, Michel (1963), *Le phénomène bureaucratique*, Paris: Le Seuil.

Duval, Christian (2006), 'L'offre communale de service public: l'exemple français de l'eau', paper presented at the first Villa Vigoni conference on The Supply of Social and Public Services on the Municipal Level – Between Public Sector and Market. A Comparison Between Different Countries, Menaggio, Italy, 3-4 March.

Feigenbaum, Harvey B., Jeffrey R. Henig and Chris Hamnett (1999), *Shrinking the State: The Political Underpinnings of Privatization*, Cambridge and New York: Cambridge University Press.

Finger, Matthias and Jeremy Allouche (2002), *Water Privatisation: Trans-national Corporations and the Re-regulation of the Water Industry*, London and New York: Spon Press.

Fitch, Kimberly (2007), 'Water Privatisation in France and Germany: the importance of local interest groups', *Local Government Studies*, **33** (4), 589–605.

Gilardoni, Andrea and Alessandro Marangoni (2004), *Il settore idrico italiano: Strategie e modelli di business*, Milan, Italy: Franco Angeli.

Héritier, Adrienne (2001), 'Market integration and social cohesion: the politics of public services in European regulation', *Journal of European Public Policy*, **8** (5), 825–52.

Istat (Istituto Nazionale di Statistica) (1999), 'Sistema di indagini sulle acque', accessed at http://acqua.istat.it.

Kluge, Thomas, Matthias Koziol, Alexandra Lux, Engelbert Schramm, Antje Veit and Selma Becker (2003), *Netzgebundene Infrastrukturen unter Veränderungsdruck: Sektoranalyse Wasser*, netWORKS papers no 2, Berlin: Deutsches Institut für Urbanistik.

Kuhlmann, Sabine (2008), *Politik- und Verwaltungsreform in Kontinentaleuropa*.

Subnationaler Institutionenwandel im deutsch-französischen Vergleich, Baden-Baden, Germany: Nomos.

Malaman, Roberto and Stefano Cima (1998), *L'economia dei servizi idrici – Indagine sulle grandezze economiche e strutturali dell'industria dei servizi idrici in Italia*, Milan, Italy: Franco Angeli.

Marquand, David (2004), *Decline of the Public: The Hollowing Out of Citizenship*, Cambridge: Polity Press.

Ochmann, Daniela (2005), *Rechtsformwahrende Privatisierung von öffentlich-rechtlichen Anstalten, Dargestellt am Holdingmodell zur Teilprivatisierung der Berliner Wasserbetriebe*, Baden-Baden, Germany: Nomos.

OECD (Organisation for Economic Co-operation and Development) (1999), *The Price of Water – Trends in OECD Countries*, Paris: OECD.

OECD (2006), *Environmental Performance Reviews: Water: the Experience in OECD Countries*, Paris: OECD.

Pollitt, Christopher and Geert Bouckaert (2004), *Public Management Reform: A Comparative Analysis*, Oxford: Oxford University Press.

Pollitt, Christopher and Colin Talbot (eds) (2004), *Unbundled Government*, London and New York: Routledge.

Richter, Peter, Thomas Edeling and Christoph Reichard (2006a), 'Kommunale Betriebe in größeren Städten', in Werner Killian, Peter Richter and Jan Hendrik Trapp (eds), *Ausgliederung und Privatisierung in Kommunen: Empirische Befunde zur Struktur kommunaler Aufgabenwahrnehmung*, Berlin: Sigma, pp. 55–84.

Richter, Peter, Werner Killian and Jann Hendrik Trapp (2006b), 'Verselbständigung kommunale Aufgabenerbringung und die Folgen', in Werner Killian, Peter Richter and Jan Hendrik Trapp (eds), *Ausgliederung und Privatisierung in Kommunen: Empirische Befunde zur Struktur kommunaler Aufgabenwahrnehmung*, Berlin: Sigma, pp. 111–30.

Schäfer, Roland and Bernd Roreger (1998), *Kommunale Aufsichtsratmitglieder: Rechte, Pflichten, Haftung, Strafbarkeit*, Bonn: Friedrich-Ebert-Stiftung, Arbeitgruppe Kommunalpolitik.

Scheele, Ulrich (2006), *Versorgungssicherheit und Qualitäts-standards in der Wasserversorgung – Neue Herausforderungen unter veränderten Rahmenbedingungen*, netWORKS papers no 23, Berlin: Deutsches Institut für Urbanistik.

UNESCO–WWAP (United Nations Educational, Scientific and Cultural Organization – World Water Assessment Programme) (2003), *Water for People, Water for Life: The United Nations World Water Development Report*, Paris: UNESCO.

West, Karen (2005), 'From bilateral to trilateral governance in local government contracting in France', *Public Administration*, **83** (2), 473–92.

10. Comparative aspects of institutional variants for local public service provision

Giuseppe Grossi, Gérard Marcou and Christoph Reichard

INTRODUCTION

This chapter addresses the various institutional arrangements for the delivery of local public services in France, Germany and Italy. It has a comparative focus but provides an analysis of how the different institutional variants of service provision have developed over time. In particular, it examines what new arrangements have been adopted and what effects may be expected for municipal governance. The chapter is intended to offer a critical analysis of the overall structures and trends rather than an analysis based on sectoral developments (e.g. water or social care). These may be found in other chapters of the book. With regard to the broad portfolio of local services, our intention is to concentrate on services usually provided by local utilities and which are mostly traded on (regulated) markets (in EU terminology: services of general economic interest), for example infrastructure services and basic services such as water, energy and transport.

The chapter is organized as follows. It begins with an overview of institutional patterns in the three countries under study. We make a comparative analysis focusing on corporatization, that is, on the ongoing process of transforming local government units into (semi-)autonomous corporations, most with independent legal status and enjoying considerable managerial freedom. We also identify similarities and differences in patterns of service delivery.

INSTITUTIONAL PROVISION AND ORGANIZATION OF LOCAL PUBLIC SERVICES IN THE THREE COUNTRIES

France

Institutional variants of local service provision: a general overview

In France, most local services are provided by municipalities and joint authorities including public-law corporations of associated municipalities (see the 'intergovernmental' chapter for an overview). Currently, municipalities and joint authorities have to be considered together as they form the municipal level of government. Since 1 January 2008, 33 636 municipalities joined forces to constitute 2583 '*intercommunalités*', for example, multifunctional joint authorities vested with the right to levy taxes, property rights and functions assigned by the law. This leaves some choice for member municipalities. *Départements* and *régions* have a more limited role for direct service provision to the public, except for specific functions. The main focus below is on the municipal level.

In discussing public services delivered to the public locally, it is necessary to distinguish between national and local public services. National public services are commonly provided locally by national agencies. The employment service, for example, is entrusted to a 'national public institution' that helps the unemployed find jobs and provides unemployment benefit.[1] There are other examples, such as education, which is constitutionally guaranteed at all levels; tax administration; public security for events exceeding the bounds of a municipality and the management and deployment of police (under the authority of the prefect of *département*); the delivery of various licences (driving, hunting etc.). A number of local public services, such as social housing and public hospitals, are provided by public corporations under the local authority that are subject to supervision by state authorities.

Lastly, numerous local public services are provided by municipalities or joint authorities either directly (in house) through municipal mixed economy companies or by contracting out. This commonly goes by the name of public–private partnership (PPP) and is no innovation in local public service provision in France. Such arrangements may be established by concession agreements of various kinds, by contracts authorizing the occupation of public-domain premises subject to specific duties imposed in the public interest, and more recently by public procurement contracts – local government has been entrusting the management and delivery of local public utilities to private companies since the end of the nineteenth century. The recently introduced 'partnership contract' (Ord. 17 June

2004, modified 24 July 2008) is a new type of agreement proposed to government authorities, notably local authorities, offering new arrangements for some matters, in particular a single contract from design to operation paid by the authority; this is, however, considered an exception to procurement law subject to specific conditions (Const. Council 24 July 2008). This was already possible in concession agreements under which the operator is paid from operating revenues. Thus the new legislation cannot be interpreted as introducing a modern form of PPP in France. It simply continues existing practice.

Many private-law organizations are involved in social care provision. There are various types, such as local public corporations or services directly managed by the local authority or, more frequently, non-profit organizations subject to authorization and regulated tariffs. A small number of public functions are performed by municipal authorities as delegated state functions. In France this is much less frequent than in some other countries. As a result, the privatization of local public service provision has been of limited influence in France. What has sometimes proved controversial is the change in delivery arrangements. One example is granting a concession for a service previously delivered directly or, conversely, returning to in-house delivery after expiry of the concession agreement. In both cases the local authority remains legally responsible for service provision.

The legal framework of local service provision
In France, local service provision is governed by the legal principle of *service public*.[2] This means that while the activity may be organized and operated under public- or private-law rules, and performed by private companies as well as by public bodies, public-law rules are always involved in the establishment of the public service and/or in control by the public authority responsible for provision (Auby, 1997; Fialaire, 1998). On this basis, the scope of local government initiative and discretion for providing public services is subject to two restrictions: the principles of commercial and industrial freedom, and that of self-government (Constitution, Art. 72). According to the first principle, local government may not engage in commercial or industrial activities in competition with the private sector. The only exception is where the private sector fails to meet the needs of the local population. According to the second principle, local governments are vested with various functions, some of them duties (e.g. water supply) and others powers (e.g. public transport). Within the limits of the law, local governments manage autonomously the functions devolved upon them by the law. Local governments are also vested with the so-called general competence: 'the municipal council rules by [its] own deliberations [over]

municipal matters' (former municipal law of 5 April 1884). Although disputed at present, the general competence clause remains an essential ground for free local government initiatives under a liberal interpretation of administrative law. This may cause some confusion about the distribution of functions among the different levels of government.

There are other restrictions on creating local public services and on contracting them out. Some activities may not be contracted out at all (e.g. police powers or child care at schools). There are other limitations that may arise from the application of competition law and public procurement law. In France, as in other EU countries, contracts awarded to local authorities are subject to tendering rules under European law. In-house awards and in-house entities are subject to very narrow definition.

Present institutional trends in local public service provision
Institutional arrangements are available for all local government levels, and at the municipal level for both municipalities and joint authorities. However, a distinction has to be made between administrative or non-commercial public services and commercial public services, the latter being required to cover most costs from operational revenues. This distinction does not coincide with that between public-law and private-law corporate bodies or between in-house services and corporate bodies (Auby, 1997; Fialaire, 1998).

Administrative public services are delivered by local government departments, by direct management units (*régie*), or by public-law corporations. Alternatively, local governments may use a non-profit organization recognized under private law. Numerous social care services are delegated to non-profit organizations belonging to national professional bodies.

Commercial public services may be provided under various institutional arrangements. Direct provision is possible by direct management units or local public corporations. Both are called *régies*: whereas the first variant (*régie directe*) has only autonomous financial management but is still integrated into local government administration (similar to the German *Eigenbetriebe*), the second variant (*régie personnalisée*) is a legal subject separate from local government, although totally under the control of the local authority. There are centralized data on these institutions, except for *régies personnalisées*, which in 2005 numbered 496 (Rapport, 2007, p. 169). However, *régies directes*, which are quite numerous, are not included. According to their sector of activity, *régies* are subdivided as follows: 170 in electricity supply, 17 in gas supply, 30 in cable communications (most of which are incorporated; see www.anroc.com). *Régies* are also quite common in the sewage sector. More than 60 per cent of municipal sewage disposal is operated by a *régie*, most of them are not incorporated (Institut Français, 2005). In water supply, the number of *régies* is likely to increase whereas delegation to private companies is still preferred in larger municipalities; this is now a much more controversial topic (FNCCR/Régie des Eaux de Grenoble, 2008). *Régies* are also numerous for school canteens, public transport and local seaports. These are therefore likely to be more *régies* than mixed-economy companies.

The local mixed-economy company (SEML) is a common form of institution in France. It comes under local government control: the majority of seats on the board and the majority of equity have to be owned by local government. At least 20 per cent of equity must be owned by other shareholders. In fact, the overwhelming majority of the capital is public. On the basis of special legislation (law of July 2006, 'National Commitment for Housing'), there are a few local public companies in full public ownership. To assemble all these local public enterprises, the former Fédération française des SEML was transformed into the Fédération des Entreprises publiques locales in April 2008 (FEPL; see: www.lesepl.fr; the following data have been extracted from this site).

In 2008, there were 1094 local public enterprises of this kind (in the legal form of a company) with more than 51 000 employees, a turnover of €10.3 billion and a total equity capitalization of €2.8 billion. The development of this variant began in the 1960s and accelerated in the 1980s after the first decentralization reform and following new legislation on SEMLs; in 2000 there were more than 1300. Since then, there has been a decrease owing to concentration. The development of SEMLs and later of EPLs led to a diversification of their fields of activities. Whereas until the 1980s the majority of SEMLs concentrated on housing and urban development, SEMLs have since been used for all kinds of utilities. Local government holds 65 per cent of total equity, with a growing share for *départements* (8.9 per cent). The Caisse des Dépôts et Consignations (a major national public financial institution) holds 6.6 per cent. Among other shareholders, private enterprises represent 8.7 per cent and private financial institutions only 6.1 per cent. This means that privatization in industry and in the banking sector has not brought a significant increase of private equity in SEMLs.

Public service delivery may also be delegated to private (or other public) operators under a tender procedure called delegation agreement, which is always an administrative contract (Boiteau, 2007). In water supply, for instance, the public sector has a 28 per cent share and the private sector a 72 per cent share under delegation agreements. In the sewage disposal sector, the figures are 45 per cent for the public sector and 55 per cent for the private sector (BIPE/FP2E, 2008, p. 16). There are several variants of delegation agreement, the best known being the concession agreement. In so far as a 'substantial part' of the concessionaire's revenue is earned from operation, the contract is a delegation agreement; otherwise it is considered a public procurement contract. This makes a difference in tendering and decision-making procedures. Under a number of delegation agreements the operator is an agent of the local government, administering the budget of the public service, and being remunerated partly from this budget and partly on the basis of operational performance; in this case most of the risks are borne by local government.

Public procurement contracts may also be used for public service provision. From a legal point of view, the service is then rendered to the local government, although in practice users are the direct beneficiaries. Such contracts for delivering services to users are concluded for a fixed term. Local government pays from tax revenues or from charges levied from users (e.g. waste disposal).

Partnership contracts, introduced in 2004, are a new opportunity for local government to engage in different activities. The concept was developed elsewhere, one major example being the Private Finance Initiative (PFI) in the UK. PFI provides an opportunity to devolve a complex task on a company or a consortium, including the design, financing, building and operating of the infrastructure. In return, local government pays for such services and activities by periodic instalment. In France this type of contract is still considered as an exceptional procedure.[3]

A number of sectors traditionally spared the influence of market forces are now being exposed to competition in France. This does not constitute a major shift in the institutional forms of local public service provision, since contractual relations with the private sector for the delivery of public services has a long tradition (Allemand, 2007).

Germany

The legal framework of local service provision
In Germany, municipalities have limited opportunities to provide services of general economic interest. According to the various local government constitutions, if municipalities wish to offer such a service, they must fulfil three conditions that considerably limit the market activities of municipalities and of their utilities:

- the service must serve a public purpose;
- it must be restricted to the territory of the municipality;
- the municipality must be able to provide the service more cheaply than a private competitor.

The in-house provision of local services is problematic because of EU rules (see last section for more details), as well as national law. There are legal restrictions on municipalities awarding contracts if their own utilities are participating in the tendering procedure. Under German procurement law, municipalities are not allowed to award contracts to their own utilities: they are required to award them to external, private bidders. Municipalities are thus in a dilemma: while obliged to be competitive and put up services for tender, they cannot award contracts to their own utilities even if they make the best offer.

Institutional variants of local service provision: a general overview
In Germany, local governments are multifunctional authorities that offer a broad and plural choice of services to the public (see Chapter 1). Local government is the major provider of services at the local level. Federal or state authorities are only marginally involved in service provision to the public. Exceptions include police services, tax administration and labour services. Local services in Germany are traditionally provided *in*-house, by a unit of the core administration or by a local utility. Social, health or cultural services, for instance, are provided either by core departments or by non-profit organizations. Services closer to the market and which involve technical infrastructure and expertise such as energy and water supply, transport and so on are usually provided by municipally owned utilities. In many municipalities there is a single multi-utility, the *Stadtwerke* ('city works'), which integrate the various infrastructure services and sometimes cross-subsidize loss-generating sectors such as transport by more profitable segments such as power.

Autonomous municipal corporations Over the last two decades, German local government has experienced strong corporatization. Although municipalities have established corporations in the past, the trend towards corporatization increased remarkably after 1990. This is in line with trends in other countries (Verhoest et al., 2004). The major motives behind the increase in corporatization at the local level are to provide more flexibility and competitiveness (arm's-length operation), to reduce (party-) political influence, and to increase efficiency. Furthermore, municipalities have seen corporatization as an opportunity to escape from various legal restrictions: for example, civil service law, budgetary law and public procurement law.

In Germany, local government as a whole owns some 4000 corporations, about 20 per municipality[4] (Edeling et al., 2004; Richter et al., 2006; Bremeier et al., 2006). The role of corporations in municipal service provision is quite remarkable. About 50 per cent of the municipal workforce is employed in corporations; the remaining 50 per cent are in core administration (Richter et al., 2006, p. 61). Municipal corporations are organized in different legal forms. There are several public-law types, for example, the semi-autonomous utility (*Eigenbetrieb*) or the institution of public law (*Anstalt*). However, the most widespread type today is the limited company (GmbH) (73 per cent). The role of joint stock companies is rather limited at the local level (4.9 per cent).[5]

Particularly smaller (rural) municipalities use various patterns of public–public collaboration to achieve economies of scale. They establish consortia or special-purpose associations (*Zweckverband*), or collaborate in more informal ways. Examples are to be found in such sectors as water, sewage and waste disposal, schools and hospitals.

Public–private partnership (PPP) In Germany, the PPP or mixed-economy corporation is of long standing. Private commercial partners are involved in 40 per cent of all local corporations (Edeling et al., 2004). Thus a large part of local utilities is not 'public' in the sense of pure public ownership but may best be described as hybrid enterprises involving both the public and private sectors. In recent years there has been an increasing tendency to sell shares in utilities to private partners. This is due to local authority financial straits. The contractual PPP is another, more recent, variant: municipalities invite private business firms to collaborate in investment projects, for example to renew local infrastructure. The private partner usually finances and sometimes manages the project, for example, under leasing or 'Build–Operate–Transfer' (BOT) schemes. Contractual PPPs are currently in fashion in Germany: every second German municipality is involved in such partnerships (DIFU, 2005). Consultants and private financing institutions promise greater cost-savings than 'purely public solutions'. The long-term effects and risks are, however, unsolved problems. It is also unclear how PPPs will function in times of economic recession.

Contracting-Out In contrast to France, contracting out local services to private business firms has not attracted much attention in Germany (apart from usual procurement activities, e.g. road construction or the maintenance of municipal buildings). It is only recently that municipalities have been more active in contracting out services, and this is likely to prove controversial. Contracting out to private non-profit organizations (NPOs) is another matter: municipalities have been contracting out services for many decades in, for example, social care. Due to the subsidiarity principle, private welfare associations and other NPOs participate in the provision of local services. This trend has increased in the past ten to 15 years.

Private providers now operate in many other local public service sectors, for example, infrastructure maintenance, housing, public transport, waste disposal, water or energy, but also in internal services like office cleaning or IT services (Bogumil et al., 2007).

Privatization At the local level in Germany, material privatization – the complete transfer of a public task to a private provider, including responsibility for ensuring provision – has been rare. Certain municipalities have indeed sold some assets in the past, and also privatized services. However, compared with other levels of government and with other countries, privatization has been relatively limited. Due to the continuing fiscal crisis, the level of privatized services has increased in recent years (Libbe et al., 2002). It is unclear what the future holds, as finance is now more limited than in the past.

As a whole, German local government has undergone many institutional changes in the last two decades: local authorities have broadened the scope of municipal corporations, stepped up collaboration with public and with private partners, contracted out some services to NPOs (rather than private business), and privatized some local services. Generally speaking, German municipalities remain the principal providers of a large variety of local services (Reichard, 2006).

Italy

Institutional variants of local service provision: a general overview

From a historical point of view, the Italian government is a unitary system with recent trends towards a (quasi-)federal system (see the 'intergovernmental' chapter). Local government is entrusted to provinces and municipalities. Municipalities are responsible for delivering services such as water supply and sewage disposal, local transport, local road maintenance, child education, services for the disabled, the elderly, and children (see Chapters 4 and 5), municipal police, building planning and control, recreational services, libraries and cemeteries. Provinces are responsible for transport services, environmental protection and control, supervision of fishing and hunting, rural and urban planning, vocational education, high-school building maintenance, and so on.

The institutional landscape of public services at the local level in Italy is as follows:

- *Corporatization* depending on their size, Italian municipalities directly and indirectly own numerous corporations. Larger cities, in particular, directly control a number of municipal corporations, many dating

far back and providing a wide range of services (transport, energy, waste collection, water, cultural services, etc.; see Grossi, 2007).
- *Public–public collaboration* has become an issue in recent years; local governments and municipal corporations have opted for various forms of joint venture, including mergers and consortia. The traditional choice, especially in small and medium local governments, have been intermunicipal associations (*consorzi*), to which member municipalities devolve the provision of public services and internal services such as building maintenance, IT services, administrative services, catering, or office cleaning (Bobbio, 2005).
- *Public–private partnerships* (PPP) are one of the latest institutional trends at the local level. Approximately 25 per cent of Italian municipalities have already been involved in 'territorial pacts' (a form of agreement between local governments and private interests designed to improve local growth); and nearly 30 per cent of all municipal corporations are organizational PPPs, that is, in mixed, private–public ownership (Confservizi, 2006), operating especially in the utilities sector (water, energy, etc.; Grossi, 2005, 2007).
- *Contracting out* local public services to private corporations and NPOs has increased remarkably in recent years. Municipalities have contracted out whole or parts of service packages to private commercial or non-profit firms (Dipartimento della Funzione Pubblica, 2006). Contracting out has been particularly important in social and cultural services, but also in internal services.

The legal framework of local service provision

The Italian legal framework for local services of general interest is complex and continuously changing. Apart from EU legislation, the local government act, several sectoral national laws (e.g. on energy, water, waste, transportation and various regional general and sectoral laws) have to be respected. In line with EU terminology, current national regulations differentiate between services that are or are not of 'general economic interest'. The law offers three options for services of general economic interest:

1. a joint stock company commissioned by public tender;
2. direct assignment to an organizational PPP in which the private partner is chosen by public tender;
3. direct assignment to a joint stock company totally owned by a local government, on condition that the local authority exercises control over the company as over its own services, and that the company delivers the greater part of the service with the local authority that owns it.

For services not of general economic interest, the legislation appears more flexible as it allows local authorities to choose among the following solutions:

1. direct assignment to institutions, special undertakings (also consortia) or wholly publicly owned joint stock companies on the condition mentioned above in case (3);
2. direct management when, due to the limited size or the nature of the service, entrusting it to other entities would not be advantageous;
3. in the case of cultural and recreational services, direct assignment to local government associations or foundations or such organizations in which local authorities participate.

COMPARATIVE ANALYSIS: FRANCE, GERMANY AND ITALY

Important Commonalities and Differences

Germany and Italy share certain past developments, the two countries having begun the in-house provision of local services in the early twentieth century when local utilities were established. For many decades, these local utilities provided the population with many services. They were loosely linked to the municipality and subject to fairly weak political control. With the rise of neoliberal thinking in the 1980s, and particularly under the influence of EU deregulation, local government and utilities came under severe pressure, having to adapt to increasing competition from private business to retain their traditional markets. Local authorities accordingly started to diversify from the established institutional arrangements for public service delivery. In France, by contrast, the private sector was early involved in providing local public services. From the beginning, private partners collaborated in delivering urban services such as public transport, gas and electricity supply, street lighting, water and so on. The usual explanation of this peculiarity is the extreme fragmentation of municipalities in France. However, this explanation is not sufficient because the development of these services took place in cities, not in rural areas. Another possible explanation is the ban on local authorities engaging in any industrial activities since the time of the French Revolution, the famous *Décret D'Allarde* that established the principle of 'industrial and commercial freedom', later developed and protected by administrative case law. This prohibition was mitigated in 1920, but by then the legal tools for public service provision by private providers were fully developed. As a result, the current 'new' ideas of PPP and the privatization component of the new public management doctrine had limited impact in France. France has also maintained its respect for the public service, and this may also be reflected in the attitude of French municipalities to change.

Increasing institutional diversity
At the first glance, similar trends in institutional development at the local level are apparent in all three countries. The first is corporatization, that is, the transformation of administrative units into self-standing corporations. This is not a new tendency: it has been in evidence for more than a century. However, in the past two decades municipalities have broadened the scope of semi-autonomous utilities by transforming not only units from the traditional utilities sector but also entities from the social or cultural sector into corporations. The proportion of the municipal workforce employed by autonomous entities is as follows: France: 16 per cent, Italy: 30 per cent, Germany: nearly 50 per cent. In France the development of SEMLs, especially after the 1980s, may also be interpreted as a trend towards corporatization. However, there are major differences: SEMLs usually work with private contractors, and as a result their workforce as well as their equity is notably smaller than those of municipal companies in, for instance, Germany.

The next institutional variant is also not new: public–public collaboration. This has been for decades a prime option for many small municipalities, which have established consortia or merged utilities. However, collaboration among local authorities in service delivery on a joint basis has become more attractive in recent years. Consortia and similar arrangements are accordingly common in all three countries. In France, for instance, SEMLs often function as a form of public–public cooperative venture, since several local authorities share in the equity and appoint a joint board. Mergers of local utilities, in contrast, seem to be more popular in Italy, where local utilities often merge to constitute large-scale corporations (e.g. the Hera SpA in Emilia-Romagna). Public–public collaboration is likely to increase in future, not least because of the potential offered by ICT, for example for a joint back office located in one authority serving front offices in several authorities (shared service centres).

Public–private partnerships (PPPs) are now much in favour in Italy and Germany; they have long been established practice in France. The main motive behind the PPP trend is the need for municipalities to access new financial sources, primarily for infrastructure projects. PPPs are strongly supported by the private sector because they offer a profitable new business field where most risk is borne by public authorities. Another argument for the attractiveness of PPP might be that partnership contracts favour big enterprises and banks, as only they seem to be qualified to organize a consortium able to handle big projects throughout their life cycle. Partnership agreements can therefore promote business coalitions on domestic and European markets with better prospects for international competition. The increasing influence of private business firms on local utilities may, however, lead to goal and interest conflicts among partners, between market-led decisions and public policy goals.

Contracting out of local services has been a well-established practice in the three countries for many decades. Ancillary services (e.g. building or road maintenance) have long been outsourced there. The same is true for social and health care services, which have been contracted out to welfare associations (according to the subsidiarity principle, although this is never referred to in France). However, service outsourcing has considerably increased in recent years, primarily because of fiscal pressure but also because of growing private competition, less in France than in the two other countries because of the different point of departure.

The privatization of local public services has so far played only a limited role in the three countries. Although there have been some important instances of privatization, the general trend has been either for municipalities to retain their utilities (Germany and Italy) or to continue the traditional collaboration with the private sector in local public service delivery (France).

After two decades of institutional diversification, the landscape of local service provision has changed considerably – however, much less in France than in the two other countries. Although municipalities still seek to produce and deliver services in house (again much less in France), the institutional options are now much more varied and complex. In Germany and Italy, many services are now provided in network structures where public, non-profit and commercial organizations collaborate and where municipalities perform new roles as stimulators, coordinators and financiers of such networks. Consequently, new challenges arise for steering and controlling them. In France, the major trend is to transfer several municipal public services to joint authorities (*intercommunalités*).

Legal framework of service provision

The national legal restrictions of public service provision are converging, although not always interpreted strictly. The German local utilities are less flexible in their business activities. They are bound by three restrictive pillars (*Schrankentrias*), which means that the services they are offering must have a clear 'public purpose', they must be restricted to the own territory and they must be offered at a cheaper price compared with private competitors. Not surprisingly, there is a continual struggle between the

Länder governments, the chambers of commerce and the utilities' associations about the interpretation of a 'public purpose' and about the pricing rules. In France, administrative case law seemed to depart from these limits in the early 2000s, but the Conseil d'Etat has reaffirmed in 2006 that public authorities, when taking economic initiatives, are bound by the limit of their competence, the purpose of their services must be in the public interest (particularly if the private initiative is failing) and they have to take care not to distort competition (CE Ass. 31 May 2006, 'Ordre des Avocats au Barreau de Paris', no. 275531).

If we compare the situation in the three countries, there is another obvious commonality: the influence of the EU legislation and of decisions of the European Court of Justice on the national legal framework. This is because all services of general economic interest, as defined under Article 86.2 of the Treaty on the European Community, are subject to the rules on competition, unless these rules impede the realization of their mission in conditions compatible with the viability of the enterprise. According to the EU Court, if a local authority decides to devolve the operation of a public service to a private company, it must use a competitive procedure. This is even the case if the authority itself has created a local enterprise to deliver the respective service, unless it is able to exercise the same control over it as over its administrative services (this is known as the 'in-house' exception). For the Court, it suffices that the said company has external shareholders, even in a minority position, to invalidate the exception (Rodriguès, 2007). As a result of these EU policies, the freedom of local authorities to choose how to manage their local services is restricted, even though this freedom has long been considered to be an important part of local self-government in many countries (France, Germany, Spain etc.), notwithstanding that some other countries have sought to restrict local autonomy in this respect to open up the market (Italy and the UK, in particular; see Marcou and Wollmann, 2008, p. 221).

Legal forms of local utilities
The general patterns of legal forms are quite similar in the three countries under comparison. In each of them we find several public-law-based forms as well as some private commercial-law-based types. In Germany and Italy there is a clear trend to transfer utilities from public-law status into a private-law form. In France, local utilities usually have the status of dependent units of the municipality, of a more autonomous public law-based corporation (*régie*) or of an SEML (in the legal form of a joint stock company) Table 10.1 presents a picture of the various legal forms used for local utilities in the three countries.

While French utilities either have a public-law status (*régie*) or are joint

Table 10.1 The variety of legal forms of local utilities

Law base	Type of legal form	France	Germany	Italy
Public law	Semi-autonomous utility	*Régie autonome*	*Eigenbetrieb*	*Istituzione*
	Autonomous institution of public law	*Régie personnalisée*	*Anstalt*	*Azienda speciale*
	Consortium (owned by several LGs)	*Syndicat*	*Zweckverband*	*Consorzio*
	Foundation of public law, public or private law based	Not relevant	*Stiftung* (mostly for cultural affairs)	*Fondazione* (for social and cultural services)
Private law	Association, private law based	*Association de la loi de 1901*	*Eingetragener Verein* (only rarely used for cultural or social services)	*Associazione* (primarily for social and cultural services)
	Cooperative, private law based	Not relevant	*Genossenschaft* (usual in housing)	*Cooperativa* (usual in social services)
	Limited company, totally or partly owned by LGs	*Société à responsabilité limitée* (legally not allowed, only with government authorization; very few cases)	*Gesellschaft mit beschränkter Haftung* (GmbH)	*Societá a responsabilitá limitata*, designed for small-scale activities (min. equity: €10 000)
	Joint stock company, totally or partly owned by LGs	SEML and a small number of *sociétés publiques locales*	*Aktiengesellschaft* (AG)	*Societá per azioni* (min. equity: €120 000)

Source: Summary by the authors.

stock companies (SEMLs), the utilities in the other two countries are mostly joint stock companies (Italy: 58 per cent) or limited companies (Germany: 73 per cent). These differences can be explained by different legal restrictions concerning the two legal types: in Italy the limited company seems not to be very attractive because it only applies to smaller utilities and is less able to raise new capital sources. In Germany, in contrast, the limited company is very attractive because it offers flexible opportunities to regulate the governance structures and promises sufficient managerial freedom. The joint stock company, in contrast, is attractive in Italy, as local utilities have the opportunity to register at the Stock Exchange and thus have easy access to the capital market. In Germany, there are only very few cases of local utilities 'going public', and furthermore, the governance mechanisms of German stock-company law are thought to be too heavily in favour of the autonomy of the corporation and thus do not allow much external influence by the owning municipality. French legislation is close to Italian legislation in this respect.

Governance issues of local utilities

Municipalities play two different roles in governing corporations: they are owners (shareholders) and they are contractors (purchasers) and regulators of services. Both roles can be conflictual. Governance mechanisms have to take account of this double role. Governance mechanisms in the three countries depend largely on commercial law, that is, the law on limited liability companies and stock corporations in Germany, the commercial code in France or the Italian Codice Civile. This legislation focuses on the shareholders' interests and provides no mechanisms in favour of the purchasers' role.

Apart from this general deficit, there are several differences between national governance systems. Italian corporations are based mainly on a one-tier board system (executive board with internal and external directors), and the shareholders' meeting is quite influential. Additionally, there is a board of auditors, which inspects the financial reports. The executive board is composed of professionals and former politicians. Germany's corporations – limited liability companies or stock corporations (*Gesellschaft mit beschränkter Haftung*, GmbH or *Aktiengesellschaft*, AG) – are governed by a two-tier system: a supervisory board (*Aufsichtsrat*) decides on general strategy and exercises oversight. This board is composed of council members (i.e. politicians) and, according to German co-determination law, of employee representatives. The second body is the board of directors (*Vorstand*). The shareholders' meeting usually does not play an important role. Financial auditing is the responsibility of the internal revision unit of the municipality and in most cases of private auditing firms, as well. The situation of SEMLs in France is very similar. Obviously, the influence of the municipal council on the corporation is much stronger in Germany and France than in Italy. While Italian council members are not allowed to sit on the board, this is the normal practice in Germany and is required in France. However, Italian politicians find ways to circumvent such regulations, for example by appointing former councillors to the board. Furthermore, in France the council itself regularly deals with utility issues, which is not so much the case in Italy. In fact, utility matters are more likely to be politicized in France and Germany than in Italy, while patronage problems may arise in all countries.

As the data have shown, holding structures in the three countries are quite complex: municipalities (in France primarily larger authorities) directly or indirectly own a series of corporations. French municipalities sometimes own a share in several SEMLs because several local governments can participate in one SEML. In Germany, it is not unusual for large cities to form a holding (*Konzern*) with sometimes several hundred corporations. Municipalities are thus 'municipal corporate groups'. The patterns of administrative steering in these holding groups are quite similar in Germany and Italy, and often show major management shortcomings in coordinating and controlling the group (see Grossi and Reichard, 2008 for details).

INTERPRETATION AND DISCUSSION

Reasons for institutional change

The various changes in the three countries are attributable to many different influences and causes. One major driver common to all countries is the never-ending local government financial crisis, which has forced municipalities to cut budgets and look for more efficient ways to provide service. They have sought to cut costs by autonomizing administrative units and integrating private capital. Second, municipalities have adopted currently popular private sector patterns (mimetic isomorphism). Private business companies have also succumbed to such influences: they have split into smaller units, outsourced much production, collaborated with others (e.g. in joint ventures). An influential consultancy industry has also influenced current fashions, persuading city managers to try the new solutions. The neoliberal mainstream that has led the ideological debates of the last two decades is another explanatory factor. Many politicians – perhaps less so in France – accepted the general conviction that the private sector was superior to the public sector. Municipalities accordingly opted for 'private' solutions wherever possible and were attracted by PPP models or contracting-out strategies.[6] Narrowly associated with this trend was the 'new public management' (NPM) movement of the past two decades, which had less influence in France (e.g. GRALE, 2008). Part of this doctrine was the establishment of autonomous and responsible, single-purpose entities and the strengthening of markets and competition. NPM encouraged a shift towards autonomous units and more competition by contracting out local services. Finally, there were strong incentives to establish autonomous entities: local politicians expected new influence and power as members of the board of a municipal corporation. They were accordingly in favour of autonomization. Even the heads of the different units expected higher remuneration if the units became autonomous corporations.

Apart from these more ideological or cultural factors, institutional change was doubtless also a result of the changes in legislation: the EU Commission and national governments gradually stepped up the pressure on local authorities and their utilities to provide local services in an open market framework. Local or regional monopolies had to be eliminated and municipalities were obliged to put out some services like energy or transport to tender. The pressure in some sectors to contracting out was thus considerable.

However, change differed in intensity from country to country. While the situation in France remained quite stable, developments in Germany and Italy were much more turbulent. To some extent this can be explained by divergent historical backgrounds and differing contextual factors: French *communes* have always been very small on average, and needed outside help to provide local services in a professional manner. They hence opted either for public–public collaboration (consortia of *communes*) or commissioned private firms to provide services. Some of these firms became very large and powerful over time and are now big global players in public infrastructure and services (for example, Veolia, Suez etc.). Interestingly, despite its well-known étatisme, the French government has never had serious reservations about large private companies providing essential services.

German trajectories of change again have their path-dependencies: German cities have enjoyed considerable independence for centuries. With emerging industrialization, they soon set up their own utilities to provide local services like water, sewage and waste disposal, energy and transport. These city works expanded over time. In rural areas, local authorities opted quite early for intermunicipal collaboration and established consortia. In the last few decades, financial straits have induced municipalities to involve private firms as partners in municipal utilities, thus developing more and more of a 'mixed economy' and institutional PPPs. The other institutional variants – contracting out and privatization – have emerged only in recent years, as a consequence of the opening of markets, the fiscal crisis and neoliberal mainstream policy.

As in Germany, current developments in Italy include corporatization, institutional PPPs, and intermunicipal collaboration through corporations or consortia involving several local governments. An Italian peculiarity is the growing aggregation of municipal corporations and their stock exchange listing.

Effects of institutional change

Although there is little empirical evidence, it can be assumed that the change to the new institutional patterns has had at least some positive effects: there is some evidence that corporatization increases efficiency and managerial flexibility, also in financial terms (for Germany, see, e.g., Bogumil et al., 2007). Some evaluations of PPP projects also show positive economic effects, for example cost-savings, shorter project duration, more professional management of infrastructure construction projects but also of the production and delivery of services (for Germany, e.g., see DIFU, 2005). In France, the new legislation on partnership contracts has so far had little impact, partly because of restrictive legal conditions. Contracting out and privatization again sometimes seem to have had positive economic effects. There is evidence that private contractors operate more efficiently, partly because of specialization advantages, partly because of lower wages in the private sector.

On the other hand, the new institutional patterns are likely to produce unintended negative effects. All institutional variants may be problematic with regard to efficiency gains. Lower production costs may be set off by higher transaction costs. Corporatization, as the first variant, may have particularly negative side effects: the establishment of a variety of autonomous corporations was an opportunity for local governments to hide their liabilities and debts. In Germany, for instance, about 50 per cent of all local debts are allocated to local corporations. As long as no consolidated financial reporting exists, these debts remain opaque and give municipalities more freedom in financial management. In Italy, corporatization has mainly been due to the need to transfer personnel costs out of local government budgets. This allows local governments to respect the limits set by the European stability pact. Consolidated financial statements are a new trend in large cities, especially in central and northern Italy. If they become more common, this may have a negative impact on corporatization.

There is also some evidence that the managers of autonomous local utilities tend to value change. They are increasingly profit-seeking and show a lack of public-purpose focus. This can mean the increasing commercialization of local services. There is also some evidence that ethical problems in municipal groups are increasing, for instance in the form of 'decentralized corruption': a municipal group with its variety of autonomous corporations offers new opportunities for unethical behaviour. Furthermore, the ethical values of managers are more 'open' to temptation (see, for Germany, Maravic, 2007). Corporatization also allows clientelism to flourish, for example, through the recruitment of 'friends' to positions in corporations. Another effect of current corporatization is the fragmentation of municipal governance structures. Steering and controlling the new complex holding groups becomes more and more difficult. Steering problems in large municipal groups are frequently reported in both German and Italian local government. To some extent this is the result of inadequate corporate governance concepts and mechanisms (Grossi and Reichard, 2008).

As far as PPPs are concerned, there is some evidence that diverging interests between partners may endanger the stability of such organizations. Another frequently reported problem is unfair distribution of risks between partners, with most risks tending to be borne by the public partner. However, it is still too early to assess the long-term economic effects of PPP projects, as most have a life span of more than 20 years. With regard to contracting out and privatization, there is a great deal of empirical evidence about their effects for customers and governments (e.g. Weizsäcker et al., 2005). The general balance is rather mixed: apart from some – often short-term – positive efficiency effects, there are certain negative impacts, including price increases for consumers, quality problems, exclusion of some population groups from consumption, and the insolvency risk of private providers.

Generally speaking, the complexity and intransparency of the extended institutional patterns pose considerable challenges for local authorities, causing severe governance problems. The future of these structures will depend on the ability of local government to cope successfully with these complexities and to steer and coordinate service networks and their own corporations as well as their public and private counterparts. A particular problem is to ensure clear and reliable accountability structures, for example the allocation of responsibilities to contractors and providers in complex service arrangements.

Future trends

There are some arguments in favour of stability: all three countries belong to the classical European administrative states and Napoleonic governance context. Etatist structures and values are important even at the local level – and this will continue. There are some signs that the current trend of institutional diversification in Italy and Germany will not persist.

People in these countries are likely to discover that services provided by their own municipality – which they can control democratically – are 'better' than private sector alternatives. Politicians and municipal managers will realize that the efforts – and transaction costs – of coordinating and controlling external providers and autonomous entities are very high. In Germany, for instance, there are first attempts to reintegrate autonomous corporations into the municipal core and to call back outsourced services. In France, the different institutional legacies with large private providers will probably continue as the population is accustomed to it, and these private companies are politically quite influential and powerful (although a reverse trend can be observed in several sectors). In some big Italian cities (Rome, Turin, Palermo), special authorities responsible for monitoring the quality of services provided directly by local government, by municipal corporations or by external corporations (in case of outsourcing) have been established. In middle-sized cities, like Ravenna and Lucca, municipal holdings have been created to control and coordinate the activities performed by municipal corporations.

On the other hand, some services traditionally provided by local authorities are likely to be delivered by private firms in future. In some service fields like energy or telecommunication, new technologies, new forms of regulation or increased opportunities for marketing services have resulted in a shift from the public to the private sphere.

Much will depend on future developments in EU legislation and on the future financial situation. If the EU continues to hinder in-house provision and institutional PPPs, and if local finance remains critical, local governments will be more in favour of contracting out and privatization. The future of institutional PPPs – including the French SEMLs – is also doubtful in this regard: if the selection of partners for their utilities has to be based on competitive tendering, many local authorities may be very cautious. Instead of an uncertain partnering adventure, they will prefer to sell their utilities.

Finally, the 'institutional landscape' in the three countries will continue to be pluralist, with distinctive characteristics. In France, private business will continue to have a strong impact on local services while Germany and Italy will probably reduce their institutional complexity, concentrating on strong local government as service provider with reliable private partners.[7]

NOTES

1. This is a result of Law 2008-126 of 13 February 2008 on the reform of the employment service. These functions had been divided between two institutions: ANPE for assisting job-seekers and AS–EDIC for the payment of unemployment benefit.

2. In the specific French perception of a public service as an activity aiming at a public interest (or reflecting a public policy) through the provision of a service under government control.
3. It has so far found little use: among 130 projects, only 17 contracts had been signed by January 2008.
4. Numbers depend on size: large German cities, for instance, have nearly 90 companies on average (Trapp and Bolay, 2003).
5. With regard to the smaller German municipalities, the relations are slightly different (Bremeier et al., 2006): only 40 per cent of corporations of the smaller municipalities (< 50 000 inhabitants) are limited companies, 25 per cent are public consortia, 20 per cent are semi-autonomous utilities.
6. There is, however, a reverse trend in the French water and sewage sector, although it is neither general nor significant.
7. In France, the law of 28 May 2010 allows local governments, for exercising their competencies, to establish local public companies in which they may hold 100 per cent of the capital. Thus they will be devised to be in house companies with regard to EU law. They can be involved in development projects or in public service provision. The legislation on local mixed economy companies remains unchanged.

REFERENCES

Allemand, R. (2007), 'Les distributeurs non nationalisés d'électricité face à l'ouverture à la concurrence', *Annuaire 2007 des Collectivités Locales*, GRALE, Paris: CNRS.

Auby, J.F. (1997), *Les services publics locaux*, Paris: Berger-Levrault.

BIPE/FP2E (2008), *Les services collectifs d'eau et d'assainissement en France*, Boulogne, France: Billancourt.

Bobbio, L. (2005), 'Italy after the storm', in B. Denters and L.E. Rose (eds), *Comparing Local Governance. Trends and Developments*, New York: Palgrave Macmillan, pp. 29–46.

Bogumil, J., St Grohs, S. Kuhlmann and A.K. Ohm (2007), *10 Jahre Neues Steuerungsmodell – eine Bilanz kommunaler Verwaltungsmodernisierung*, Berlin: Sigma.

Boiteau, C. (2007), *Les conventions de délégation de service public. Transparence et service public local*, Paris: Dexia/Le Moniteur.

Bremeier, W., H. Brinckmann and W. Killian (2006), 'Kommunale Unternehmen in kleinen und mittelgroßen Kommunen sowie in Landkreisen', in W. Killian, P. Richter and J.H. Trapp (eds), *Ausgliederung und Privatisierung in Kommunen. Empirische Befunde zur Struktur kommunaler Aufgabenwahrnehmung*, Berlin: Sigma, pp. 25–53.

Confservizi (2006), *Annuario associate 2006. Le gestioni del sistema Confservizi*, Rome: Confservizi.

DIFU (2005), *Public Private Partnership Projekte. Eine Bestandsaufnahme in Bund, Ländern und Kommunen*, Berlin: DIFU.

Dipartimento della Funzione Pubblica (2006), *L'esternalizzazione strategica nelle amministrazioni pubbliche*, Catanzaro, Italy: Rubettino.

Edeling, T., C. Reichard, P. Richter and S. Brandt (2004), *Kommunale Betriebe in Deutschland. Ergebnisse einer empirischen Analyse der Beteiligungen deutscher Städte der GKI-4*, KGSt-Materialien 2/2004, Cologue: KGSt.

Fialaire, J. (1998), *Le droit des services publics locaux*, Paris: LGDJ.
FNCCR/Régie des Eaux de Grenoble (2008), *Séminaire des régies d'eau et d'assainissement*, Grenoble, France: FNCCR.
GRALE (2008), *Annuaire 2008 des collectivités locales*, Editions: 'Où en est la gestion locale?', Paris: CNRS.
Grossi, G. (2005), *La corporate governance delle società miste. L'esperienza in Italia e negli altri paesi europei*, Padova, Italy: Cedam.
Grossi, G. (2007), 'Governance of public–private corporations in the provision of local utilities in the Italian case', *International Public Management Review*, **8** (1), 130–51.
Grossi, G. and C. Reichard (2008), 'Municipal Corporatization in Germany and Italy', *Public Management Review*, **10** (5), 597–617.
Institut Français de l'Environnement (IFEM) (2005), *Les services publics de l'assainissement en 2004*, Paris: IFEM.
Libbe, J., S. Tomerius and J.H. Trapp (2002), *Liberalisierung und Privatisierung kommunaler Aufgabenerfüllung*, DIFU-Beiträge zur Stadtforschung, vol. 37, Berlin: DIFU.
Maravic, P.V. (2007), *Verwaltungsmodernisierung und dezentrale Korruption. Lernen aus unbeabsichtigten Konsequenzen*, Bern: Haupt.
Marcou, G. and H. Wollmann (2008), 'Europe', in CGLU (ed.), *Premier Rapport Mondial sur la Décentralisation et la Démocratie locale*, Barcelona/Paris: L'Harmattan, pp. 126–65.
Rapport de l'Observatoire des finances locales (2007), *Les finances locales en 2007*, Paris.
Reichard, C. (2006), 'New institutional arrangements of public service delivery', in C. Reichard, R. Mussari and S. Kupke (eds), *The Governance of Services of General Interest between State, Market and Society*, Berlin: Wissenschaftlicher Verlag, pp. 35–47.
Richter, P., T. Edeling and C. Reichard (2006), 'Kommunale Betriebe in größeren Städten', in W. Killian, P. Richter and J.H. Trapp (eds), *Ausgliederung und Privatisierung in Kommunen. Empirische Befunde zur Struktur kommunaler Aufgabenwahrnehmung*, Berlin: Sigma, pp. 55–84.
Rodriguès, S. (2007), *Les services publics locaux face au droit communautaire. Les exigences du marché intérieur*, Ministère de l'Intérieur, Travaux du Centre d'Etude et de Prospectives, Paris: La Documentation Française.
Trapp, J.H. and S. Bolay (2003), *Privatisierung in Kommunen – eine Auswertung kommunaler Beteiligungsberichte*, DIFU-Materialien, Berlin: DIFU.
Verhoest, K., B.G. Peters, G. Bouckaert and B. Verschuere (2004), 'The study of organizational autonomy: a conceptual review', *Public Administration and Development*, **24** (2), 101–18.
Weizsäcker, E.U. v., O.R. Young and M. Finger (eds) (2005), *Limits to Privatization: Report to the Club of Rome*, London: Earthscan.

11. From public sector-based to privatized service provision. Is the pendulum swinging back again? Comparative summary

Hellmut Wollmann and Gérard Marcou

The research group set up by GRALE with the support of the Villa Vigoni programme has investigated reforms and trends in municipal services in four European countries that reflect very different administrative traditions. The shift from public sector to privatized service provision is common to all countries, although it is less salient in France, where the private sector has been involved for a long time. Nevertheless, there is some indication that we might once again be at a turning point, with the pendulum swinging back to the public sector. This development can be summarized in four steps.

First, in line with the historical approach referred to in the introductory chapter, the historical roots of public/social service provision in the local government tradition and their profile in the advanced welfare state in the 1960s and 1970s are briefly recalled.

This is followed by summaries of the findings of the policy field chapters.

Convergence and divergence in institutional developments since the 1980s are then discussed on the basis of the sectoral policy chapters.

Finally, we consider whether traditional local government has been replaced or essentially modified by local governance.

HISTORICAL BACKGROUND OF PUBLIC SERVICE PROVISION

Historically, public utilities and social services were largely provided by local government or local charitable organizations. From medieval times, local authority responsibility for the 'local poor' made social assistance and care a crucial local commitment. In the face of the mounting sanitary and infrastructural problems caused by rampant industrialization and urbanization in the course of the nineteenth century, local authorities also came to play a key role in the provision of public services (e.g. water and energy supply, sewage disposal). Critically labelled 'municipal socialism' by contemporary conservatives, the multifunctional profile of local government amounted to an early form of a 'local welfare state' (*den lokala staten*, Pierre, 1994) that foreshadowed the emergence of the national welfare state.

There were three main aspects to the advance of the national welfare state, which, showing the handwriting of social democracy, climaxed in the 1960s and early 1970s in most countries.

First, the public sector in the advanced welfare state had extensive functions and responsibilities centred on a broad range of public and social services.

Second, functions were expected to be carried out by the public sector, that is, by public sector organizations and personnel, with the non-public non-profit and private for-profit sectors playing at best an ancillary role. The fixation on public sector delivery came first from a belief that public administrative structures and personnel were equipped (by 'self-sufficiency'; see Stewart, 2000, p. 51) to carry out the tasks in a professional and trustworthy way. Furthermore, the rationale was that elected representative bodies (parliaments and local councils) could thus best guide and control activities for the common good and in the best interests of the public (see Wollmann, 2004, p. 255 ff.).

Third, welfare state policies and services were implemented by a Weberian bureaucracy bound externally by legal rules, with hierarchical internal structures and professionalized personnel.

Whereas the institutional development of the advanced welfare state and its public sector exhibited these three aspects, which from a cross-country perspective constitute an ideal-typical, convergent macro trend, the countries under study showed significant divergence in institutional development at the micro level, mainly attributable to differences in historical tradition and path-dependence (as suggested by 'historical institutionalism') and country-specific actor constellations (as proposed by 'actor-centred institutionalism') (on the variants of 'neo-institutionalism'; see Chapter 1).

Few examples are needed to illustrate such divergence within the generally convergent macro trend.

After 1945, the macro trend towards public sector delivery of a broad range of functions and services was particularly pronounced in the UK, where, under a ('semi-socialist') Labour government, energy was nationalized in 1947, water supply in 1948, and the National Health Service was introduced in 1958. In postwar France, too, energy was nationalized (in 1946) by establishing state-owned monopolists (EdF for electricity and GdF for gas). In striking contrast, energy provision in Norway has remained the exclusive domain of a multitude of municipal hydropower companies. In Germany the energy market has been dominated by largely private capital energy companies, with municipally owned companies (*Stadtwerke*) playing a considerable role.

There is also significant divergence between the countries under study in the provision of social services within the institutional framework of the advanced welfare state.

The UK was again at the forefront in putting the public sector (local authorities) in charge of social service delivery by in-house administrative units and personnel. Until decentralization in 1982, social services in France (funded by *aide sociale légale*) were similarly delivered mostly by state employees and non-profit organizations at the level of the *département*, although largely financed by the *conseils généraux*, the elected assemblies of the *départements*. The situation has differed in Germany, where, under the 'subsidiarity' principle (a compromise between State and Church in the nineteenth century) the lion's share of social services have been provided by non-public, non-profit organizations.

Finally, the countries under study also differ in public/municipal administrative structures. The common law and civil culture tradition of Anglo-Saxon and, to some degree, Scandinavian countries and the Roman law and rule-of-law tradition in continental European countries differ strongly, each providing a quite different cultural and legal setting for public administration (see Wollmann, 2000, pp. 4 ff., Pollitt and Bouckaert, 2004, pp. 52 ff.).

In the following analysis of institutional developments, the starting conditions in each country, the given mix of commonalities and differences between countries need to be taken into account to ascertain the rate and direction of convergence and divergence in policy and services.

CHALLENGES TO THE ADVANCED WELFARE STATE AND SERVICE DELIVERY SINCE THE 1980s

Since the 1980s, the model of the advanced welfare state and public sector service provision that had developed between 1945 and the early 1970s largely under social democratic auspices has been challenged and partly dismantled in three crucial dimensions:

- the functional scope of the advanced welfare state has been criticized as an excessive burden on public finance and hence on private business, and lean government has been propagated, involving the transfer of major functions to the private sector, with government limited to an enabling role in service provision;
- public sector dominance, if not monopoly of service provision, has been criticized for causing inefficiency; the introduction of market, or market-like, structures and privatization to provide competition has been promoted as the key to efficiency;
- the traditional Weberian model of administration has been criticized for giving priority to externally legal correctness over cost-efficiency and to internal hierarchical routine over responsiveness.

Three overlapping political and conceptual currents have driven change since the 1980s:

- 'neoliberalism', first promoted by the Conservative Thatcher government from 1979, aimed at replacing the allegedly 'excessive' welfare state by 'lean government';
- the new public management (NPM) movement which, again originating in Anglo-Saxon countries, sought to replace public-sector-focused Weberian administrative structures by private sector managerialist concepts;
- finally, and most importantly, EU moves to introduce market competition in key public and social services in the single European market.

SUMMARIES OF POLICY CHAPTERS

Against this background, the following summaries of the chapters on policy outline institutional convergence and divergence trends.

Pre-school child care (Chapter 4)

Pre-school child care displays strong similarities across the four countries (for example, similar approaches in child protection involving the courts and key roles for public agencies; a low level of child care provision in the early years with strong independent sectors; strong emphasis on pre-school education, with the main institutional provision linked with the regular education system, except in Germany).

In many respects, dissimilarities arise from differences in local government systems and/ or the relationship between central and local government, such as relatively uniform systems in France and the UK (with different kinds of control and monitoring in the two countries, and stronger emphasis on this kind of service in France), variations between *Länder* in Germany, greater autonomy at the regional and local levels as a source of diversity in Italy.

The strong central policy drive towards pre-school education and child care to facilitate parental labour force participation is causing some convergence. In this respect developments in Italy, the UK and Germany may be reducing differences between their systems and that of France (action against de facto diversity in Italy despite central legislation, increased central control of local authorities in the UK and federal government intervention in family policy in Germany).

Long-term Care (Chapter 5)

Until the 1970s, the UK maintained an elaborate version of the advanced welfare state, with local authorities exercising a quasi-monopoly in social services delivery, including long-term care, through municipal personnel. The self-sufficiency rationale (Stewart, 2000) of in-house delivery was backed by the assumption that local authority personnel were best equipped to provide these services. This delivery pattern changed dramatically in the 1980s when the Thatcher government adopted the neoliberal procedure of 'compulsory competitive tendering' (CCT), obliging local authorities to put service provision out to tender, which resulted in extensive outsourcing of services, including social care, to external non-public, mostly for-profit providers. Although New Labour formally revoked CCT in the late 1990s, competitive outsourcing has persisted, replacing in-house provision by contracted-out delivery by a multitude of external providers.

Until the early 1980s, social services in France, funded by *aide sociale légale,* were delivered almost entirely by government personnel and non-profit private organizations under state supervision (at the *département* level). After 1982, responsibility for social services was transferred to local authorities (*collectivités locales*) at the *département* level in a major move to decentralize traditionally centralist government. These *collectivités locales* both stocked up human resources for direct service provision and increasingly contracted them out to external providers, mostly in the non-profit (*à but non-lucratif*) sector; but this has not been a dramatic change. Indeed, decentralization in this case has involved the horizontal transfer of functions from the *préfet* and field agencies of the social affairs ministry to the *département*, included transfer of human and other resources.

In Germany, social services provision has traditionally been shaped by the 'subsidiarity principle', under which it was primarily assigned to private, non-for-profit organizations (so called 'welfare organizations', *Wohlfahrtsverbände*), which in the past divided local markets among themselves to form virtual oligopolies. Given the traditional preponderance of non-profit organizations, local authorities have played an 'enabling' role (in current NPM parlance), ensuring that such services are delivered at the local level and, where necessary, delivering them directly. In 1994 the federal Long-Term Care Insurance Act (*Pflegeversicherungsgesetz*) abolished the *Wohlfahrtsverbände* oligopoly in long-term care provision, opening the market to all providers: non-profit, for profit and municipal. This has profoundly changed long-term care provision. Domiciliary care, in particular, is now mainly delivered by private/commercial providers.

In Italy, too, personal social services were traditionally provided by non-profit, charitable organizations, often affiliated with the Catholic Church. Since the social reforms of 2000, which failed to clearly define institutional responsibilities in the intergovernmental setting, a plurality of providers, *comuni, province, regioni*, as well as the traditional non-profit organizations, have been involved.

Health Care (Chapter 6)

Health care is the sector under study where decentralization has probably been most problematic. In most countries with well-developed welfare structures, the health system as a whole has tended to be managed centrally, with other actors, among them local and regional governments, being involved in various ways and to varying extents. However, decentralization in the health system does not mean devolution to local or regional governments, although this may have been the case, as in Italy; it can also mean decentralized sectoral service delivery organizations, with local authorities participating, as in France, albeit only as stakeholders, not policy-makers, and for specific functions within the system.

It might be useful to consider the three countries under review and the role of local government in a wider, international context. Bruno Palier (2008, 2009) distinguishes three main types of health system: tax-financed national health systems; health systems based on health insurance and a mix of public and private infrastructure; and liberal health systems based on mainly private delivery and private health insurance, with only minimum public service provision. Systems do, of course, change, and countries may display features of several systems. In France, for example, the share of social contributions in the financing has diminished from 97 per cent in 1980 to about 56 per cent in 2007, whereas most of the rest has been covered by tax revenues. In Denmark and Sweden, in contrast, where health care has been financed mainly by tax revenues, the share of social contributions increased significantly from 1990 to 2005 (Cour des Comptes, 2008). Of the countries under review, Italy belongs to the first category, and France and Germany, despite their differences, to the second.

Tax-funded national health systems ensure free access to health care for all citizens, and health care is organized by the state, but they may be centralized or decentralized with respect to local or regional government. In the UK it is centralized through the National Health Service, and was recently recentralized in Norway. In Sweden and Denmark it is decentralized at the county level (regions instead of counties in Denmark since 2007), and in Italy and Spain at the regional level. Systems based on health insurance may also be more or less decentralized. France and Germany belong to this category, as well as Belgium and the Netherlands. In these countries, services are decentralized to local health insurance agencies, and not to local governments, which play only a marginal role. In Germany, the system appears to be more decentralized because of the responsibilities assigned to the *Länder*, since they manage most government functions of domestic scope. In Europe, there are traditionally few countries with a liberal health system: Ireland is one, but this system was widely adopted in Eastern Europe after the collapse of socialism. However, common to all systems is the marginal role of municipal government and the upper tier of local government (*département/ provincia/Kreis*), even if there is some room for local initiative.

This situation is a departure from historical practice and is the result of central government expanding social protection in all three countries. Where decentralization has been addressed in recent reforms, it is in managerialist terms rather than in terms of territorial decentralization.

However, the three countries differ basically in four regards: financing (taxation in Italy; insurance in Germany and France); the scope of the public sector (high in Italy and France, medium in Germany); the degree of centralization in decision-making (high in France, medium in Italy, mixed in Germany); the role of professional groups (strong in Germany, medium in France, low in Italy). But all three are under constant pressure to reform to cope with demographic developments and financial constraints. They are in search of a new balance between competition (with quasi-market procedures) and cooperation (for greater economies of scale), between centralization of health system management to meet financial challenges and decentralization of delivery to increase provider efficiency. The three countries also differ in the relationship between social and health care: whereas the two are quite separate in the UK, they are closely interlinked in Italy on the basis of health districts; and in France there is a move to link these two functions, with the *départements* in charge of social care and the new regional health agencies established by the new law of 21 July 2009 in charge of both regional health care and regional medicalized social care.

In Italy, regions (*regioni*) are now the main players, with responsibility for financing, planning and organizing the provider network, subject to central regulation to enforce constitutional rights and supervise expenditure. However, municipalities are only 'consultants', directors of local health authorities subordinated to the region. In France, hospitals were originally local public corporations headed by the mayor; over time, mayors have lost all control of hospitals, but have opposed redundancies in the health system. Decentralization has transferred mother and child health protection (*protection maternelle et infantile* – PMI) to *départements*, as well as the fight against 'social plagues', but the latter was recentralized some years later. Municipalities may be in charge of several public health tasks through their 'hygiene boards' (vaccination). The law of 2004 transferred several areas of health personnel training to the regions, and made it possible to co-finance hospital investment, but this has not been successful. For Didier Truchet, the main trend in the health system is centralization, which decentralization reform will not reverse (Truchet, 2004). This view has been confirmed by more recent reforms, even if municipal ambulatory health care is supported by the new law, especially in deprived urban and rural areas, and despite the fact that municipalities are sometimes involved in local initiatives to overcome the lack of health practitioners in their area. In Germany, too, few service areas are organized and financed by local government; following recent reforms, their main roles are in supporting local psychiatric health care and planning ambulatory nursing services. The chief future role of municipalities will probably be to coordinate health and social care.

Provision of Electricity (Chapter 8)

In the UK, where in 1947 the Labour government nationalized the entire electricity sector, both local power plants and private power companies, placing the sector under the control of a government central board, another dramatic shift took place in 1989, when the Conservative government handed the public energy sector over to private companies in a wave of asset privatization. The 1989 legislation also introduced the concept of 'unbundling', namely, the institutional separation of the three key functions of energy provision (production, transmission, distribution/supply), establishing competition in the energy sector by ensuring competitive (discrimination-free) access to transmission grids. While the neoliberal shift from public to private sector electricity supply was exceptionally abrupt and complete, it provided a conceptual and institutional model for subsequent similar, albeit less radical, moves in other EU member countries in 'marketizing' energy provision.

In Norway, where electricity had traditionally been provided entirely by the municipal sector, that is, by a large number of municipally owned hydropower companies (this exceptional circumstance being the reason for Norway's inclusion in the study), major changes in the system occurred in 1990. The hydropowered plants and short-distance transmission grid continued to be owned and operated by municipalities, but a national electricity agency was established as a key market mechanism that collects local power production, which it then sells to consumers at 'market-regulated' prices. Although Norway has formally remained outside the EU, the Norwegian marketization formula in the electricity provision concept has provided a model for EU member states.

As early as 1989, the Conservative UK government turned to wholesale asset privatization and competitive unbundling in pursuit of neoliberal innovation, and in 1990 the non-EU member Norway 'invented' a national market mechanism on the institutional basis of municipal hydro plants (see above). It was only in the course of the 1990s that other EU member states moved to make electricity provision in national energy markets more competitive. The EU played an increasingly active role in promoting this development, particularly by way of directives that EU member states were required to transpose into national legislation. The Acceleration Directive (2003/54 of 26 June 2003 and 2009/73 of 13 July 2009) obliged member states to unbundle transmission grids to ensure competitive, that is discrimination-free, access and establish national regulatory agencies to 'watchdog' competition.

The countries under study differ significantly in the timing and extent of measures taken in the course of the 1990s, depending on national particularities, especially specific starting conditions.

Since nationalization of the French energy sector in 1946, the electricity market has been dominated by the state-owned electricity company (EdF), while the small number of municipal energy corporations exempted from nationalization have played a marginal role. During the 1990s, the French government, arguably keen to maintain the position of the state-owned EdF in both national and international markets, was tardy in transposing EU directives. Although EdF was formally privatized in 2004 as a stock company (with a 30 per cent ceiling on private participation) and unbundling has been legally stipulated, EdF remains the dominant actor on the national energy market, whereas municipal companies may not expand and no new such enterprise may be established.

After nationalization of the Italian electricity sector in 1962, the energy market came to be dominated by the state-owned ENEL, while the traditional municipality-owned, often multi-utility companies (*municipalizzate*), which were exempted from nationalization, continued to play a significant role. In 1992, in response to the EU's market liberalization drive, the Italian government transformed the formally privatized ENEL into a state-owned stock company, obliging it to sell shares to outside investors (material privatization). Also in line with EU directives, an independent regulatory agency (*autorità per l'energia elettrica ed il gas*) was set up in 1997 to monitor market liberalization. The municipal companies that avoided nationalization in 1962, particularly in big cities, have not only defended their position in the energy market but have recently extended it by, for example, buying into ENEL and expanding production and transmission resources. A certain degree of remunicipalization is thus in evidence in the electricity sector.

In Germany, electricity was provided by largely privately owned stock companies with the lion's share of the market and by municipality-owned, mostly multi-utility enterprises, in first place *Stadtwerke*. In the early 1990s, the first phase of EU-promoted market liberalization had the paradoxical effect of accelerating concentration in the energy market and ushering in the market dominance of the 'Big Four' (E.on, RWE, EnBW, Vattenfall, the latter being Sweden's state-owned energy company), which increasingly acquired *Stadtwerke* by way of 'asset privatization' (*Stadtwerkesterben* = *Stadtwerke* decline). Particularly in reaction to the EU Acceleration Directive of 2003, federal legislation required unbundling from the mid-1990s, and a federal regulatory agency (*Bundesnetzagentur*) was established in 2005 to oversee developments. Despite the continuing market dominance of the 'Big Four', the *Stadtwerke* have consolidated and even reinforced and expanded their role for a number of reasons. First, they have adapted to market competition. Second, most were not required to unbundle, because the federal government – intent on protecting them against additional competition – exempted companies with fewer than 100 000 customers. Third, and politically perhaps most important, a new coalition formed between the EU Commission, the federal government and German local authorities to check the dominance of the 'Big Four' by strengthening small companies, especially *Stadtwerke*. In fact, a trend towards remunicipalizing energy provision appears to be gaining momentum as *Stadtwerke* have expanded their operations, new *Stadtwerke* have been established, and local governments have been increasingly motivated to re-enter direct service provision upon expiry of concessions. At the same time, the 'Big Four' appear increasingly disposed to give up the minority holdings they had acquired in *Stadtwerke*. In sum, although the 'Big Four' still dominate the German energy market, the municipal sector appears to be regaining ground through remunicipalization and expanding its market share, as evidenced by the recent spectacular acquisition of an E.on subsidiary by a *Stadtwerke* consortium for €3 billion.[1]

Water Provision (Chapter 9)

In the UK, water provision was transferred from a multitude of local enterprises to ten public regional water authorities in 1974, thus coming under indirect state control. In 1989, in line with the Conservative government's neoliberal faith in the private sector and market forces, water provision was privatized, being sold to private British and international companies.

In France, the municipalities (*communes*) have been traditionally responsible for water provision. Since the late nineteenth century, urban services have been developed primarily by various kinds of concession agreement, in particular for water supply. This was stepped up in the late twentieth century in the prevailing enthusiasm for private sector service delivery, despite disputes about payments to political parties. In 1993, legislation enforced transparency in contracting procedures. Direct water supply by a municipal enterprise is more widespread in smaller communities or joint authorities or in those with local resources. Seventy-two per cent of the population are served by private suppliers, among which three companies hold over 95 per cent of the market.

In Germany, water supply, also traditionally a local government task, is still highly fragmented, being operated by some 6500 enterprises, mostly in-house municipal administrative entities or formally privatized municipal companies, the latter primarily in the form of multi-utility *Stadtwerke*. Particularly for budgetary reasons, municipalities began during the 1990s to sell off their water facilities either fully or in part to both domestic and international private companies, such as RWE and E.on, Veolia Water – previously Vivendi – and Suez. One much-publicized example was the 50 per cent sale of the Berlin waterworks to RWE and Veolia in 1999. However, more than 80 per cent of the German population are still serviced by municipal water facilities. In the municipalities and cities concerned, for instance in Berlin, a public debate about the remunicipalization of water supply has recently been gaining momentum.

In Italy, too, water provision was a traditional responsibility of the individual municipalities (*comuni*). Because of the great number and comparatively small size of municipalities (8100 municipalities averaging 7200 inhabitants), this has caused the organizational 'pulverization' (Citroni's term) of water supply. In reaction to this development, in 1994 national legislation (*Legge Galli*) sought in 1994 to overcome this organizational fragmentation by a scheme for the technical and economic optimization of water supply. 'Agencies of optimal territorial scope' (*autorità di ambiti territoriali ottimale*, ATOs) were established throughout the country with four main institutional features. First, they generally coincide territorially with the 110 *province*, with competence to define their territorial coverage lying with the *regioni*. Second, they are organized on lines similar to those of the intermunicipal bodies, *consorzi*, whose decision-making bodies are composed of the mayors (*sindaci*) of member *comuni*. Third, each ATO is expected to integrate the entire water provision cycle (source, transmission, supply, and wastewater disposal) horizontally in a single enterprise, private or public. Fourth, the commissioning and contracting out of these services is to be subject to competitive public tendering. In sum, the ATO concept is complex but remarkably innovative in that it aims to overcome the territorial and functional fragmentation of the entire water cycle, involving local actors (mayors) and introducing NPM-inspired competitive tendering. In view of the novelty and complexity of the scheme, it is no surprise that the ATO architecture has so far had a relatively slow start. By 2006, 91 ATO (of the 103 *province*) had been established, in a considerable number of cases with foreign companies as minority shareholders (see Chapter 9). As a result, there has been a privatization effect as the ATO scheme has opened up to the private sector and actually invited private companies, not least international water companies, to become involved.

Waste Management **(Chapter 7)**

While waste collection and disposal was another classical local government responsibility prompted by sanitary and health concerns, waste-related issues have been on the national policy agenda since the 1970s, along with growing environmental concerns, and have also increasingly been taken up by the EU by way of directives with a particular focus on landfill reduction.

In Germany, the 1972 Waste Management Act (*Abfallgesetz*) introduced a distinction between household and industrial waste – with counties (*Kreise*) and county-free cities (*kreisfreie Städte*) being responsible for household waste, while industrial waste management, particularly recovery, was to put on the market as proposed by the EU. Municipalities have usually outsourced operations to municipal corporations and to mixed or private sector companies, the latter becoming more and more prevalent (see Bogumil and Holtkamp, 2006, 2008).

In France, waste management is the responsibility of municipalities, which outsource to municipal companies, often in the form of intermunicipal bodies (*syndicats*), and to external, mostly private, companies. While just 13 per cent of waste management is handled by municipal companies, the lion's share goes to private companies, essentially two large private enterprises, Veolia-Environnement (formerly Compagnie Générale des Eaux) and STA-Suez (formerly Lyonnaise des Eaux).

In Italy, too, waste management was traditionally handled by municipalities (*comuni*) and intermunicipal bodies (*consorzi*). In response to widespread inefficiency, the Italian government introduced an entirely new institutional scheme of ATOs in 2006 on the same lines as those introduced in 1994 in the water sector. The territorial coverage of waste management ATOs is hence defined by the regions (*regioni*), and organized in intermunicipal form (*consorzi*), horizontally integrating the full waste management cycle and operated by a single company selected by competitive tendering. So far, the strikingly novel and complicated system of waste management ATOs has been slow in getting off the ground (see Citroni and Lippi, 2009). Inefficiency and corruption in waste management in the southern region of Campana prompted central government to install a special regime (*poteri commissariali*) in 1996 to regain direct control of waste management in the region (see Iannello, 2007).

In the UK, responsibility for waste management lies with counties and unitary authorities. Since 1990, they have established ('arm's-length') local authority waste disposal companies which have outsourced waste management to waste disposal contractors, either local government-owned entities or, in most cases, private commercial companies. In 1995, a country-wide regulatory quango, the Environment Agency, was established.

CONVERGENCE OR DIVERGENCE?

The trends discussed invite a somewhat ambivalent, if not contradictory, conclusion. On the other hand the model of the advanced welfare state with its essentially public-sector-centred concept of service delivery has been profoundly affected by the combined onslaught of neoliberal concepts ('lean government'), NPM tenets ('marketization') and EU policy ('market liberalization'). Both the extent of public sector involvement and its organizational forms have changed enormously. A convergent mega trend is apparent from public-sector-based service provision to privatized, in part marketized, provision.

On the other hand, there is significant divergence between the countries under study in developments at the micro level within and notwithstanding this general trend with the role of local government differing significantly from sector to sector and country to country.

In key analytical dimensions, these shifts can be summarized as follows.

Material/Asset Privatization

The public sector has retreated most conspicuously where government has abandoned public ownership and operation, and transferred assets to private ownership. The UK offers the most pronounced example. After nationalizing the energy and water sectors after 1945, Britain, in pursuit of neoliberal policies, led the way in the 1980s in selling off these sectors.

When, from the 1990s, France and Italy – having transformed their market-dominating, state-owned electricity enterprises into private stock companies – sold holdings to private investors, they fell short of significant asset privatization, particularly in the case of France.

Formal/Organizational Privatization

Under formal/organizational privatization, also referred to as 'corporatization' (see Chapter 10), public services are transferred to organizations, which, while still publicly owned, particularly by local authorities, are organizationally and financially self-standing. In the past, local authorities often used such 'para-public' or 'para-municipal' entities to gain a measure of organizational flexibility. The Italian *municipalizzate* and German *Eigengesellschaften* (*Stadtwerke*) – often multi-utilities – are cases in point. This also applies to mixed or hybrid, public–private enterprises such as *sociétés d'économie mixte locales* (SEML) in France, which enable municipalities to establish cooperative ties with the private sector.

While corporatized forms of municipal service provision have long been well entrenched in local government practice, they have recently expanded significantly as local authorities, in obedience to NPM concepts, have sought to increase organizational and budgetary flexibility by transferring in-house activities to corporatized, municipality-owned entities. In German municipalities, for instance, up to 50 per cent of personnel were formally employed in corporatized units (see Chapter 10).

Outsourcing, Contracting out, Commissioning

Outsourcing or contracting out describes an organizational form of public service provision in which the local authority is responsible for providing the service (in NPM parlance: 'enables' provision), which is, however, delivered by an external, non-profit, for-profit or public operator under a short- or long-term contract.

Outsourcing has long since been established local practice, particularly in France, where *gestion déléguée* now covers a wide range of contractual arrangements deriving from the former concessionary model with the purpose of contracting out service delivery and eventually investment costs. Common to all variants is that a substantial proportion of the operator's earnings must come from operational results, so that the operator bears part of the risks. Such contractual arrangements have been used since the end of the nineteenth century for all urban services, especially water and energy supply, sewage disposal and urban transport. Public procurement contracts have also been used in contracting out service delivery under direct local government responsibility, in particular for refuse collection and waste management.

Since the 1980s, neoliberal policy and NPM approaches, introducing the imperative of competitive tendering, have reduced local authority in-house delivery of social services in favour of competitive outsourcing to external, preferably private, providers. After devolution of social services to the *département* level in France, contractual outsourcing also expanded. In Germany, too, the market for long-term care has been oriented on competitive outsourcing since 1994.

Such forms of contractual, in part competitive, outsourcing have been extended to an array of public services originally provided by local authorities themselves either in house or in corporatized form, and have increasingly been taken over by outside providers, often operating on a commissioned/contractual basis. Italy's ATO schemes for water supply and waste management, under which services are outsourced to outside providers by competitive tendering, have created a notable opportunity for outside providers.

Intra-administrative Managerialism

Finally, mention should be made of local authority intra-administrative reforms since the 1990s, embarked on under the influence of the international NPM debate (see Chapter 3). To overcome shortcomings attributed to the traditional, Weberian model of administration, private sector managerialist concepts were introduced, such as 'de-hierarchized' resource management and control. In France, discourses on the 'entrepreneurial city' flourished in the 1980s, but failed to take root, probably because of the traditional involvement of the private sector in municipal service delivery. Nevertheless there was a genuine, albeit piecemeal, trend towards performance management, partly under the influence of state budgetary reform. In Germany, municipalities revamped their internal organization, adopting a 'holding model' (*Konzernstruktur*) borrowed from the business sector – with traditional departments treated as 'profit centres', the traditional mayor as 'CEO' and the local council as a kind of stockholder meeting (see Bogumil and Holtkamp, 2008, pp. 93 ff.).

ASSESSING PROS AND CONS OF SERVICE PROVISION PRIVATIZATION

Ideal-typically, traditional multifunctional service delivery by the public sector was premised on the assumption that the public was best served if services were delivered by public personnel and if elected local councils were thus able to act as guardians of the common good and the interests of the local community. Local providers operated essentially for and within the community, constituting a 'protected' territorial market, if not a quasi-monopoly.

Since the 1980s, this model of public service provision has been increasingly confronted by the assumption, promoted by EU market liberalization policy, that the common interest would best be served by a single European market for goods and services that would eliminate the price inefficiency and quality distortions inherent in service provision by local markets. Service provision by the multifunctional, quasi-monopolist municipal sector and its Weberian bureaucracy was to be replaced by a plurality of single-purpose outside providers selected by competitive tendering, each intent on making a profit but ideally competing in price and quality (for a discussion of multifunctional, public-regarding versus single-purpose, private-regarding logic see Wollmann, 2004; Wollmann and Bouckaert, 2006).

Since the 1980s, the transformation of the public sector, which has affected service provision in the countries under study in various ways, has undoubtedly had a number of positive effects. For one, the scope of service providers has become broader, now going beyond the one public/municipal provider to both non-profit and for-profit commercial providers. Second, competition has been introduced in service provision, so that the consumer can now choose between different providers, for instance in the energy sector.

On the other hand, serious drawbacks have emerged. First, there is empirical evidence that consumer prices have been rising despite competition. Certain developments in Germany indicate that private providers, having made price concessions to secure a market position, tend to raise prices.

Furthermore, the privatization of public services in its various stages and types tends to depoliticize them in the local arena, eroding the influence and control of local authorities and the elected local council.

This holds true for formally privatized or corporatized municipal companies, which are increasingly disposed to operate as single-purpose organizations intent on pursuing and optimizing their specific interests, while ignoring the common interest postulated and defended by elected councils (see Wollmann, 2004; Bogumil and Holtkamp, 2008, pp. 96 ff.).

As these corporatized units (in Germany also called *Beteiligungen*, 'holdings') have developed their own entrepreneurial and centrifugal dynamics, controlling such holdings has become a critical challenge for councils.

This also applies to contractors of outsourced services, which local authorities often have difficulty defining and subsequently monitoring, owing to a lack of staff and time. Finally, once the municipal service provider has been sold (asset privatization), the local authority has practically forfeited all influence.

The increasing pluralization and expansion of single-purpose actors 'in orbit' around local authorities has been described as the 'satellization' (Huron and Spindler, 1998; Chapter 3 in this volume) and even 'atomization' (Dieckmann, 1999) of the local arena.

IS THE PENDULUM SWINGING BACK?

Sober assessment of service privatization – particularly by material/asset privatization, which constitutes a full retreat of the public sector – has provoked some rethinking about the pros and cons of this strategy, most notably among the local authorities concerned. In Germany, an increasing number of local authorities appear to be interested in reversing the trend they had themselves initiated in the 1990s. Realizing that it is in their financial and political benefit in both the short and long run to retain and expand municipal corporations (*Stadtwerke*), they have begun to invest in the economic basis of their assets, establishing new *Stadtwerke*, even for power generation, particularly of the renewable and environment-friendly sort. The term 'remunicipalization' (*Rekommunalisierung*) appears to have captured not only the political imagination of local politicians, but to have made it onto the practical local agenda (for the 'pilot city' of Bergkamen, including energy, waste management, see Schäfer, 2008; Verbuecheln, 2009).[2]

In Italy, too, municipal corporations (*muncipalizzate*), particularly in big cities, have recently shown an interest and the economic potential to expand their role in the national energy market. Such a debate is also growing in the French water supply sector, some cities having decided to resume direct municipal operation on expiry of concessions; the decision of Paris to move in this direction had a big impact. In public transport, the municipal enterprise and the SEML are still competitive alternatives to *gestion déléguée* (see Baldersheim et al., Chapter 8 in this volume).

An international trend towards reversing the privatization wave of the 1990s appears to be gaining momentum, water supply in the USA being a recent instance (see Hefetz and Warner, 2007).

Finally, intervention by national governments and supranational organizations to combat the global economic crisis signals a conspicuous comeback of government and the public sector, which might well silence the neoliberal battle-cry 'private is better than public', ushering in a profound and lasting reappraisal of the public sector and the public good.

Similarly, reappraisal of NPM-guided modernization of public administration has begun. During the 1990s, NPM, championed not only by Anglo-Saxon countries but also by influential international organizations, appeared to be triumphing worldwide. However, continental European countries, notably Germany and France, rooted in the Roman law and rule-of-law traditions, have exhibited considerable resistance to NPM radicalism while integrating useful elements into traditional structures. The resulting mix has (with positive connotations) been called 'neo-Weberian' administration (see Pollitt and Bouckaert, 2004; see also Chapter 3 in this volume).

Similarly, the pendulum of change has swung back from NPM-inspired attempts to reshape local government to a 'holding' design borrowed from the private sector. Experience with such innovation has been discouraging, so that a return to the traditional organizational fabric appears to be under way.

GOVERNMENT AND/OR/VERSUS GOVERNANCE?

Making allowance for differences between countries, the transformation of the advanced welfare state has been marked by institutional differentiation and 'fraying out' owing to the multiplication of institutions and actors beyond the formal institutional structures of government, comprising self-standing, municipally owned or mixed corporations, non-profit and for-profit companies, whether or not under contract to local government. While such institutional fraying out has a long tradition in local government operations, corporatization, outsourcing and asset privatization have lent it unprecedented dimensions.

To capture – heuristically, analytically and possibly theoretically – the maze of actors and networks that have evolved beyond the formal structures of traditional local government and to conceptualize how this new multi-actor world relates to traditional government, the term 'governance' has found its way into the current social science debate (see, above, all, Rhodes, 1997). Notwithstanding definitional and conceptual uncertainties, it is widely agreed that, in a descriptive understanding, the term governance can serve heuristically and analytically to identify the institutions and actor networks that have emerged at the fringes of and beyond traditional formal government structures. In a prescriptive/normative understanding, it refers to the capacity and strategy for steering and directing governance (in its descriptive meaning) structures (Marcou, 1996a, 1996b, 2006).

Government and governance – the constellation, juxtaposition and coexistence of these two worlds are marked by pronounced tension (see Wollmann, 2004; Wollmann and Bouckaert, 2006). Whereas traditional, elected local government is based on a multifunctional model and, ideally and normatively, is politically mandated and democratically legitimated to define, advocate, decide and, if necessary, enforce the common good and the best interest of the local community, the governance world is made up of actors disposed to pursue their own, single-purpose interests and profit from the externalization of costs in conflict with the interests of other actors.

How then can local government systems cope with the coordination problems endemic to single-purpose governance networks (in the descriptive sense)? To cope with such problems, caused by the multiplication and expansion of governance actors beyond the immediate influence of local government, recent reforms have introduced another, essentially political, strategy, namely to strengthen the institutions of traditional local government. Under differing historical circumstances, local political and administrative leadership has been strengthened since the 1990s in both Germany and Italy by introducing the direct election of mayors (*Bürgermeister, sindaco*) (see Wollmann, 2008b, pp. 288 ff.; 2009a, pp.124 ff.; Bobbio, 2005, pp. 40 ff.). The aim has been to enhance the democratic legitimacy and accountability of the mayor and governability in local politics and the local arena. In France the mayor (*maire*), whose position in the *système local* has traditionally been very strong (see Mabileau, 1994), is still indirectly elected by the council, although, in the reality of French local politics, he is for all practical purposes elected directly (see Kerrouche, 2005; Thoenig, 2006, p. 55). Following the unexpected territorial reform in intermunicipal cooperation with the establishment of intermunicipal bodies (*intercommunalité*) empowered to levy taxes, the next step will be their institutional reform to give them democratic legitimation. Attention will have to be paid to the reform contemplated by the government in autumn 2009 to introduce such reforms and establish so-called *métropoles* with additional responsibilities withdrawn to the surrounding *département*.[3] The mayor (*Bürgermeister, sindaco, maire*) is plausibly in a position of local leadership that lends him significant influence, as a key player and 'key networker' ('reticulist', Friend, 1977), in the governance networks outside local government proper.

Returning to the distinction between descriptive/analytical governance and prescriptive/normative governance, it can be argued that, by reinforcing traditional political local leadership in local government, recent reforms have strengthened its (normative) governance capacity to coordinate (descriptive) governance networks of single-purpose actors in the local arena beyond local government. It could be claimed that, in institutional fabric and operational logic, government and governance are functionally interrelated, interdependent and complementary – reminiscent of 'old' and 'new' economy (see Wollmann and Bouckaert, 2006, p. 33).

NOTES

1. See *Süddeutsche Zeitung*, 13 August 2009: 'Energy rebels on buying trip: Consortium of Stadtwerke acquires the E.on subsidiary Thüga for €3 billion and is braced to compete with the established energy companies in Germany'.
2. For the recent spectacular purchase of an E.on subsidiary by a consortium of *Stadtwerke* see note 1
3. See speech of the French Minister of the Interior in Senate, 30 June 2009.

REFERENCES

Bobbio, Luigi (2005), 'Italy after the storm', in B. Denters and L.E. Rose (eds), *Comparing Local Governance*, New York: Palgrave Macmillan.
Bogumil, Jörg and Lars Holtkamp (2006), *Kommunalpolitik und Kommunalverwaltung*, 2nd edn, Wiesbaden, Germany: VS Verlag.
Citroni, Giulio and Andrea Lippi (2009), 'Pubblico e privato nella governance die rifiuti in Italian', *Revista Italiana di Politiche Pubbliche*, **1**, 71–108.
Cour des Comptes (2008), *La sécurité sociale*, Paris: Journaux Officiels, accessed at www.ccomptes.fr/fr/CC/documents/RELFSS/RALFSS2008-.pdf.
Dieckmann, Jochen (1999), 'Die Städte im Bundesstaat', in Hellmut Wollmann and Roland Roth (eds), *Kommunalpolitik*, 2nd edn, Opladen, Germany: Leske + Budrich, pp. 292–305.
Friend, John (1977), 'Community and policy: coordination from above or below?', *Linkage*, **2**, 4–10.
Hefetz, Amir and Mildred Warner (2007), 'Beyond the market versus planning dichomy. Understanding privatisation and its reverse in US cities', *Local Government Studies*, **33** (4), 555–72.
Huron, David and Jacques Spindler (1998), *Le management public local*, Paris: LDGP.
Iannello, Carlo (2007), 'L'emergenza dei rifiuti in Campania: i paradossi delle gestioni commisariali', *Rassegna di Diritto Pubblico Europeo*, **2**, 137–78.
Kerrouche, Eric (2005), 'The powerful French mayor: myth and reality', in Rikke Berg and Nirmala Rao (eds), *Transforming Local Political Leadership*, Basingstoke: Palgrave Macmillan, pp. 150–67.
Mabileau, Albert (1994), *Le système local en France*, 2nd edn, Paris: Montchrestien.
Marcou, Gérard (1996a), 'Metropolitan governance. Patterns and leadership', in United Nations DDSMS–Governance and Public Administration Branch, *Metropolitan Governance. Patterns and Leadership*, New York (ST/TCD/SER.E/30), pp. 37–57.

Marcou, Gérard (1996b), 'Gouverner les villes par le droit?', in CURAPP, *La gouvernabilité*, Paris: PUF, pp. 174–205.
Marcou, Gérard (2006), 'La gouvernance: innovation conceptuelle ou artifice de présentation?', in GRALE, *Annuaire 2006 des Collectivités Locales*, Paris: CNRS, pp. 5–18.
Palier, Bruno (2008), *La réforme des systèmes de santé*, Paris: PUF – 'Que sais-je?'.
Palier, Bruno (2009), 'Quelle régulation pour la santé? Un regard comparatif', *Annales de la régulation*, 2, Paris: Bibliothèque de l'Institut de Recherche Juridique de la Sorbonne, pp. 387–96.
Pierre, Jon (1994), *Den lokala staten*, Stockholm: Almqvist & Wiksell.
Pollitt, Christopher and Geert Bouckaert (2004), *Public Management Reform*, 2nd edn, Oxford: Oxford University Press.
Rhodes, Ron (1997), *Understanding Governance*, London: Macmillan.
Schäfer, Roland (2008), 'Privat vor Staat hat ausgedient. Rekommunalisierung: Modetrend oder neues Publikphänomen?', *Öffentliche Finanzen*, Sonderbeilage, 3.
Stewart, John (2000), *The Nature of British Local Government*, Basingstoke: Palgrave Macmillan.
Thoenig, Jean-Claude (2006), 'Sub-national government and the centralized state: a French paradox', in Vincent Hoffmann-Martinot and Hellmut Wollmann (eds), *Comparing Public Sector Reforms in France and Germany*, Wiesbaden, Germany: Verlag für Sozialwissenschaften, pp. 39–58.
Truchet, Didier (2004), 'Santé: la centralisation inéluctable?', in GRALE, *Annuaire 2004 des Collectivités Locales*, Paris: CNRS, pp. 139–42.
Verbuecheln, M. (2009), *Rückübertragung operativer Dienstleistungen durch Kommunen am Beispiel der Abfallwirtschaft*, DIFU Papers, January.
Wollmann, Hellmut (2000), 'Comparing institutional development in Britain and Germany', in Hellmut Wollmann and Eckhard Schröter (eds), *Comparing Public Sector Reform in Britan and Germany*, Aldershot: Ashgate, pp. 1–26.
Wollmann, Hellmut (2004), 'Local government reforms in Great Britain, Sweden, Germany and France: between multi-function and single-purpose organisations', *Local Government Studies*, **30** (4), 639–66.
Wollmann, Hellmut (2008a), 'Comparing local government reforms in England, Sweden, France and Germany. Between continuity and change', accessed at www.wuestenrot-stiftung.de/download/local-government.
Wollmann, Hellmut (2008b), 'Reforming local leadership and local democracy. The cases of England, Sweden, Germany and France in comparative perspective', *Local Government Studies*, **34** (2), 245–66.
Wollmann, Hellmut (2009a), 'The ascent of the directly elected mayor in European local government in West and East', in Herwig Reynaert and Kristof Steyvers (eds), *Local Political Leadership in Europe*, Bruges, Belgium: Vanden Broele, p. 147.
Wollmann, Hellmut (2009b), 'Les systèmes communaux européens en mutation: Etude comparée de la France, de l'Allemagne, de l'Italie, du Royaume Uni et de la Suède', *Pouvoirs Locaux*, **81**, 57–72.
Wollmann, Hellmut and Geert Bouckaert (2006), 'State organisation in France and Germany: Between "territoriality" and "functionality"', in Vincent Hoffmann-Martinot and Hellmut Wollmann (eds), *State and Local Government Reforms in France and Germany. Convergence and Divergence*, Wiesbaden, Germany: VS Verlag für Sozialwissenschaften, pp. 11–37.

Index

Chapter headings are written in bold letters. The country abbreviations are DE, Germany, FR, France, IT, Italy, NO, Norway. We thank Dipl.-Pol. Michael Opitz, M.A., Assistant at Deutsche Hochschule für Verwaltungswissenschaften Speyer, for compiling the index.

à but non-lucratif sector (FR) 245
accrual accounting
  DE 59
  FR 58
  IT 63
affermage (FR) 207
agences de l'eau (FR) 207
Agences Régionales de l'Hospitalisation (ARH) (FR) 127, 135, 140
aide sociale légale (FR) 28, 32, 245
Ärztekammer (DE) 126
ATO (*autorità di ambiti territoriali ottimale*) waste (IT) 157, 158
  water 38, 204–6, 250, 251, 253
Autorità per l'energia elettrica ed il gas (independent regulatory agency) (IT) 182
aziende sanitarie locali (ASL) (local health agencies) (IT) 35

Berlusconi government (IT) 113
Blair government (UK) 106, 107, 114
budget, budgeting 50
  DE 59, 60
  IT 56, 64
Build-Operate-Transfer (BOT) scheme 224
Bundesnetzagentur (Federal Network Agency) (DE) 178
Bundesrat (Federal Council) (DE) 18

Caisse Nationale des Allocations Familiales (FR) 87
Central Electricity Generation Board (CEGB) (UK) 171
Centres communaux d'action sociale (CCAS) (FR) 32

charities
  DE 76
  IT 77–8
  UK 78–9
child care 4, 10
child health 76, 78, 86
child protection
  DE 76–7, 79–80, 84–5, 94
  FR 76, 79, 83–4, 94
  IT 77–8, 81–2, 85, 94
  UK 78–9, 82, 86–7, 90, 94
churches 77, 78, 82, 91, 92
Cité entrepreneuriale (FR) 254
clientelism 236
combined heat and power technologies (CHP)
  DE 177, 179
  FR 181
  UK 175
Comité Balladur (FR) 30
commercialization 235
commoditification 168
communalisation *see* municipalisation
communautés à fiscalité propre (FR) 30
communes (FR) 135
comparative approach 8
comparative summary 240–60
competition 254
competitive tendering (IT) 205
compulsory competive tendering (UK) 6, 244, 245, 253
concession 218, 222, (FR) 170
consolidated financial reporting 235
consortium 226, 227, 228
contract
  concession 299
  gestion déléguée 253, 256

261

contract, contractual arrangements 50, 51, 69
  contracting out 4, 12
  DE 53
  FR 53, 55
  IT 56
  outsourcing 7, 8
  public contracts 11
contracting out 224, 226, 229, 233, 234, 235, 236, 244, 249, 251, 253, 254, 255, 257
convergence 9, 240, 252
corporate governance 236
corporatization 12, 13, 50, 65, 228, 235, 236, 252, 253, 254, 255, 256, 257
  DE 52, 53, 223–4
  FR 220–22
  IT 56, 57, 225–6
corruption (IT) 203, (FR) 210
country selection 5
cross-subsidization (DE) 174, 178

Daseinsvorsorge (provision of public services for well-being) (DE) 2, 23, 169
day care, day nurseries
  DE, 76–7, 87–8
  FR, 87
  IT 88–9
  UK 79, 82–3, 89–90
decentralization 124, 131
  DE 125
  FR 101–2, 125–6, 135, 139, 142
  IT 125, 136–8
declining birth rates 81
delegation agreement 221
de-municipalization of energy provision 168, 186
département (FR) 79, 83, 84, 87, 135, 139
disability benefits
  FR 102
  IT 104–5
  UK 99, 106
disparities, regional and local 98
  DE 104
  FR 102, 108–9
  IT 104, 113–14
  UK 100–101, 108
divergence 9, 240, 252

E.on (DE) 177, 201
early years education, *see* nursery schools
EC Acceleration Directive 2003/54/EC 176
EC Directive 1996/92/EC 176
écoles maternelles (FR) 91
Eigenbetrieb (DE) 231
Electricité de France (EdF) (FR) 171
electricity 4, 5, 10, 11, 241, 242, 247, 252, 254
  EDF 242, 248
  ENEL 248
  hydropower 247
  Norway 247
  unbundling 247, 248, 249
Electricity Act of 1989 (UK) 175
en régie
  FR 170
  IT 170
enabling role 243
enchevêtrement (functional overlap) (FR) 30
ENEL (IT) 172, 182, 248
energy provision 168–90
Environment Agency (UK) 160, 161, 252
établissements publics de cooperation intercommunale (EPCI) (FR) 30
Environmental Protection Act (1990) (UK) 162
EU (re-)regulatory policy 187
EU Acceleration Directive (2003) 248
EU Landfill Directive (1999) 146
EU legislation 147, 230, 234, 237
EU market liberalisation 6, 23, 243, 252, 254,
EU Urban Waste Water Directive 208
EU Waste Directive (75/442) 149
EU Water Framework Directive 191
European multi-level-governance 187
European single market 4

federal government (DE) 80, 81, 87, 88, 92
Federal Recycling Waste Management Act (1994) (DE) 153

Federal Waste Management Act 1972 (*Abfallgesetz*) (DE) 152–3
female labour market participation 75, 76, 79, 81, 83, 89, 91
formal/organizational privatization 252
foster parents, fostering 76, 84, 85, 86
foundation 227, 231
fragmentation 227, 236

GDR (German Democratic Republic) 195
Gemeindepsychiatrie (DE) 132
general competence 219
gestion déléguée (FR) 32, 253, 208, 211
Gesundheitsämter (health offices) (DE) 23
governance 232, 240, 257, 258
government and governance functionally complementary 258
grey care markets 97, 114
guardianship 76, 85

healthcare 4, 5, 10, 11
  National Health Service 242, 246
health care coordination
  DE 132, 142
  FR 135–6, 142
  IT 133–4, 142
health care financing 121, 122–3, 125, 126, 140, 141
health care providers' nature
  DE 128, 129–30, 143
  FR 129–30, 131, 143
  IT 129–30, 131, 143
health care-social care divide
  DE 103
  IT 105, 111, 112
  UK 100
health insurance 122
health policy regulating and planning 125–8, 142
health services 120–45
historical approach 5, 240
holding structure (*Konzernstruktur*) (DE) 233, 237
hollowing out of local government 115
hydro-based local power corporation (NO) 173

in house 218, 223
informal care
  DE 110
  IT 114
institutional care for children 78
institutional variants for local public services 217–39
institutionalism 6
  actor centred 7, 241
  discursive 7
  historical 7, 50, 51, 68, 168, 241
  new 50, 51
  sociological 50, 51
Integrated Water Resource Management (IRWM) 191
integration of social and health care 133, 134, 143
intermunicipal bodies
  DE 21
  FR *(intercommunalité)* 29, 218, 229
  IT 37
interregional disparities
  FR 29
  IT 34, 36, North/South 159–60
introduction 1–14
isomorphism 7, 233

joint stock company 226–7, 231, 232
joint venture 233

key networker (reticulist) 258
kindergartens 76, 77, 80, 85, 87, 93 (*see also* nursery schools)
Konzernstruktur (of local government) (DE) 254
Konzessionsverträge (concession contracts) (DE) 179
Krippen (DE) 81, 87, 88

Land/Länder (regional state/s) (DE) 87, 91, 93, 94, 18, 126, 133
lean government 243, 252
Legge Galli (IT) 204
liberalization 3, 6, 9, 12, 13, 252
Lisbon Treaty 3
limited company 231, 232
Local Government Act (1999) (UK) 107
local government modernization 49–74

Local Health Authorities (LHA) 125,
    126–30, 131, 134, 137, 138,
    142–3
local mixed-economy company
    (SEML) 221, 228, 230, 232, 233,
    237
local welfare state (*den lokala staten*)
    241
long-term care 4, 10, 97–119, 243–4,
    253

marketization 6, 8, 10, 13, 51, 98, 115,
    247, 252
    DE 111–12, 115
    FR 115
    IT 115
    UK 115
    double marketization in DE
        (111–12)
material/asset privatization 252
mayor 258
mixed companies
    DE 197
    FR 207
    IT 206
multi-level institutional setting 15–48
municipal corporation *see* municipal
    enterprise
municipal enterprise
    in house, 242, 249
    local mixed economy company
        (SEML) 12, 253, 256
    municipal energy corporation 247,
        248
    public corporation 12
    stadtwerke 12, 242, 248, 250, 252,
        254, 256
municipal socialism 5, 193, 241
    DE 169
    FR 170
municipalization 12, 13
municipalizzate (municipal
    corporations) (IT) 37, 170, 182,
    201–4, 252, 256

Napoleonic state
    FR 26, 27, 33
    IT 33, 38
National Health Service (NHS) (UK)
    41

nationalization 5, 242, 247, 248, 252
nationalization of the energy sector
    IT 172
    UK, FR, IT 171
neo-institutionalism 7, 241
neo Weberian (administration) 59, 68,
    69, 256
neo-liberalism 243
network regulation theory 187
Neues Steuerungsmodell (NSM) (DE)
    57, 58, 59, 60, 66
New Public Management (NPM) 5, 6,
    8, 9, 10, 13, 49, 50, 51, 52, 57, 66,
    67, 68, 69, 234, 243, 244, 252, 253,
    254, 256
    DE 52, 59, 138–9, 142–3
    FR 60, 61, 62, 139–40, 142–3
    IT 57, 62, 63, 64, 65, 136–8, 142–3
    lean government 5, 13, 243
    performance 10
nidi d'infanzia (IT) 88, 89
non-profit organization (NPO)/-sector
    98, 115
    DE 103–4, 111–12, 115, 224
    FR 102, 110, 115, 220
    IT 105–6, 113, 115
    UK 99–101, 108, 115
Nord Pool (NO) 175
nuclear energy generation (FR) 180
nursery schools
    DE 76–7, 80–81, 92–3
    FR 76, 79, 91
    IT 81–2, 91–2
    UK 79, 82–3, 93

opere pie (IT) 77, 78
output oriented steering, output
    steering 50, 51, 57
    DE 60
    IT 63
outsourcing contracting
    commissioning 253
outsourcing (of service delivery) 49, 51,
    52, 229, 237
    DE 52
    FR 29, 53, 55
    IT 56

partnership contract 218, 222, 235
partnerships 12

public–public 12
public–private 4, 12
path dependency 7, 8, 9, 11, 51, 66, 168, 234, 241
performance management 50, 51, 57
   DE 60
   FR 60, 61, 62
   IT 57, 63
personal budgets (UK) 107
Pflegekonferenz (DE) 132
Pflegeversicherungsgesetz (DE) 245
Plan Laroque (FR) 102
Politikverflechtung (policy-interlocking) (DE) 18
pre-school child care 75–96
private finance initiative (PFI) 11, 222
privatization 6, 12, 13, 50, 52, 65, 219, 229, 234, 235, 236, 243, 248, 250, 252, 254, 256
   asset (water) (DE) 200
   material privatization 225
   DE 52, 53
   FR 55, 195
   IT 56, 57
   organizational privatization 225
procurement contract 218, 222
protected local markets (DE) 174
provision of energy, gas and electricity 169, 247
public interest 230
public purpose 229, 230, 235
public sector personnel 19
public sector personnel by level of government over time 25
public service(s) 1, 3, 4, 241
   economic services 1, 4
   obligations, 3
   social services, 1, 4, 5, 6
   universal service 4
public utilities (UK) 41
public utilities 1, 2, 5, 6, 7, 240
public–private mix, *see also* welfare mix
public–private partnership (PPP) 218, 228, 233, 236
   DE 224
   FR 219
   organizational PPP 224, 226
   contractual PPP 224

public-public collaboration 226, 228, 234
purchaser-provider split (UK) 106–8

quangoization (UK) 42
quasi-federal state
   IT 34
   UK 40

re-communalisation see municipalization
régie 220, 230
   régie autonome 231
   régie directe 220
   régie personalisée 220
région (FR) 135, 136, 140
regionalization (IT) 105, 113–14
regione (IT) 125, 126, 129, 137
regulatory agency 247, 248, 249, 252
   Bundesnetzagentur 249
remunicipalization 4, 6, 13, 256
   DE *(Rekommunalisierung)* 23, 156, 178, 179, 180, 249, 250
   IT 182, 248
Revenu minimum d'insertion (RMI) (FR) 28
Re-Weberianization *see* Neo-Weberian 59, 68, 69
RWE (DE) 173, 201

satellization (FR) 255
school medical service 79
scuola dell'infanzia (IT) 88, 91
scuola materna (IT) 81
service of general economic interest 226
service of general interest 3
service public (FR) 2, 3, 4, 219
services of general economic interest (EU) 2
service public administratif 2
services publics industriels et commerciaux (FR) 2
services publics industriels et commerciaux (SPIC) (public services of industrial and commercial character) (FR) 32, 207
servizi pubblici (IT) 2
Servizio Sanitario Nazionale (SSN) (national health service) (IT) 35, 125, 129, 130, 131, 136

sewage disposal 220, 221
social assistance
 DE 103–4, 111
 FR 101–2
 IT 104–5, 112.
 UK 99–101
social care provision 219
social democracy 241
social insurance 114
 DE 103, 110
 FR 101–2, 109–10
social services 240, 242, 243, 244, 246, 247
social state 2
social work 82, 84
sociétés d'économie mixte locales (SEML) (FR) 171, 253
Sozialstaat (DE) 15
Sozialstationen (DE) 132
Stadtwerke (city works) (DE) 23, 169, 174, 177, 211, 223, 242, 248, 252
Statnett (NO) 176
subsidiarity principle 224, 242, 244
 DE 103
 FR 102
 IT 114
syndicat (FR) 231
 á vocation unique (SIVU) (FR) 208
sytème local (FR) 258

taxation and management of waste 150–51
territorial reform, 9, 258
 DE 21
 FR 29
 IT 36
 UK 42
Thatcher government (UK) 100, 106, 108, 114, 174, 243
transaction costs 235, 237

unbundling 175, 176, 247
 of generation, transmission and distributions 168
unitarischer Bundesstaat (unitary federal state) (DE) 15

Vattelfall (DE) 177
Vivendi - Générale des Eaux (FR) 210
voluntary organizations, voluntary sector 75, 85, 86, 88, 91, 92

Wächteramt (DE) 84
Wasserverbände (DE) 198
waste 4, 11, 251
waste management 146–67
waste management 251–2
water 4, 5, 11, 241, 242, 249
 Ambiti territoriali ottimali 250, 251
 sewage 241
water provision 249–50
water services 191–216
Weberian administration/bureaucracy 6
welfare associations *see Wohlfahrtsverbände, freie*
 DE 103–4, 111–12
welfare mix
 DE 111, 112
 FR 110
 IT 105–6
 UK 99, 100, 107–8
welfare state 5, 13, 241, 242, 243, 252
 local 5
 social democratic 5
Wettbewerbsföderalismus (competitive federalism) (DE) 18
Wohlfahrtsverbände, freie (free welfare organizations) (DE) 23, 224, 245

youth offices 77, 80, 84, 85, 88

Zweckverband (DE) 231